For all t...

The Seasons of a ...

Richard E. Taesch

My Remembrance

Edited by Stephanie Pieck

To my mom & dad,
Lloyd, my stepfather...

And,

Dr. Ernest M. Burgess

- CONTENTS -

Winter

Early Spring

Mid Spring

Late Spring

Early Summer

Mid Summer

Late Summer

Short Stories

The Coda

Photo Gallery 349

INTRODUCTION

As an author primarily of music textbooks and journal articles, I could never envision a day where I might begin to write about myself. Within the isolated world of private music teaching, one may appear obsessively concerned only with the welfare of his or her students; and yet we are always willing to bathe in the joy of becoming the creative medium through which they will succeed.

Suddenly, in an unexpected moment of inspiration – many of which occur during my early morning practice sessions – I became oddly aware that I am the fortunate one; my students have been my children and my teachers. Why not then celebrate my own life as though somehow observing the pathways through their eyes – sighted and blind – watching and guiding us through *seasons*, ever reminding me that their investment in themselves is only as rich and complete as we have all made it – together.

Have I placed too much importance on my role in their lives? After all, there are many music teachers. Heaven knows I make more than my share of mistakes, and often try to explain things far too much. Within my writings and lectures in the field of music and visual impairment, I frequently remind myself of the quote by a man that I have never met, nor know anything about:

"The great teacher never tries to explain his vision; he simply invites you to stand beside him and see for yourself."
                                                                            - The Rev. R. Inman

Always learning from the mistakes of each day, most teachers do not seem to consider themselves necessarily *great* at their craft; like educated engineers, we continue to learn by trial and error. I am told that Andres Segovia, until his death, considered himself to be *a student of the guitar*. The Maestro he was to his followers, but his greatness was in a gentle simplicity within which he was willing to perform even the most basic of etudes in concert. He too was a student who learned from his teaching. He always seemed to play to the people, and never over their heads. Have I always remembered to imitate such ideals? Hardly! Mistakes yes, but too late to learn, never.

As the days went on, more and more forgotten recollections of my own experiences and how they have shaped the way that I live and work came to mind; I began to write them into a notebook. As thoughts would flow, I couldn't help but to amaze myself at this stranger – an emerging storyteller who was about to venture toward what seemed to be very far from himself; but then was it really?

I began to feel that perhaps my little stories could be told; and no, they were not all just about day-to-day life. Although not those of an exotic world traveler, many are adventuresome and perhaps to some, may not even seem real: the little calf who was saved by her mother's incredible sense of geography; the young rattlesnake who decided to curl up next to me while I napped under a bush, and his inspiring contribution to Chapter 28; my fears of airplanes changing when I learned to fly; the life-long friends that I made as a result, and what I learned then about teaching music by being an adult student; the blind child who proved his teachers wrong when they said that he would never learn to read braille; the school in Vietnam for orphaned blind boys; truly real and intriguing tales, all playing some part in everyday life, while proving to me that *even the nighttime darkness of a remote forest trail can become a very magical, friendly, and warm place.**

As short stories and little vignettes unfold, be prepared for a little of the best and the worst of me: sadness, wonder, pain, and even raw humor – a part of any story. At times dialogue might carry an edge; at one time, some would probably have been censored. But as one who is sometimes prone to question what is now called *"politically correct,"* be prepared for my best attempt at honesty for things as I saw them, and as I lived them at that moment.

Kindly take heart dear students, friends, parents, and anyone who may have thought that I was never capable of an expletive, or expressing occasional stubborn rebellion and resentment. However, I do rest well believing that I made my sincerest effort – always learning day to day – striving to live my professional life with dignity, integrity, and with the highest respect for you and for my work.

*Explained in "Late Summer"

But alas, I could not rest well knowing that in my remembrance, I *politically* tweaked my own outcomes of human emotion, defects, fears, and insecurities that often remain hidden on the dark side of all our proverbial moons. A more marketable story was never my intention here.

A highly regarded friend and blind colleague – having lost patience with the title controversy of "handicapped" vs. "impaired" – once expressed to me that, *those who feel they must champion politically correct, seem to lack courage to face the truth.* I have chosen to write about my experiences as I lived and felt about them *then*, while remaining ever aware that this is *now*.

For those who may read politics into my opinions, be it known that Richard does not bear a label of any kind; I tend to remain motivated by what I believe to be right for me, and what I have learned from those whom I respect, regardless of which so called category an idea may happen to fall within at any given time.

And as to what this work has taught me in 2011 [and well beyond], I believe now more than ever that we become what we are only by accepting the good, the not so good, and by learning all that we can from the *other* person we were in the past. Leave the past behind as we were sometimes taught in childhood, and you might well risk stumbling into your future.

For my dear friends and colleagues who passed away after writing about them, I've left the text as I wrote it while they were living. I felt it fitting to share the time of their passing with you as I learned of it later, and in the order of my story as it unfolds. Consequently, do expect to take frequent trips forward into later seasons, in particular, summer. Such is my way of connecting *real time* lessons from the past with their impact on the future story. Such is what it might be like to see into the future from beyond our winters, and to imagine how one's life, and others', might, or might not, have been changed by doing so.

However, my own lesson learned is that, considering one's exposure to life at a younger age, to see into the future would be no more than just entertaining, as we would not recognize its meaning. The uniqueness of a remembrance, as opposed to fiction, is the ability to compare one season to another in real time, without the need for an imagined prophesy intended to design outcome.

Richard is by no means a novelist, although I can proudly say that I have known respected and well-published colleagues and friends who are. Having only written music instruction books and courses, I will undoubtedly make many trespasses upon the nerves of good journalists. However, I have decided to forge ahead bravely, as time is too short to go back to school and waste time with unfamiliar protocol.

Some names and identities have been changed as I believe to be appropriate; others have requested that their own names be different.

What to leave in and what to leave out is always an author's dilemma when others occupy special and sensitive places in his or her heart and personal story. I have done my very best to contact those I've included as part of my own life story, and to comply with their wishes. I apologize sincerely if I have unintentionally opened wounds or that which may have been put away *intentionally*. Embellish, dramatize? Yes in some cases for fun, but most are as I recall them, and believe them to have been.

The inclusion of referenced quoted material in one's own remembrance is – to me – an author's way of recognizing those special places from within – places where someone else who has gone before does in a far better way. I have conducted extensive research, obtained permission where possible, and eliminated much for which I could not. For those that seemed inseparable from my story, and where communication with sources was unsuccessful, I have made my sincerest effort to give attribution and full credit under fair use.

I have written about my own three seasons thus far: *winter* – the beginning years at the end of World War II; *spring* – an awakening during and following the Cold War years; *summer* – overture to *fall* towards the September of my own years. And yes, always inspired by the *Chairman of the Board*, I will venture to say that, *Richard did it his way too!*

THE SEASONS*
By Richard Taesch

Winter

    I am often dark and cold – I am here to remind you of your own self, but I am also here to give you the gift of spring ...

Spring

    *I am peace – I am your new life – spend time with me in the green quiet places, **for all too soon,** I will be gone ...*

Summer

    I am quiet – noisy – hot – cool – a time for different things – a time to remember the coolness of winter, and to anticipate the new beginning ...

Fall

    I am mature, stately, and proud – my beauty can only be seen by those who walk with me in solitude – I am summer's memory ...

*Quoted by permission from: *"Introduction to the Piano for the Blind Student,"* Book 1, Repertoire, by Richard Taesch (2000) – Southern California Conservatory of Music – Braille Music Division [Published by Dancing Dots, www.dancingdots.com]

The broken promise*
*Explained in "Summer's Memory" - the fall sequel

*I have walked hundreds and hundreds of miles with nary the need to be any
particular place other than where I am -R. Taesch*

WINTER
I. *In the beginning*

"Dickie: just watch for the little red light on top of the water tower; when it comes on, you'll know when it's time to come home."
And so it was for a little boy of five years old. I would play in the dirt streets of that dusty trailer park only a tumbleweed or two away from the little home on wheels; as dark would begin to surround me, the once rustic community of *Hawthorne* – near Los Angeles International Airport – became a warm shelter.

Although still unknown to us, Hawthorne California was just one stopping place for the transient family of three during dad's employment in the post-war aircraft industry. And how strange it is that, as a man of now 70-something, I can still vividly remember the first journey to that trailer park coming from my birthplace in San Diego – a place where the celebrated Mission Bay still lingers in my memory as a watery swampland and home to deteriorating World War II ships; a place to which I would one day return for a honeymoon, seeing it having transformed into a tourist paradise.

Looking back for a moment

We had many friends and adopted families in San Diego; one hardly needed a car, and we could walk daily to the busy little town of Santee (a suburb of San Diego), warmly waving to Aunt May and others as we passed their homes. One early morning as my mother was proudly walking us to town as she did so many times, she couldn't help but to wonder why the traffic at the cross street seemed to be so very confused and disorderly. The little boy kept annoying her while she tried to navigate the noisy crossing:
"Mommy, the switch, the switch, I turned the switch."
"Dickie, please be still for a moment!"
"But Mommy, I turned the switch – see!"
At that time, the little traffic lights in Santee were supported on steel posts upon concrete mountings. The control for each light was thoughtfully hidden from sight well beneath the base of the structure, but apparently not concealed quite well enough for a

precocious child of four. I had somehow managed to spot a curious little switch below the box. All of the intersection suddenly turned into a cacophony of horns; although the times were somewhat less harsh, I am now quite able to imagine the exchanging of the venerable *California Salute* among the aggravated vehicular participants.

"What switch, what switch?" mother asked in a panic. Well, I regret that the outcome of the adventure has slipped away, but the story and the fun (and embarrassment) that it provided to my mother over time has never faded.

Dad was a fine young pilot, well trained while serving in the Army Air Corps. Days away from his job on the flight line, he would proudly fly with his wife and young son to places he enjoyed frequenting. The hot springs in the desert was a favorite along with other routine pleasure flights. He had once fallen from the wing of a DC-3 in his work as an aircraft mechanic, and earlier was accidentally caught in the mechanism of a military gun turret while training as an aerial gunner; the warm water of the mineral springs was soothing relief for the painful backaches that he endured for the remainder of his short life. My mother really didn't enjoy flying as it frightened her, and altitude aggravated an equilibrium problem. But she would bravely go forth with my father, knowing that flying was – next to us – the most important activity in his life.

We were far too poor to own our own aircraft; however, dad was always fortunate to have a club plane available to him, and I suppose that being a part-time instructor gave him some special privileges. The adventures were many to say the least, and in those days one could fly most places locally, landing on a dirt strip with little need for any traffic control.

The hot springs was generally my father's first choice; that is until one day while en-route from San Diego airport to Warner Hot Springs, we suddenly became aware of what seemed to be very loud explosions near to the little Piper Cub plane. I'm not sure just what the discussion on the radio was; however, it soon became evident that dad, in his navigational expertise, had wandered into a military gunnery range! "Oh no, now I've done it." Following a few wireless exchanges, an agreement had been reached and our yellow spy plane was more than willing to leave the area. Well, so much for aeronautical ego on that day.

San Diego never removed itself from my mother's warm memory. The weather was gentle and forgiving, while the culture was rich with summer plays, concerts, friendly people, and exciting museums. Dad was working hard as an aircraft mechanic, and looking forward to a new and fruitful life in SD.

Unfortunately, the uncertainty of his industry would soon cause us to leave our adopted family who owned the quaint apartment built above a garage, which was my first home. We would then venture on to Los Angeles with our small house trailer towed by a 1937 Chevrolet, to that rather short residency in the Hawthorne trailer park. *For all too soon*, we would be on the road again.

In the early morning darkness I opened my sleepy eyes from the back seat of the Chevy watching Highway 99 unfold ahead to the north: Culver City, Palms, West Los Angeles, Westwood – again onward toward what would become another new home, the San Fernando Valley. Married twenty years later, I would still recall a Route 99 landmark, *Johnny's* famous pastrami cafe, which my wife and I so often frequented. Amazingly, that icon is still located on our same historic route, now known only as Sepulveda Boulevard.

Life in the San Fernando Valley

The move from dad's American Airlines job near LAX was a short journey to another trailer park, in what is today known as North Hollywood. Witnessing my father being beat up by an irate neighbor there, was my first exposure to violence, as video games with sport killing were not yet among socially *acceptable* pastimes for a child in 1947.

Still I was keenly aware of my father's roots being born and raised in France. I had seen many photos of my grandparents and bombed-out buildings near their homeland during the Great War. They were very poor, but very proud. A vision of the Gestapo pounding on someone's cottage door was not reserved for TV stories and comic books. These were very real things that I knew of when

3

hearing my father read his parents' long-awaited letters aloud to my mother and me. I knew their fear, and even as a child awoke every day dreading the possibility of such a day in America.

It was rumored that my grandmother had cooked a grand meal for the great poet and playwright, Victor Hugo, when he had passed through their little town of Mulhouse in France long ago. I loved the stories of the good times there. I would see photos that I still treasure to this day of the long tables with food served out-of-doors for village friends; there was always music, and everyone played an instrument. Dad himself was a fine violinist, although he never performed professionally; perhaps it served as a prelude to my own musical life later.

Mother, father, and I would make a special trip into Van Nuys each Christmas holiday season to send gift fruit packs to dad's family, as they had very little food after the war. I was frightened of the Nazi dagger that my father brought home to show us after one of his last trips to see the family in France (ca. 1951). In my vivid memory, the very ornate relic still appeared to have traces of dried blood on it. The military dagger was a kind of grizzly heirloom belonging to a family member who never spoke of it again; he would not respond or discuss it when my mother wrote, wanting to return it to him after my father had died.

As the story was told, he had bravely taken the issued knife from a German Officer in WWII; overcoming him with his own dagger, he managed to help captured American pilots escape by means of the French underground. Violence was not a stranger to my young mind, but it was never a personal reality – not until that frightening day in North Hollywood.

Living in North Hollywood: Showdown at the (not-so) OK Corral

As such things go, one will seem to put away the painful experiences while embracing the pleasant ones; but as clear as I can remember, I see a mischievous child throwing paint on my little wagon as I rode through the trailer park. "Son, how did this happen?" dad asked, as I wheeled myself back to our space.

"Oh, that little girl in Space 10 threw it at me."

4

I was relatively undaunted by the incident, as even then I was becoming conditioned to ignore everyday altercations. Dad was angry at the hostility of the child who would do such a thing, and went walking off to find the neighbor family. I think that he must have felt it his duty to inform the child's father of his daughter's unacceptable behavior, and to request an apology from her.

A short while later he returned obviously even more angered, and describing what could have been a western movie showdown about to occur at an arranged time. Neighbors gathered as I hid from sight, well knowing that this was really not a good thing that was about to happen – "over what, a little paint?" I thought. I can remember peeking out from behind tall people gathering to be entertained by the big confrontation; a blow was thrown, another, another, and how well I still see my beloved father falling to the ground again and again – blood running down his face while the angry father of the little girl bent over waiting for him to stand up for more.

He slowly stood once again; however, this time ducked a punch, ducked another, and what seemed a heroic maneuver from his army days, swung around and skillfully decked the man – but not for long. The man sprung back quickly after being forcefully propelled by a friend, whirled around in what seemed to be a boxer's punch, and it was quickly over.

The next thing that I remember after coming out of hiding, was watching my mother helping my dad in our kitchen with wet cloths gently wiping blood and dirt from his face. Strangely enough he looked rather unharmed; he smiled at me, and just kept wiping his wounds; "Hi Dickie! Are you OK?" was all that he said.

Dad was a slight man, and although quite tall, he was somewhat light in weight. He must have been a well-trained soldier in his youth, but he was still no match for a heavy bully who did not fight fairly. The event faded, neighbors went back to their trailers, and all became a memory. But mostly that event became a very poignant lesson for a five-year-old boy.

I learned then that one can take a stand against what may seem to be an injustice: a blind child who has been denied music; a little boy who will remain illiterate because of the ignorance of his advisors; the little girl who will sit idle with her violin in hand, and whose mother was told that it is not practical for blind children to read music in braille. But without proper preparation, expect to take the blows and suffer the humiliation.

A lesson learned for the year 2000 – peeking ahead into summer

Every experience plays a significant part in how we relate to others in our work. No, Richard did not become a fire-breathing Karate expert, although the thought had crossed my mind at times. Yes, the stories and lessons from our childhood definitely seem to remain; we must all look at the good, the not so good, the mistakes, the compassion, forgiveness, and the victories of our lives as part of where we have been and where we will and must go. As teachers, how do we turn these harsh lessons into pedagogical gain for the future? (The following story is by permission; names changed.)

Natalie's mother wrote to me in the early days of our *Music Education Network for The Visually Impaired* (capital "T" in *"The"* is correct for this title). I was so taken by the story of this blind child that I immediately swung into action, calling upon expertise and reinforcement from the more experienced professionals in our field.

Having founded the once renowned *Braille Music Division* at Southern California Conservatory of Music in 1993, I was beginning to see the program gather great respect nationally. Feeling quite well prepared to go into battle for paint that had just been thrown on Natalie's wagon, I marched defiantly forward.

During the time that Natalie was in elementary school, she was able to write out her orchestral violin parts on her brailler in basic music braille notation while her mother, Tracy, dictated the simple print music to her. The mom and daughter team did quite well in the beginning as long as the music was relatively basic. As a result, Natalie became well liked and a valuable asset to her school orchestra. As time went on the music became more difficult, particularly as she entered middle school. The team could no longer keep up the pace of the advancing repertoire and higher level of orchestral arrangements.

One evening Tracy wrote to me; she described her request to the school VI resource teacher that she now needed the services of a professional music transcriber, and the process of faxing music and sending braille files back to her by email. Natalie's mother owned a braille embosser, a rather unusual luxury for most families of blind children, considering that one can cost anywhere from $3,000 more or less.

She then expressed that the teacher felt music braille is *far too complicated*, and had indicated that even if one can have music transcribed, there is no way that print music can be faxed and remain legible.

Such information is the result of many years of passed down myths, and no fault of the teacher. There is no way to assess the number of blind children and adults who have been denied music in their lives through ignorance. Playing by ear for Natalie was not an option, nor would it satisfy her family well knowing that she was music literate, and clearly becoming the victim of a serious injustice. Needless to say, my French-Italian blood began to boil, as this was only one example of many other children I knew of while becoming an advocate in my then new career.

"Tracy, let's try an experiment" I said while on a late Friday night phone call from the frantic mother. "Fax three of the parts to me now. If it takes all night, I will complete them then email the braille files to you by next day. Let's just see what happens."

Without my crystal ball being well polished, my ego hoped for the best and that all of the pieces of this puzzle just might fit: was the resource teacher willing to admit error? How proficient were Natalie's reading skills? Would the rehearsal situation provide a clear example on the girl's behalf? All had to fit exactly right, and at the right time if the paint was to miss the wagon and a dusty street fight avoided. As once expressed to me by a loved and respected mentor: *avoid the fight if you can, even if you feel that you could win; but when given little choice, respect your opponent, and give it your all!*

The music was faxed, transcribed into music braille, transmitted by Internet, and embossed by Natalie's mother late the following day. The outcome was no less than glorious! Came Monday morning's school rehearsal, there Natalie sat in her section: music in hand all memorized, and while she patiently waited for the sighted children to catch up. Win we did, and with vindicated joy! (*Sorry dad that you couldn't have been there to see four generations of struggling pay off.*)

No one will ever convince me that my father didn't recognize a lesson that I was about to learn that day. He made no effort to spare me from that horrible sight in the dusty trailer park street; I will always believe that wisdom is earned, and somehow he knew that I was not too young to learn such a lesson then and there, and at age five. One could certainly debate the possibility, but then why is it that I still can see the faces in that crowd some sixty-three years later? Someone doesn't always need to get hurt; winning can sometimes become the right thing for everyone. The resource teacher was delighted, Natalie was a very happy camper, and her school took first place that year in the regional orchestra competition.

Richard and dad in circa 1947, posing with the "little home on wheels"

II. Life as a Texan

Prelude

Dad was now making trips to the state of Texas while working for the Flying Tiger Line, a freight and shipping airline based in Burbank, California. My father's division was commissioned to convert large passenger aircraft into freight carriers then fly them back to Burbank to be put into service. Later, my mother and I would join him there for a short, but never-to-be-forgotten life in a wonderful place.

Just prior to that time, we had moved from one trailer park to another, but were now among the fortunate few to move into a lovely apartment in the valley.

Before our introduction to TV, mom and I would lie in our beds in the darkness listening to old radio shows while my father was away on his trips. In those days one could clearly *see* the faces, the expressions, and easily visualize the scenery simply by listening to the carefully written dialogue. Little did I know then, that time spent listening to those broadcasts would remain with me as firsthand experience for my work later in life. And yes, blind people do go to movies.

Another myth, another lesson: "The blind cannot <u>see</u> as we know it." Time out for another peek ahead into summer

It is always amusing to watch the reaction of those not accustomed to working with blind colleagues or students. "Have you *seen* the movie…?" is likely to produce an uncomfortable twitch in some folks when the question is directed to a blind person.

Ten rules of courtesy when you encounter a blind person describe a list of do's and don'ts published by a leading organization for the blind. Some young people tend to resent such things, as they may feel patronized as though inferior. To them, they just do things differently. In a reprisal effort, there is a list written by someone that points out *ten things to do when you see a sighted person.* It is an enormously funny spoof on the unintentional demeaning of intelligent blind people. Among related discussions is the definition of a light bulb: *"A low-tech device for vision-dependent individuals."*

During the height of my music-teaching career, recitals were regular and always pleasant events at our conservatory. The mixture of blind and sighted students was unique indeed. My older students had become my friends, and many were among those mentioned above. They would often tell humorous stories without offending each other. Blindness is part of who they are; they are not ashamed or sensitive about it. They feel that they are unique and special, but not only in spite of the fact that they are blind, but often because of it.

Richard, why don't you read the ten rules for a sighted person in your opening talk before the recital; the audience will just love it! Such prompting came from a young lady later to become the bride of one of our first blind students – now a university graduate, and a gifted jazz pianist since age seven. Somehow I didn't notice them giggling behind my back when I accepted the assignment, and in my naiveté I gladly obliged them.

As I stood behind the podium explaining how *we* felt about patronage, I eagerly began to read the list. When I glanced up, I could see many very nervous adults looking at each other in what was obviously great discomfort. As I peeked in the direction of my blind pranksters, I could see shoulders shaking silently in hysterical laughter while holding braille programs over their faces in order to hide their expressions from me. They had set me up knowing what the reaction of the parents would be; poor folks, they felt, who just really *didn't get it.*

You see, once upon a time we would listen to radio shows; video was completely unnecessary to "see" the visions produced by the well-written dialogue. In this graphic (now virtual) world that we have submitted ourselves to live in, real vision is lost. Is it so difficult to grasp a concept that vision is only a presentation to the brain? It can enter the mind's eye from more than one of our senses, and often the eye is clearly not the best one. The blind truly *see*, and yes, they even go to movies! To this day I can still see the faces, colors, and places described in those old radio shows even from age seven, and in total darkness. Have you ever been deeply disappointed in a movie after having read the same story in a book?

As I began to stumble on that ill-fated prologue to our recital that day, I stopped after number six of the ten, wiped my sweaty brow and said something I once heard from a comedian long ago while getting no laughs from his audience: "Well, how 'bout a hand for the suit?"

The recital commenced, and my embarrassment showed through anxious, but light-hearted looks directed at the culprits. *"But Richard,"* offered Kia, *"can't you see that they have the problem, not you!"*

On the road again – the family moves to Texas with dad, circa 1949

This relocation was not like the others. It remains to this day as one of the most memorable and happy times of my young life. Dad flew home to us in California, excited to return back to Texas along with his family. We were able to retain our new apartment until our later return, traveling together this time in the 1937 Chevrolet to the Lone Star State. It was to be a short stay of only two years, but for me it seemed like a lifetime, and was an enormous part of my childhood.

The trip itself is still quite vivid in my mind some seventy years later: The Grand Canyon; The Painted Desert; Carlsbad Caverns; seeing real American Indians selling blankets along the highways well before the tourist boom, was a privilege that I wish every child could share. As we stopped along the way to gas the car, we would later practice the sound of Texas accents that we heard from the locals; I loved the funky motels in New Mexico with light bulbs hanging from the ceilings by their wires; even remains of the old wooden plank roads in the desert sand were still visible at that time.

Burma-Shave™ advertising in the form of six to seven delightful little signs spaced apart over about half of a mile along the highway displayed wonderful rhymes, entertaining both drivers and passengers alike. Thousands of these marvelous and historical signs lined the roadways, and were never considered to be an eyesore. The signs graced American roadways from about 1927 well into the sixties*.

Sadly, I was unsuccessful in locating a publisher to request permission to share a few of the verses with you; consequently, I have donned the hat of a very poor poet, in an attempt to share a facsimile of how the little signs appeared to me as I peered from the back seat of my dad's car. (Each line represents one of the signs; the last was reserved for the company's name.)*

> THOUGH SPRING
> HAS SPRUNG
> AND GRASS IS RIZ
> THE SIGNS ARE NOW
> GONE FROM
> THE WHISKERS BIZ
> - Richard Taesch

We arrived at journey's end to find a town strictly out of western folklore: *Western Auto* stores, *Montgomery Ward*, and catalogue stores where no merchandise was stored, only a way to order then wait for deliveries. Residential streets were even still dirt roads. As we drove into what was to be our new home, dad admonished us not to laugh at the landlady's name of *Mrs. Oats*. An old wooden two-story apartment building graced the dusty willow tree-shrouded grounds.

As we went upstairs to enter our unit from the old fashioned veranda, we were taken aback with the rear door from the kitchen. It was a door that opened up to no porch landing at all, and a scary drop to the ground below. Apparently that part of the building had never been completed, although it seemed to be at least a century old even then.

---

*Be sure to read *The Verse by the Side of the Road"*- a delightful story of true Americana. [By Frank Rowsome, Jr. – S. Greene Press, 1965, 1979]

Music taught as a language skill? How preposterous!

I have heard it said by many that Texas schools are among the best in the nation. Having experienced it myself at least as to elementary school, I can now easily see why. As an educator of many children myself, and through our MENVI network while working with teachers and parents across the United States, I can very fondly speak of that time, and proudly say that I attended grade school there (Uh, well, at least for the second grade).

Having left California at age seven, as clearly as I can remember, I was just about to pass from third to fourth grade where we were progressing from printing to actual handwriting skills. One can imagine the letdown for my parents to be told by the Texas school principal, Mrs. Watson, that their brilliant son would be placed back into the second grade commencing immediately.

Although I was admittedly never much of a scholar, the school was actually well ahead of California in some ways. They felt that we were erroneously learning to write without understanding the meanings and usage of the language through the medium of printing. Back to printing it was, and to the awakening of word usage missed by focusing on the technique of forming letters rather than understanding the words and phrases that they represented. They believed that writing without comprehending content was no less than academically distracting (not unlike learning to read music only by playing an instrument: instrument = toy = major distraction). (See: *The Literacy Movement – What does Braille Music Have to do with It?* www.menvi.org - Articles section)

The school grounds thoughtfully consisted of no asphalt to skin ones knees on, just soft and clean sand. Many times we would tumble from an airborne swing, only to land on soft forgiving sand unhurt. At my school back home, such an event would have most likely produced paramedics, ambulances, possible disabilities, and of course, the usual litigation.

Each classroom had a nature display of aquariums for children to observe metamorphic phenomena while engaged in normal book learning. Much the same as in traditional European schools, each child was required to attend a music class twice a week; no instruments were provided to us – we learned how to sight sing, yes in real solfege, and a true appreciation that music is an academic language with many benefits.

It mattered not if we could sing or play an instrument; we learned the basics of interpretation, transposition, pitch, and interval recognition; the school believed that we would be able to carry the skill into all other learning throughout our lives. (See: *"A Blind Music Student's College Survival Guide,"* Labor Statistics [*Appendix*] www.menvi.org)

Yikes! Praying Mantises everywhere!

I was delighted to observe many lessons of life in that memorable time. I loved going to school and never felt the competitive pressure of mandatory sports and peer issues that I remembered from my school at home. In our little classroom, we watched the complete process of the praying mantis cocoon until it hatched with baby mantises. We read about nature and learned to appreciate by observing it.

One warm afternoon while playing in the yard of our apartment grounds, I spotted what appeared to be one of those interesting little cocoons. "Neat," I thought! "I'll take this home and show my mom as it's just like the one we saw in school!" I carefully placed the item in my pocket and continued to play for hours. Later that evening before supper, the dreaded Saturday night bath became imminent. I emptied my pockets and proceeded to anticipate the event.

Somehow dinner had to come first, and on the way to the kitchen I remembered the little cocoon in my shirt pocket. I hurriedly removed the item and placed it in a nearby drawer, unaware that it was where my mother stored her underclothes. We had no separate bedroom section in the small apartment, and all took to their cots and beds in various personal corners of the convertible front room. (The connecting common bathroom to the next apartment was always interesting, to say the least.)

Weeks went by, and typical of a child of seven, the stashed cocoon totally slipped my mind – until that is: One fine afternoon mom came screaming into the kitchen seeking my dad; "My god, my God! There is a horrible invasion of bugs coming out of the drawers! They are coming from everywhere!" Well, one can see the climax of this metamorphic event as the warm Texas springtime cooperated very well with nature, and with the proliferation of the praying mantis species. Mom was right, they came from everywhere in what seemed to be legions and legions of them.

"Uh, mommy, I think I know what happened."

"What?"

Once the threat of the monster invasion had been analyzed and the schoolteacher scorned in fun, a very careful rescue operation began. One by one the little mantises were rounded up, and as I remember several hundred were relocated out into the garden from whence they had been taken. Mom was ecologically proud to announce that not one casualty was discovered anywhere in her shorts, stockings, or other places in our Texas zoological center. Perhaps the Smithsonian should have been contacted, but imagine the stigma of a story describing how dozens of praying mantises were hatched in your under-shorts!

Entertainment – Texas style, 1950

As did my mother and I back home, we all listened to radio shows while living in the Lone Star state. However, movies were also very important to us, and the only two theaters in the little town of Monahans just didn't seem to change features quite often enough for us Californians.

Dad and our friends, being somewhat adventuresome, would often travel to Odessa in the same day to see another feature following the usual Roy Rogers flick in Monahans. This was always fun, and far better than TV could ever be. Potluck dinners at the airport officers' club, barbeques, and family picnics were typical – not unlike those we've all read and heard about in warm and wonderful stories of long ago. Trips to the families of dad's co-workers in Dallas and Fort Worth to spend Christmas time are all part of the fond memories of those years.

A work in progress, Texas Style!

III. Back to California

After returning to our California home, life was somewhat normal although still a culture shock of sorts. My father then made his last journey to see his family in France, returning with the Nazi war dagger; it was a rather unwelcome relic, yet a sobering reality check to family history. Nevertheless, his return was always a special event for me, and in 1952, a fine family dinner at the *Hangman's Tree* restaurant in Tarzana was such fun.

"Daddy, Daddy, what did you bring for me?"

"Son, tell you what! Wait till we get back home and I'll surprise you."

"Oh boy, I can't wait."

He would always come home with some gift from his family in France: collectors' stamps, coins, or a special keepsake of some kind. But a toy to delight any nine-year-old would always make my day. However, this would be a short time together for the family, as fate would soon present us with a different future.

One afternoon following his day back at work, dad returned with a rather bizarre package in the form of a live lobster wrapped in wet newspapers. A lady aviatrix, Dianna, often made flights into Mexico and returned this time bearing a gift. The live lobster was given to him as a token of appreciation for his work on her aircraft. My mother shrieked, I went into hiding, and our black cat yowled with eyes wide as dad allowed the lobster to crawl upon our kitchen floor, all of this prior to the inevitable boiling alive and carnivorous feast.

Not familiar to me as to what was about to happen, I couldn't help being amused at the antics and slow mysterious behavior of the cat. He would walk round and round the lobster as the creature would pull back then snap with its claws. The cat's eyes would become even larger with ears pitched forward, and very, very cautiously reach slowly with one paw, then the other. Dad howled with laughter as the cat walked in what must have been fifty circles around the lobster, while it reached and snapped back threateningly attempting to defend itself. Our good friends, a co-worker family of my father, were called to share the feast. The lobster was lured to sleep in warm then boiling water soon to be consumed. "Is this all there is?" I remember sadly thinking to my silent self.

Soon after, although unrelated to family military history, we mounted a journey to J.C. Penney's in order to fit my frame into an official Cub Scout uniform. I wore it with great pride, and eagerly attended weekly meetings while becoming involved in earning badges along with arts and crafts projects. The uniform was certainly much more intriguing to me than the one I would later be required to wear in parochial school, however.

Scout meetings were held every Wednesday at the nearby home of a school chum named Michael. This was also the day that my mother routinely cooked a large pot of clam chowder then kept it in waiting for when my dad came home from his work at the Flying Tiger Line. The chowder was prepared earlier, and maintained on the stove to be warmed for our dinner that night – it was my father's favorite.

Everything must change

It was quite windy this particular evening as we attended our scout meeting in early February. The weather was typical of Santa Ana conditions in South California, generally rather pleasant, warm, and familiar. My mom was a scout den mother at that time, and was tending to the boys and their projects. She couldn't help but to notice the seemingly disconnected chatter among the other mothers, and the fact that they had left her to attend the activities alone.

Following a mysterious phone call, I remember seeing the ladies far across the room in a kind of conversational huddle, glancing often toward my mom in what was reminiscent of a childhood gossip session. Intuitively looking toward her while busy with my creations, I could see her rather pale appearance and what seemed to be a puzzled and serious kind of energy. Something was wrong there was no doubt about that.

A flashback

Dad loved to fly, and would often take short "hops" on evenings that followed his day's work. Wednesdays were particularly good, as he would finish early and use the opportunity to give flight instruction to a young woman who worked with him in office duties. His company had formed a flying club, and the members collectively owned a Cessna 140 aircraft.

I would often take rides with him in that little brown plane from his airport in Burbank to Van Nuys, and back. Even then the term, *small plane*, seemed an oxymoron to me. As a little fellow, I would stand next to the craft, and there was clearly nothing small about it. I would sometimes imagine landing one in an emergency on a roadway, and comparing its size to cars or even some trucks.

On one memorable Fourth of July, we spent the day at a family friend's home in the valley to feast, followed by the fun of our own fireworks display. In some areas at that time, such activities were legal, but not so now, as public displays are much safer.

As we walked outside, we heard the sound of a light plane immediately overhead. Dad had taken the man of the house – his friend – for a short afternoon ride before planning to return for the evening's events.

"Paul, you come down from there right now!" his wife Marge yelled toward the sky, waving a matronly finger at the plane as if they could hear her. Well knowing that the antics would produce such chaos on the ground below, the plane circled over very low, waved its wings then zoomed off again toward the airport from whence it came. Soon the two playful men returned in an earthbound vehicle, withstood the chastising in fun, and a great time was had by all. That holiday was typical of the fine friendship that we always shared with them, as the acquaintance dated back to our trailer park days. The young daughter of the family and I were best of playmates, although she was a few years older.

Dinner was getting cold

Mom and I returned home from the Cub Scout meeting just before dark on that windy Wednesday, both somehow feeling strangely alone.

My mother and I were close then; she was always my defender when dad's rather frightening temper would flare. One morning in our small kitchen, I must have aggravated him as I would sometimes seem to do. At my age, he seemed like a veritable monster hovering over me and screaming with anger. I can see him far above me, waiting for a fatal blow that would extinguish my young life. However, he would never place a hand on me, as his love was far greater than his anger.

"Dickie," my mom would say; "remember that your father loves you; his back hurts him constantly, and I must now tell you something about him that will help you to understand why he becomes so angry. It's not something that you have done; he just can't control his temper at times; he has a very serious injury that he doesn't want us to know about. I know this through a letter sent from his brother Carl in France.

"You see, as a boy of about your age, he was tending a large dog while its owners were away. He fed the dog and became good friends with him. They would play, and he would water and feed the animal every day. The dog was a particularly unpredictable breed, but of good nature normally. The food was brought late that day, and the young dog was extremely hungry. He jumped over your father who was not more than your size then – knocked him to the ground and attacked. The animal accidentally took a large piece of flesh and bone out of your dad's skull; doctors were able to save him, but to this day he has a steel plate in his head that was used to patch the wound. So perhaps you can understand the uncontrollable temper that happens at times. Please, please, love him; but especially try not to make daddy angry for heaven's sake!"

I felt great sympathy for him, and always loved him; but never have I been able to adjust to anyone (other than my father) with such a temper. But alas the events would pass, and he was always just *daddy* to me, no matter.

A knock on our door after the Cub Scout meeting

Upon returning home from our scout meeting, mom and I felt rather uneasy but didn't know why. I was a boy of barely ten years, and she could only converse with me as such. Having been raised as an orphan in a Catholic convent, she had limited knowledge of communication skills but held a deep wisdom and a unique spiritual awareness. As she went into our kitchen to tend the clam chowder that had been prepared earlier that day, she seemed uncomfortably aware of the gusty warm winds blowing outside. Suddenly there was a knock on the front door.

I can clearly see myself walking toward that door which, somehow, still seems to tower above my head like the giant steel gates of an ancient citadel. My mom was walking a few feet behind me. She came along side as I opened the door, and there stood three of the den mothers that we had left just a short while before. There was a cold silence that seemed to last an eternity; I looked up to them and saw their hard and somber faces while waiting for one of them to speak; somehow I knew that they were about to change both of our lives forever.

"There has been an accident" Michael's mother said. I have never been able to forget the warm wind that turned suddenly into a cold chilling fog filling the room as in a ghost story.

"Oh my God!" said my mother, "what do you mean? Is it Ed?" she asked.

"Yes, I'm afraid so."

As they came into the house, they told us that his airplane had gone down just before dark. My mother, somehow knowing the worst, responded: "Is he dead?" Those words will echo in the mind of every child and parent who has ever had to face them. Only a somber nod was what I can remember. She didn't scream or cry; she only seemed to turn around, and walk quietly and slowly toward the kitchen. She sat down while the mothers gathered around her in comfort as she then began to weep; I remember quietly crying, daddy; daddy.

Shock is a strange emotion for a ten year old, or for anyone of any age for that matter. It almost seemed like I was supposed to act differently, but could only grasp at whatever response I could find. How was I supposed to know? How was I supposed to act? I had never lost anyone before – not like this. I was paralyzed with fear, uncertainty, grief, and most of all no way to express any of it.

"Can I see him?" Mom asked.

21

"I'm afraid not, Ann; as you see, there was fire. Ina Mae, his student, was with him; they are both gone beyond recognition."

Family and relatives soon gathered in the little apartment to comfort us, and an evening that seemed to last for weeks followed. Aunt Frances, my godmother, would gently say to me: "Dickie, now you must become the man of the house." What did she mean by that? Did she mean a ten-year-old man of the house perhaps? "Try to understand it this way: Your father did not desert you, or leave your mother for another woman; he died doing what he loved, and he is now with God."

Aunt Frances stayed with mom and I for several weeks to help with adjustments, but the most comfort that I can remember was from Charlotte. She was my childhood companion and make-believe sweetheart from the family of the Fourth of July get-togethers for so many years. I can remember leaving the others that evening and wandering off with her to rest. Charlotte and I retired to the back bedroom, as we were both weary and sad beyond description; she was kind and loving to her adopted little brother, but always favored him, remaining quite aware and respectful of the gender difference that we shared. She hugged me warmly in the darkness, talking sweetly while we both fell off to sleep.

As she grew and began to meet eligible young boys, I can remember seething in covert jealousy; I was certain that I was in love with her, but alas at age ten, it was not unlike the poodle and the Great Dane. I was clearly a child watching my best friend become a woman, while I was still a little boy – drat! Two years later, I would comfort Charlotte and her mother while her father, Paul, lay dying of pancreatic cancer at the Queen of Angels Hospital in Los Angeles.

"He loved cherry pie; I wish that I had made it for him more often"

My mother would often say how much she regretted not baking the cherry pies that my dad so loved. She hated to bake and would put such things off.

We always want to do the things that we feel were neglected *after* the passing of a loved one or a friend. I suppose the lesson to be learned is to simply love and be loved; share one's feelings and resent no one – or oneself – for trivial and unintentional trespasses.

Typically, if someone you are angry with, or have neglected in some way dies, you will tend to hold such things against yourself. Conversely, try NEVER to hold yourself responsible for a reaction to what seems an abuse or neglect coming from a friend or loved one. Whether it was deliberate or not, remain aware that the reason is the reason, and un-predicted outcome such as a death has nothing to do with it. Love them for who they are now, and what they meant to you before. But mostly, be sensitive to their feelings as well; from someone who has experienced heartaches from friendships that have hurt deeply, to feel what you feel is not abnormal or evil. Confusing? Do read on.

My father's good friend and his wife were very close to us. Both were with dad and my mom during our memorable Texas venture, as Peter was a fellow aircraft mechanic on that project. Upon the return to California, he and my father were both up for promotions to higher positions at the *"tigers,"* as was fondly called the *Flying Tiger Line*. Dad never really concerned himself with status, but was certainly hopeful that he would succeed well beyond his earlier San Diego and LAX position in the aircraft industry. His friend was also young, and hoping to advance himself in his career.

One warm evening my dad walked into the little kitchen after his work – so very unaware of the cold grizzly drama that would unfold before his family months later – and announced: "Ann! Dickie! I have been promoted! I am now a *Foreman*!" We were overjoyed to say the least. A new beginning for the family; perhaps a home of our own was in the future; what joy we shared! But not for very long, as dad's friend was apparently outraged at the appointment. He felt that he should have been in line for that foreman position. Both my father and his friend were qualified for the job, but dad was the choice for whatever reason.

The family voiced great disappointment, and felt anger and animosity towards both my father and my mother. The tension grew stronger, and what had been a life-long friendship suddenly became

23

hostile, followed by a severance of the family relationship. For them and my father, it was never to be reconciled.

The news of my dad's death and the surrounding circumstances came as a tragic shock to them. It was too late, as they felt that instead of celebrating his joy, they had resented him. My mother and I were now a duo and had worked through major adjustments, but not yet healed.

Peter's wife called us one day expressing extreme sorrow for what happened and for how they had felt; they invited my mom and me to join them in a dinner, and so much wanted to heal those wounds. We were very glad to hear from them.

One need not expound much further upon this lesson, but yet what was I to learn from it? A lost friendship can hurt quite deeply; and just as the joy that my father shared on his promotion becoming scarred by the resentment of his best friend, my own life's work would someday bring sadness and disappointment in a very similar way. I too would know the joy of a long-awaited dream; I would then see it vanish, and feel defeated as well. But mostly, lost friendships could have become the greatest casualty.

Join me now in Chapter 4; try to imagine being able to see ahead to your own summer from perhaps age nine or ten. Summer will tell more, and perhaps then you will see why it mattered to Richard to share some of the future with you now, as Chapter 3 will always remain a living legacy about the value of friendship, and triumph over adversity.

IV. Stories to be told and friendships renewed
An unsettling preview for summer

So many of life's compositions, such as the regretful heartache that my father's friends experienced turning into a happy ending in the major mode, seem to repeat themselves but in different keys; as though a sonata with different interpretation and a different performer, the music of our life experiences can also turn from *giocoso* to *doloroso*: joyful to sad; major to minor; happy to perhaps quite melancholy. Would you still wish to see ahead into seasons to come?

After building my guitar program at SCCM over a twenty-year period, the even longer-awaited dream of our founder had finally become imminent. Southern California Conservatory of Music was at last to have its own facility and a well-earned expansion into a fine campus with living quarters for resident students. Our newest program, the *Braille Music Division,* was only a small part of the near forty-year old institution; however, in many ways its tail was definitely beginning to wag the musical dog.

The new facility occupied a five-acre parcel in a somewhat rural part of Southern California. Even before applications for special permits were completed, planning authorities seemed comfortable allowing us to begin work in a limited way, as a kind of satellite under development. As a result, blind students began coming from everywhere. Concerts and recitals graced the halls of the beautiful building, while students and wildlife could be seen resting on the lush grounds out of doors. Clearly, the school reflected a productive lifetime overall, yet courted a constant uphill struggle for survival. Spring will bring more of the *story yet to be told,* and even some *giocoso*.

Our director's brother, Ernie, as we fondly called him, generously supported the new facility including funding for scholarships aimed at attracting gifted students. Ernie was a world-renowned orthopedic surgeon, and saw to it that the facility was funded during the time special permits were being sought.

The school spent every last ounce of reserve trying to secure the CUP (Conditional Use Permit) in order to formally open the new satellite; but after six years of trying and being turned down, SCCM was completely broke. Ernie passed on at age 89, and no choice was left but to place the facility up for sale at an enormous loss.

Some teachers migrated back to the humble storefront school where it all began in 1971; others pulled out and abandoned ship. Attempts were being made to salvage the leftover funds into a leased building; during that process, all of the school's furniture, supplies, instruments, and such, had been moved into storage at a cost of over sixteen thousand dollars not including monthly rent.

Old friendships nearly damaged

My colleague and I began a frantic search for some kind of interim classroom where limited instruction for a few blind students could be conducted on Saturday mornings. Our sighted enrollment managed to be absorbed into home lessons and private studios, and those that had not yet moved from the original school continued as usual. By then, my own student roster had completely collapsed.

At the closing of the estate, there were over thirty blind students who came from many faraway places each week, along with eight paid faculty and staff assistants. The resident students were turned away, and many of them were in great need of special academia that we were uniquely equipped to provide. Staffers were let go, and students sent home with no promise for future resumption of classes.

We then began expanding the search for different kinds of options, including some churches and schools. Upon closing the sale of our campus, there were enough funds to pay well for a few hours of temporary rental time for perhaps five to ten students on a Saturday morning; door upon door continued to close on us, as all attempts failed.

Our inability to acquire a backup facility then resulted in a major collapse. Students were lost, thousands of dollars were spent while searching for a building to lease, and nearly two years passed before we could re-open the new satellite facility. My co-director and I survived on some small retainer funds, while our personal debts mounted into the tens of thousands of dollars. Friends would call; feeling betrayed by the unknown, I would ignore their calls, but always with a deep sadness and a desire to reach out to them.

Many tried to help, but without success. I now realize that perhaps I must have resented some of them for a part in our discouraging situation, but was not even aware of it at the time. To me, the greatest hurt came from those who believed that the school must have profited immensely from the sale. How could they have known the deep loss, as we regressed 30 years in faith and hope in our dream, while emerging with empty hearts and funds?

I once heard, regarding a student and friend, that in his culture when the hurt of a situation is so deep, the only way to cope with it is to simply remove the source from one's life; pretend that it never existed, and cleanse the pain is the only logical remedy. Cleanse the pain I could not, but remove myself from any reminder of it, I tried. 1953 to 1954 lived again, but this time it was a composition with quite different performers, not to mention an unacceptable interpretation.

Inserted October 28, 2012

Last evening a delightful reunion, dinner, and a wonderful visit brought three old friends together once again.

Richard's "vicious" raccoons *(The kitten in the back is the boss though.)*

27

Charlotte, myself at age 11, and my mom

V. Late winter

A never-forgotten friend; the Cold War; parochial school and a new uniform ...

Doc, as his friends all called him, had been my dad's close acquaintance even before I was born. His real name was Archibald, so one might see why he preferred *Doc*. Most people thought that he was tagged that name due to his very good technical and "fix-it-all" talents. If it is possible for an infant to remember a visual image at less than a year old, then I can honestly say I remember seeing him looking down at me in a crib: he seems to be smiling in a way that only he could, and singing softly the song, *Danny Boy*. Doc had learned to fly with my dad's instruction, and they shared a common friendship with Peter; all three were employees of the same airline.

My mom and dad would generally invite Doc to spend holidays with them, and my second Christmas in San Diego was no exception. As the story goes, I came toddling out to the Christmas tree, stopped dead in my wobbly tracks, eyed the brightly wrapped gifts and began to cry. Apparently, I must have thought that the new toys were supposed to replace my old ones. I ran over to where my old playthings were kept, made a careful inventory, and returned to enjoy the new gifts knowing that what was familiar to me was safe. My self-admitted resistance to change was clearly developed quite early.

Doc became a kind of adopted uncle of sorts, always bringing a warm and welcomed presence to our household. He would later become the best companion a young boy could have upon the loss of his father. Model aircraft, target shooting, music, Amateur Radio,[1] and many other hobbies became a lasting bond between us.

Doc spent much time with my mother and me following the loss of my dad in 1953. He and mom never quite made it as lovers, and although they spoke of marriage at times, never took that step. Mom re-married much later in 1961, and Doc then married for the first time rather late in his life. Our contact suffered some, but later resumed following my own marriage in 1968. He was always there, and could always be relied upon when my mom and I were stranded in one way or another; even after beginning both of their new lives, he was still happy to help me maintain my old automobiles.

> *"Just remember that wherever you go, there you are!"*
> - A.E. *"Doc"* Nelson

Ina Mae's family – a new friendship and a new family

Ina Mae was only 21 years old when she died in the fiery tragic accident along with my father on that windy Wednesday night. Soon after the event, and still grief-stricken by their loss, her family sought to befriend my mother and me, becoming somewhat of a new family. They owned a large home in Van Nuys and we would spend quality time there. Doc was always nearby, and would often join with us in the visits.

Emma and George, Ina Mae's parents, were religious people and felt that they could help us by encouraging mother and me to become more active in our church; mostly they wanted for me to attend the Catholic school, and offered to pay for the first year's tuition. This was another setback for me, as I was just about to enter the fifth grade in public school. The nuns looked suspiciously upon that, and decided I should enter late in the fourth grade semester instead. I suppose that it was a good thing, as the regimentation, discipline, and strict religious studies were somewhat of a difficult adjustment for me. I was beginning to think that I might become the only child to never graduate from the fourth grade!

My mother and I then moved from the apartment that our now-smaller family occupied after trailer park days, and into a wonderful detached house. There were two bedrooms, and one was gifted exclusively to become my sanctuary until I married some thirteen years later. It was my playroom, music study, and later became my ham radio *shack*.

The little house was conveniently across from the new school where an interesting paradox sometimes took place: the church bells tolled pleasantly several times a day, sometimes for funerals, and others for the joys of weddings. On the corner, however, was constructed an air raid siren as graced many corners in our valley at that time. The church bells would often yield to the horrific sound of air raid tests from the sirens; awaking deep in the night from their warning cries was not unusual.

Following my own experience with aircraft turning into fiery endings, I was with the constant fear that – one day – the siren would be for real. The sound of piston engine aircraft terrified me beyond description, and nightmares were routine. In my own professional work with children now, I often wonder how they would react to such a thing today. I am reminded of my grandparents' life in war torn Europe, and pray that they may never have to experience such things; and, that they may never witness a parent who served his country nearly beaten to death while defending them over a trivial domestic matter.

While in the process of adjusting slowly to the new school and being taught the rigors of salvation, Sister Marcella announced to the class that we should stop and say a prayer for something that had just happened. It seems that an airplane had just crashed into a schoolyard in nearby Pacoima, and we were to now pray for the children and others who had just perished.

Sometimes while walking from school with my young friends, we would find ourselves taking cover at the sound of a plane overhead. It would seem that we lost years off of our lives whenever the air raid sirens would scream their grisly warnings. In the school training, we were also drilled that when the word "DROP" was un-expectedly and loudly exclaimed by the teacher, we were to stop what we were doing, drop to floor, and try to take cover close to, or under our school desks.

The Cold War took its toll on all of us, and younger readers may be tempted to think: No, no; this is just a dramatization; this could not have happened in your generation, Richard, could it? Make no mistake; it could, it did, and pray that it never happens again.

Time out to look ahead again: "But you know that I don't like to fly!"

During the later years of my decade-long marriage, I had the opportunity of flying with my wife's mother and her fiancé, Jim. He owned a four-passenger Beechcraft Bonanza, the type with a V-tail rudder assembly. Even though I would sometimes take the controls myself and enjoyed the trips we took, I was nonetheless always glad to get back on the ground.

My marriage ended after ten years, and eventually I began to date again. My friend at the time was a wonderful and caring girl, some twenty years my younger. To this day, we remain as soul friends and a special kind of family.

She must have decided that it was about time I put those silly flying fears to rest; for my birthday that year, she purchased two tickets on an airliner for a fifty-minute flight to San Francisco to spend the weekend. She was so excited and happy when she surprised me with the gift. I looked at it, growled, and said "Victoria, I thought you knew I hate to fly." She smiled mischievously, and undaunted by my obvious displeasure, went about making the remainder of the plans. Needless to say, I was on the edge of the seat for the entire trip but somewhat fascinated by it at the same time. We spent a wonderful time in S.F., and even surprised old friends that I knew lived there. The flight back was un-eventful, but little did I know what she had in mind later.

No, the fears of planes hadn't vanished quite yet. However, my young friend wasn't quite through either. She was aware that during my marriage I had become intrigued with the idea of sailplanes while visiting a soaring facility with Jim and my wife's mother. Somehow the thought of flying in a sailplane seemed safe, as long as I didn't actually have to get into it. One lovely Christmas morning after awaking with her, we proceeded to open our mutual gifts. The first one for me was in the shape of a curious tubular item, not unlike that which one finds a poster inside. I opened it, and to my amazement there was the most curious gift! I thought how nice, she has given me a huge poster of a glider in flight for my wall at home.

She smiled sweetly and then said, "Richard, open the envelope now." I proceeded to follow directions, and after glancing inside promptly turned pale! She had made a special trip all the way out to Crystal Soaring in the high desert to purchase a glider ride for me.

"Aw drat!" I said in my thoughts of course. "Now I've got to go through with this."

I procrastinated for some time before taking the ride, but the result was no less than a new life and friendships that will last always. The instructor was somewhat of a musical-appearing fellow with a kind-looking beard. I immediately felt comfortable around him; when it turned out that he was an amateur classic guitarist, the bond took hold. I took my ride, went back in secret about two weeks later for another ride, and became hopelessly hooked. It was then that I decided I would take instruction and become a pilot myself. Upon telling my mother about *that* plan, all she could say was: "Oh God, just like your father!"

Time passed, and I logged over 100 hours of solo flights along with about $10,000 of credit card debt to boot. Was it worth it? You bet it was; the dreams of crashing airplanes stopped, and my tow pilot, 13 years older than I, became one of my best friends. He is now [was then] 80 years young, and although not flying real planes any longer, he is [was] just as hooked on radio-control model aircraft and helicopters – truly living his flying time again, and again. There are no air raid sirens on street corners any longer, but interestingly enough when I finally ran out of money and some time passed after my last flight, those dreams did return at times.

How I discovered something about myself: teachers can learn new things too

Among the many things one learns during training to be a sailplane pilot is that of emergency procedures, such as what to do if the towrope from the power plane pulling your aircraft upon takeoff breaks. Training gliders can easily weigh 1,000 pounds or more, and are well equipped with instruments just as with any aircraft. The world's altitude record in a sailplane is about 50,000 feet, and high altitude flights and aerobatics are not at all uncommon.

When under a tow, the power plane is pulling the glider up with at least a 175-foot-long special towrope. An instructor might require the student to say the altitude aloud incrementally upon takeoff, and particularly at 200-400 feet above ground. If the rope should disconnect below 200 feet, there is no alternative but to land ahead in the desert most likely damaging the aircraft, as there is not enough altitude to turn around for a safe return landing.

Students would learn to connect their own cables from the tow plane when there were no "wing-runners" available. I had done that many times, and was quite comfortable with it. One simply fits the hook into the nose of the glider, reaches back into the cockpit, and opens the release. Once seated back inside, signals are given and off you go. This particular day a kind gentleman offered to hook my rope up for me. I accepted and off I went … well, not quite. I acknowledged the usual 200-400 feet to myself as I had been taught, but never in my training had the instructor surprised me with an actual unexpected rope disconnection.

Suddenly there was a loud popping sound, and I was quite aware that I was no longer under a tow. Perhaps the tow pilot had done that on purpose; perhaps it was supposed to be a test. Well, no time for figuring that out now.

The experience was not unlike a scene in a movie being shown in slow motion. Apparently the training paid off, as there was no panic, no fear, just reaction: *"Check the altimeter; lower the nose; put the wing down steep and turn back, keeping nose down; and for heaven sake don't lose airspeed or you'll stall and spin for sure"* echoed the words of my instructor. I turned back downwind, picked up speeds of up to 100 mph, landed in the dirt and stopped less than ten feet from the chain-link fence.

I then sat there quietly for a moment while people came running from the distance; I opened the cockpit, stepped out, and just walked away mumbling: "I'm kind of glad that happened; always wondered what I'd do in a life-threatening situation; whew!" The $60,000 aircraft was un-harmed, and for some reason I could even talk in a calm voice. Imagine! So now what's the worst that can happen? If the son of a pilot who perished while teaching someone to fly can learn to fly himself, then yes, blind people can teach music.

My first landing …

First solo!

"If the son of a pilot who perished while teaching someone to fly can learn to fly himself, then yes, blind people can teach music."

My Dad's last completed flight: 2-2-53

This is the last page entry in my dad's pilot logbook, dated February 2, 1953 ... The blank row at the bottom would have contained the flight that he was unable to complete; it would have been dated: (Wednesday) 2-11-53.

[1] The *Amateur Radio Service* is stated with capital letters, as it is viewed as a public service entity regulated by the F.C.C. It also serves as a hobby to licensees.

VI. Blind people cannot teach the piano?

I was now in the fifth grade at my new Catholic school, and becoming somewhat adjusted to the black-garbed nuns. However, certain aspects of fitting into this world as a child of about 12 were not quite making it, so to speak. Sports were mandatory there, and no you could not just sit at lunchtime and chill out. One must play ball of some kind whether one wants to or not. Military disciplines were in force, and unless a student had authorization to return to his or her home for supervised lunch, out to the chain gang it was.

Needless to say I was not the sports type, and would generally be the one that none of the captains would want on his team. But they usually felt sorry for me, and would put Richard somewhere he couldn't do them too much damage.

"Enough of this crap," I says to my pubescent self; "I'm going to go home for lunch and to heck wid'em." I was at an unusually young age to earn an FCC radio license, and have embraced Amateur Radio as a hobby all of my life. While the fools were running around chasing balls and getting scrapped up on the asphalt play yard, I was home faking lunch and working foreign countries by radiotelegraph. "Ta' heck wid'em."

Altar boy selection: "Taesch, sit down!"

While the indignities continued my skin grew tougher, and today I am reminded of a saying that goes: "Sticks and stones can break my bones, but names just piss me off!" And so it went that morning when the pastor of the church came to recruit new altar boys for the church services.

Father O'Dwyer was a stern-looking Irish priest who always had a twinkle in his eye. Somehow you knew he loved all of us, and I highly respected and loved him. It was he who was among the first to visit my mother and me the day following our tragic loss.

In walks Father to visit our classroom one fine morning; "girls," Sister announced, "please continue reading quietly while Father selects new altar boys. Boys, those of you who would like to be considered, please stand up." Well, perhaps half of the boys in the room stood up proudly for Father to survey. He looked over to Sister and whispered something to her; she began filtering out several of the *less-desirable* candidates, at least those that she considered not quite fit to serve the Lord in the holy mass.

"Jones, sit down! Schotbe, sit down; Taesch! Sit down!" she said with a little extra nuance. After all, how dare I think that I might qualify for such a calling? No problem, just more time for me to go home and do my hamming. Ha!

My secret wish was always to play the church pipe organ. I sang in the children's choir for morning mass, and would longingly watch the very pretty lady caress the organ console foot pedals with her stocking feet. "Oh what I'd give to be one of those pedals," I would think to my sinful self.

Sister Dominica was a cheery little nun, and remained the music teacher for the school most of her life. One day I decided that I would take a chance and approach her *un-approachableness* to ask how I could get lessons on the organ. Sister looked sternly down at me and said: "Young man, that's not possible; besides, you would have to take years of piano lessons first."

Yuk! I thought – I hate the damn piano. Later I discovered that she knew I was a guitar player, and probably thought that I was just too unmusical to study the piano under her tutelage, much less the pipe organ. Ah well, I'll just go home and build my own make-believe organ. And so I did: two suitcases, a kitchen table center-insert with keys drawn on it, and several croquet mallets served very well as facsimile foot pedals. "Ta' heck wid'er too!"

Guess What? – Blind people (and guitar players) can teach the piano! Another unavoidable peek into summer

If there was one thing that I learned from becoming a uniformed parochial school student, it was how to effectively remain a rebel while avoiding as many bruises as possible. After it was all over, and Notre Dame High School was in my Chevy's rear view mirror, I must proudly say that I was given the best education that a young man could ever hope for. Complaining was just plain fun, and had it not been for the strict discipline of the nuns in grade school and for the brothers in high school, yours truly would never have made it past that fourth grade. They were wise, competent, and wonderful. In all of my years as a growing schoolboy, vulnerable as any child could ever be, never once was there anything that even came close to resembling the sad claims of abuse that have emerged in recent times.

I have no valid opinion of things I know little about, nor discount the possibilities, as abuse is never acceptable; but having lived close to the clergy as my beloved educators, they were never less than wonderful to me and to my classmates. I would advise anyone to exercise caution when forming opinions based on what is heard in the media. Where there is money to be made in litigation and a giant to topple, there is evil lurking to destroy what is good. In today's world, often what was good is now bad; and what was bad is now strangely OK. Could this be what the nuns meant as *"The Anti-Christ"*?

Music Education Network for The Visually Impaired was born in circa 1997. It has been a networking source for blind individuals interested in music education, related careers, and the cause for braille music literacy from its beginnings. I have been the primary moderator of the network, and as its founder, a vigorous advocate for the rights of blind children and adults to pursue music as a career. Labor statistics clearly dispel myths that music degrees are only useful for performers and music teachers. The music industry is not a friendly place for competitive performers, and making a living as such is difficult at best. However, many other forms of employment are possible for blind music people. A recent prominent magazine article clearly indicates that some corporations look favorably upon music degrees in their hiring policies.

Richard, please help me to find information for my friend in Indonesia. Her piano teacher tells her that it is not practical for her as a blind person to consider teaching piano. She says that since you cannot see the keys, you will not be a good teacher. Such was content of an email plea that came to me one evening while monitoring those who would often write to the MENVI listserv for information.

Once again I could see the bloody street in North Hollywood, and was defiantly inspired to stop the paint that was about to be thrown on this girl's wagon. Up to the discussion list I went – well armed with my computer keyboard and my well-earned rebellion learned in parochial school. Sister Dominica, I said to myself (most respectfully), Ta' heck wid' you too!

The young lady's situation was posted on the MENVI list, and within 24 hours protests poured in; blind music teachers came forth, and I almost began to feel somewhat sorry for this sadly misinformed piano teacher who was about to learn her own lesson about covert discrimination. Over the next two days nearly forty people, among them blind educators, responded.

A happy ending: Maria completed my published courses under Stephanie Pieck, went on to pass her Associated Board (United Kingdom) exams, and is now in college learning to be a piano teacher. The Natalies, the Marias, and so many others like them should not have to travel that road alone – never again! (Maria graduated college as a music educator in 2013.)

And for me...

Vindication is often a very personal victory; but it need not be a crusade, and it should not become hostile or vengeful. Natalie's story clearly proved that, and so many more have followed. I can remember in my eighth grade classroom being required to pass written exams on football tactics. I hated sports with a passion, and always resented being forced to play. Once in high school it was quite different, as the athletes were actually very real gentlemen. Passing the elementary or middle school level somehow reveals the more sensitive side of us, and we begin to realize that the better we are at something, the less we need to prove it.

But I must admit that as an adult, I am guilty; many a daydream would find me thinking: "Oh how I wish now that I could get one of those football stars out on a mountain trail." I could just envision them at middle age huffing and puffing, bald heads and smoker's cough. I have my own form of sports, and could never have imagined such a thing when being forced to play in grade school. I guess it's really best that we don't see the future, as there are enough ways to be unkind; *and as for me,* none of us need spend time, nor indulge the patience it takes to waste on vengeance. Ta heck wid'em anyway.

Winter

I am often dark and cold – I am here to remind you of your own self, but I am also here to give you the gift of spring ...

Winter
Richard Taesch

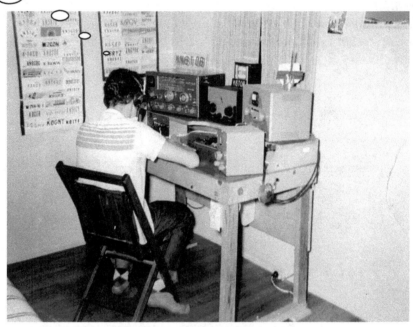

Home faking lunch and working foreign countries by radiotelegraph (ca. 1957)

EARLY SPRING

VII. "Spend time with me
in the green quiet places ..."

"Marc, look out! Mahoney's right behind you and she's waving her cane!" cried the young boy.

My friends in the Catholic school were many, but one – among others – stands out in a unique way. Marc was somewhat of a slow learner, not unlike some of the special children that I have encountered in my professional work. He was the only 16-year-old student in the eighth grade, and yet the envy of us all. You see, Marc had his own car! Imagine the 13-year-old boys going to their bicycles at 3pm, while Marc drove away in his new (old) wheels. Humiliating it was, at best. He was considered to be good-looking by the feminine set, tall and husky, and one might never guess which amongst us the girls noticed first.

He was such a pleasant young man, and his maturity somewhat balanced the typical teen bravado edge that most of us in the all-boys class professed. He was truly the big brother and elder to all of us; we felt fortunate to have his friendship. If a bully were to assault one, simply call for the "enforcer." He knew that he was liked and respected in spite of the fact that he seemed somewhat academically challenged by parochial school standards.

Now Mrs. Mahoney was an elderly Irish lady who walked her little dog each day along the same route to the school. Her stature was almost frightening: straight as a rod, short and trim with hair cropped quite short in a man's style – 1950's, that is. She held her head high and righteous while walking her dog near home on the same street that many of the children walked daily. The sidewalk jutted out conspicuously around the large tree in front of her house, and must have produced quite a problem with the city when sidewalk easements were requested. Apparently, she was the only one who had never granted one.

"Mahoney" would peer out of her window with a paranoid and hostile air; if one of the children would pick a leaf from the green hedge that curved around the tree, she would come running out to chastise the intruder. Needless to say, Mahoney-teasing became a

great sport, but one best be well prepared to go like the wind, as she could outrun just about any kid that accepted the leaf-picking challenge. Out the door she would rage, cane waving madly, and the pursuit would begin. Had the church not been within reach as a sanctuary, perhaps many a young violator might have risked a well-deserved rap on the head from Mahoney's scepter.

Marc was a peace-loving boy and tried never to aggravate the lady; he would avoid the temptation, often walking on the opposite side of the street. This particular day he must have been late and decided to jog past Mrs. Mahoney's house as his car was not working. She saw him running and assumed the obvious: *little devil; I know what he's up to*, she must have thought. The description of our harmless six-foot-tall Marc running down the street with a *seventy-something* lady half his size hot on his heels, was a thing of art, indeed! As I remember, it went something like: "There was Marc – *ass n' elbows* – probably running faster than his old car could go."

Mahoney was closing in fast, cane swinging with true aim that only she had. Somehow Marc lost his footing and fell on a grass lawn, stumbling head over heels. But this was not just any lawn; it was the front of the priests' rectory! Well, even an angry Irish lady in hot pursuit was not going to carry out a hostile act while the good Father peered out the window. Now imagine her going into the weekly confessional and telling that one to the same priest.

A future peek into summer: how the west was (not) won
A story of courage, and undaunted faith

Marc's narrow escape took place in about 1957, and in 2000 our Mahoney was most likely peering out of her own heavenly window while making sure that no one picked roses from the front of her pearly gate. Now there's much yet to be told when summer officially arrives, but we must take a moment to indulge ourselves once again for a short stage-setting look into the future.

The director (and founder) of our music conservatory was still running the original site of the school in year 2000 while a new campus was under development. The location was in somewhat of a

44

rundown part of the city, and altercations in the alley behind it were commonplace. Miss B bravely fought the graffiti and trash dumping day to day; approaching eighty years of age herself, she was becoming a very tired warrior. Everything from mattresses to leftover food from the sub shop next door would turn up lodged against the back door of the conservatory, making life very difficult at best. Miss B would force open the back door then tirelessly proceed to drag the items away from the building, closer to the alley. The police were very understanding, but the neighbors were not as tolerant. She became quite vigilant with these activities, and even the children rehearsing for musical theater would join her on the "front line;" after all, the boss was always right – uh, well …

The Sun Valley *cold war* seemed somewhat harmless, other than that the culprits became even more motivated and just intensified their illegal dumping. But when the graffiti became difficult to cover, she decided to post a skull and cross-bones on the back door in retaliation. No, Miss B, not a good move, indeed. You see, this was considered to be a serious act of war by the local gangs, and the party began to accelerate: the trash got worse, the graffiti increased, and when a bullet finally came crashing through the rear door of the conservatory, the *fun* really began. In order to maintain some humor in a tragic situation, Miss B now became playfully known as "Mahoney 2000." And so it was from then on; but only to those of us on faculty and staff who really understood her frustration, and underwent so many other battles along with her.

She would often drive down that back alley to view the extent of the mess at her beloved school's back door; this particular day, a young gang stood firm in the alley and confronted their adversary with what appeared to be serious intent. However, Miss B was driving a 9-passenger van – a gauntlet for certain. She peered out the front window, knuckles white on the steering wheel, and a look that would have made Clint Eastwood's day. She proceeded driving at a snail's pace waiting for the gang members to step aside; they did not. (You see one of her brothers had been an aerobatic pilot, and another owned a sports car.) From behind her glasses and gray hair she glared menacingly at the flank in front of her, raced her engine pretending to take aim while bodies ran left and right in mortal fear. Now we don't know quite how that affected the outcome of the war, but it certainly made things clear as to who had taken the hill on that day. (Story may be dramatized slightly as inspired by Miss B's colorful accounting.)

Owen, the peacemaker

Miss B's heart was about as big as the Mormon temple that she frequented monthly; and as stern and hard as she seemed, could not turn away the homeless little man who had taken up residence in the war zone behind the school.

One quiet afternoon before children's musical theater rehearsal began, she opened the back door to lift a heavy bag of trash into our dumpster. As the bag descended into the rusty chasm, up from the bottom of it came this voice: "Hey lady, what the hell are you doing?"

Miss B drew back, peered down into the bin not unlike a bear looking for food in a forest campground, and said: "Excuse me! This is a school here; what do you think you are doing in there?"

"Lady, I live back here, and I'm just trying to find whatever I can to recycle."

"This is unacceptable, sir! There are children in here and we can't have you lurking about in the back alley."

Now Owen was an elderly black man of small stature, and no match for any *Mahoney* (either one); there was certainly no mistake about that. But she just could not be angry with him, and we now had what is known as a standoff.

Time went by, and Miss B would cautiously open the back door each day only to find the mess cleaned up. Owen minded his own affairs, and tended a sweet little flower garden that he had made on the dirt strip across the alley next to the neighbor's fence. Well, a friendship began but not with a happy ending; a neighbor reported the homeless little man, and the do-gooders made sure that he was arrested and taken away. Following that, the alley returned to its prior filthy condition and the gang war resumed. Owen, the little angel of Sun Valley, was never to be heard of again.

All of the children and the professional music faculty called Miss B, "Miss B." But the few of us who knew the inside track, still sometimes refer to her as (very respectfully), "Mahoney" to this day – long after her regretful passing in 2005.

Outtake

Unsung heroes come in many different packages, but most often are forgotten and rarely immortalized. Our Miss B was someone who, at times, was not always liked. But then great leaders who make impossible things happen, are seldom liked by everyone. They are often patronized by those who agree with them, or loved *and* respected by those who have the courage to stand up to them.

Under her leadership, within the first ten years of its life, the tiny SCCM earned one of the highest ratings attributed to new degree-granting schools by state authorization at that time.

Our director not only made impossible things happen, but she stood gallantly on the side of those whose lives were the better for remaining an integral part of her dream; that is, what she believed a conservatory should be, and what it should stand for. Consequently, students and faculty were put at the very top of her loyalty and respect list. Yes there were differences among beliefs, and tragic "fallings out" due to conflicts, but even with advisors and faculty who sometimes opposed her, she stood by them, deeply respected their opinions, and always considered their points of view. This then, is what makes a great leader, and the catalyst for SCCM's unexplainable longevity! [RT]

VIII. Springtime,
and a young man heads to high school

But first, a philosophical interlude performed in "Rubato" tempo

The Mahoneys, the Marcs, and the Owens will always remain a permanent part of my life – past, present, and future. Each of us experience life's seasons differently; each episode provides intricate and significant lessons, while every day of a season brings new and uniquely distinctive opportunities. Some will say to never look back; others will say that the past is even more important than the future, as the future can only be reached by means of the road (including its current condition) that has been paved directly to it.

As each season and its new surrounding unfolds, there seems to be a tapestry of different colors molding attitudes that bear significant effects upon each day within it; some will be positive and others will not; some will give us hope, others will bring disappointment and can sometimes harden us. But each time I take myself back into the stories that my own seasons have provided, I often see new and different ways to solve problems. I do hope that the experience of the past as I relive and share it here will somehow prove to be a positive force as well as entertaining. It is with this purpose that I offer you – my reader – some humble insight as seen through my own eyes; perhaps it might provide a benefit similar to that of my own learning experience when writing curricula for students.

"It is the unknown that is unavoidably the weakness, and a key factor in man's quest for education. Enlightenment can only be expected to 'light' the way of our journey — it can make no promises!"*

- Richard Taesch

*From: *"The Guitarist,"* Jelloian Publications 1993 – used here by permission

Hopefully the reader might now see that it would be impossible for me to move logically forward with each of the seasonal accountings and little tales told in this book – chronologically and orderly – without the distraction of looking ahead, looking back, and peeking into certain specific places within the seasons ahead. For example, the bloody battle scene with my father and the impressions of a child provided a very powerful catalyst for my own responses as an advocate for blind students; Natalie's story from summer had to be told as the turbulence of that winter day was fresh. Every day of each season must be treated as a lifetime unto its own. Mrs. Mahoney lived in winter; Mahoney 2000 lived in summer; they are now most likely chuckling at us. However, both had to be presented together even though separated by half of a century.

Such lessons often become a part of one's character, or can sometimes contribute to his or her weaknesses. If we can continue to learn as we teach, then and only then will those we educate respect our accumulated wisdom and benefit from our efforts. And alas, pretend as I might to be a real storyteller, I cannot seem to escape the habit of creating lessons out of living parallels.

* * *

Grade school segued into high school, and life for me continued to be a musical score always undergoing development and re-harmonization. Elementary school in the parochial system consists of first through the eighth grades. Middle school is not recognized, and high school begins at the ninth grade without parole.

The transition into the cold stone walls of the (then all boys) Notre Dame High School was no less than traumatic, indeed. More football: Yuk! Going from class to class was at least different than sitting for hours with the same boring nun. But alas, I must admit that it led to such a nice time holding hands with a special girl while watching the Friday night teams perform in the well-lit ball field. Our Homecoming dance was my first entrance into the world of courtship, and the joy of asking my admired grade-school crush, Judy, to be my date was an exciting event. It was enough to awaken any young man's hormones, there is no doubt about that!

A new friend

Amateur Radio continued to be a primary therapeutic companion throughout Richard's struggle through his teen years even though music remained a mainstay of self-identity and amusement; but the thought that music might one day become a career never entered my mind at that time.

I tended to be somewhat of a loner with respect to friends in high school until I met Greg. His family had just moved to California from Indiana, and he too seemed to keep to himself. Both of us had just entered our sophomore year, and soon began to chat a bit during lunchtime. He was my first acquaintance in quite some time that was not involved in ham radio, and I was reluctant to make friends with an "alien." Although Brother Nivard headed an active radio club at Notre Dame, I just never seemed to fit into the typical social networks, and never attempted to join the club.

As mutual interests grew, my new friend would quietly watch as I escaped into a mysterious world that many only heard about in adventure novels or on news programs. Unfortunately, I was unable to flee to my secret place during lunch as I had done in grade school; nonetheless, most of my friends became quite familiar with it. Come with me now for just a moment as we flee together.

A brief escape to that other world

Radio was my personal escape and daily adventure into a world that few young people will ever know. Today our Internet takes us into a strangely virtual (sometimes bewildering) commercial world. Long ago the Beatles wrote in a song about a place where *nothing is real*; my world on the airwaves was quite real and nothing that I do now on today's virtual reality can compare. I often feel a great sadness for those who will never experience the joy of hearing one's own licensed call letters coming back to them from a faraway place; a place where there is no satellite or cable intermediary required, nor anyone to send a monthly invoice for the *privilege* of communication – simply point to point global contact with only the air between you and the other station.

51

It is sad to think that most folks now really believe that they are talking directly to someone on their cell phone using "wireless." They have no way to know that they are only using the equivalent of a cordless phone connected to a relay within a mile or so; true wireless has been with us since the early 20th century. Internet servers of today are not unlike a computerized version of the old-time central telephone switchboard.

"This is the yacht Compromise departing from St. Thomas in the Virgin Islands" was the voice signal heard clearly in the headphones of my communications receiver. The *Compromise* was a small ship staffed with marine, as well as Amateur Radio operators. Each night I would warm up the tubes of my old station, and tune to hear where the yacht was at that time. I "virtually," excuse the term, followed the Compromise around the world for several weeks, making nightly contact with the operator that I had grown to know well.

At other times, contacts were made using radiotelegraphy: a skill that was required in order to earn the FCC license. Mom would say, "Dickie, go to sleep!" as I snuck over to my *rig* in dark of night. I soon learned to place a towel at the base of the door to my room so that she could not see the glow of the dial lights under it. Headphones and a J-38 military surplus hand key seemed silent, and hid my secret venture. I never knew then that she could still hear the tapping of my sending, and smiled mischievously as she went off to sleep. My little antennas waved in the cold night winds outside, and magic was always in the air.

A joy it was is an understatement, and an experience that contributed to who I am now from those growing years. Even in adulthood, so many years after many similar experiences, I occasionally awake from a wonderful dream of a large backlit radio dial; not one with digital numbers and no visual meaning, but an analog one where I can somehow see images of exotic places inside the dial and beyond, as though it were a window to the world that was at my fingertips. Those joys were too many to tell, as hundreds of pages could be written and most likely not of interest to everyone. However, one trophy does still hang in a picture frame on my wall today.

The Admiral Byrd Antarctic Expedition was quite a catch for a novice licensee's radio station; the call letters were: KC4USA. Radio was the only communication that the men on the ice-capped wilderness had. The station was making contacts daily with high-powered stations in America, and those of us with small rigs would sometimes get lucky. I had made the contact with a subsequent expedition whose call was KC4USB. Later I acquired the coveted "QSL" card from them by mail confirming that contact.

Interestingly enough, the Soviet Union had later established a similar expedition and radio station on the same location; the call letters were, UA1KAE. Then our sunspot cycle propagation was at a high, so distant and rare contacts were quite common even with low power stations. I bagged the Russian expedition, and today proudly display both QSL cards of the United States and the Soviet stations as partners in the same frame. (See Page 58)

Considering the delicate and dangerous cold war relationship of the United States and the Russians at that time, frequent contact with them was a major point of good will and a warm expression of friendship. Few know what effects ham radio operators may have had on the hearts and attitudes of potentially destructive forces that existed then. Even fewer are aware of the role that we played in so many world communication and technological advances.

An early National Geographic magazine article shows pictures of one of the Christian family – descendant of the ill-fated ship, *Bounty* – on Pitcairn Island at the controls of a small ham station; that station was their only tie to the outside world, and the article told their story. (Tom Christian – call letters VP6TC – died on July 7, 2013. Tom was the last living grandson of Fletcher Christian who led the mutiny on the *HMS Bounty* in the year 1789.)

One famous actor was himself a licensed Amateur Radio operator. He lived in French Polynesia at certain times of the year, and found that by communicating with fellow hams he could become "just one of us," escaping the shackles of notoriety for short periods. Monarchs, celebrities, scientists, and statesmen of all walks would surprise many to know of this common bond that has been shared through the Amateur Radio Service; even the Vatican in Rome always maintained an active station. And yes, hams used and developed the equivalent of cell phones long before they became commercially marketable.

* * *

Back to our original frequency, and to where our digression began

Alas, it was always more fun to have a buddy to double date with for our dances and such, and somehow Greg and I found common ground and a lasting friendship. His father would drive us with our dates to the formal dances, and it was then that both of us became fascinated with the dance bands that would perform at the events. Greg knew that I had studied the guitar from age seven, and began hinting that he would like to play (we were both around age 16 at this time). I hadn't taken lessons in many years, and just dabbled in the instrument for quite some time.

After much discussion, we decided to take lessons together at the same academy that I had attended as a child. It was within walking distance from my home, and we would waltz to the lessons together each Saturday. Our teacher, Mr. Raymond, – later to become a bandleader that I worked for – would peer at us over his heavy black glasses, dazzling us with his experience and musical knowledge that we so much wanted to gain. We would take bets that his nose would most definitely come off along with those glasses; however that was not to be, but it did make for fun conversation on our double dates.

Sometimes we would brag to our dates that we were "musicians," and that we played in a band in hopes that they would find us more attractive; little did we know that there would be a time when the musician's lifestyle might become somewhat less than attractive to some; ah but that's for another season.

As time went on, we met other friends in the school who were involved in music, some of which went on to brilliant professional careers: Chad, who could out-sight-read all of us, played hundreds of shows in a row for a successful musical. He served in the army at West Point, and was a guitarist / arranger for the U.S. Military Band. Others we met outside of our own school later joined the symphony; another became the most recorded drummer of the seventies, and the list goes on. But the best part of those associations was the many social times that we shared simply because we all had a common interest in music.

"River's End" – a paradise near home … one of my first "green quiet places"

Well, *"Ocean's Eleven"* – the famed *Rat Pack* from the movie starring some of our favorites, we were not to be compared. But *"River's Six"* often ventured out to a wonderful canyon resort called River's End. Sometime well before I entered high school, my mother, Doc, and I would explore new horizons while sporting about in Doc's still new 1956 Ford Thunderbird. River's End was discovered quite by accident on one of our Sunday explorations. It was a delightful kind of rustic oasis unlike any of the commercial parks today. It was off the beaten path, tucked away along a country mountain road only about a 45-minute drive from our home in the San Fernando Valley.

I yearned to return to River's End one day in my own vehicle, as it was indelibly etched in my fond memories; and so I did, but much later with my new companion, Greg. Other comrades: Chad the guitar player, Mitch, Pat the church organist (that I never became – drat!), later to become an NBC audio engineer, and others within our musical circle, soon joined us for many a fun day at *Rivers,* as we came to know it.

It was an unusual place, in that it truly was at the *end* of several similar resorts in Soledad Canyon that existed along the small river that made its way eventually into what is known today as Santa Clarita. A small natural lake was formed as a swimming hole – not a paved pool, but the real thing surrounded by grass and trees. A little creek ran through the park, and a miniature golf course and lunch bar also graced the grounds. Geese roamed freely, creating a challenge for us to outrun them as they nipped at our bare legs while running through the park on our way to the swimming hole. And yes, a real wooden raft just like in Tom Sawyer was an inseparable part of the dark waters in the little lake. Later, our parents or girlfriends would sometimes join us for weekend outings at our secret discovery.

"Yikes," yelled one of the parents! "There's a snake in the water … oh my god!" Well, it was a somewhat busy day at Rivers that Sunday, with a number of families and children enjoying their newly discovered treasure. Somehow a family of delightful little water snakes found their way into the swimming lake and decided to share their presence with swimmers. They were about a foot long, and quite easy to spot if one would swim under water along with them.

The boys soon found that they were quite harmless, and much fun to handle for a time before returning them safely to their adopted environs. So the day's entertainment would often include carrying one of our slithery friends up to one of the girls or an unsuspecting parent. The usual screams and laughter went on until we convinced ourselves that we had successfully driven most of them to depart to the safety of their homes. "Ah, solitude; *Rivers* is ours once again."

Ken was the caretaker of the place, and somewhat of a mature, fatherly type of man to us. Weekdays were nearly deserted at Rivers, and he would always welcome our descent on the park with a warm smile, sometimes overlooking the little fee that was generally charged for admission. He lived in a small trailer on the premises, and his two sons would often visit to help with chores and such.

Now the *River's Six* was not always six strong, but anywhere from 2 to 4 culprits was not unusual. Ken would often retire to an early bedtime at dark, and was quite comfortable allowing us to stay for as long as we wanted, well into the warm summer nights. There were several special events that we looked forward to, but the most exciting one was the hike at dusk up the creek into the canyon above the park. We would venture in our bare feet and swimming shorts, wading through the creek to confront the "monsters." Such was a bit of an exaggeration, but a true adventure to where hundreds of bats would emerge at near dark.

Of course, the usual myths of bats getting caught in one's hair and other Halloween-type of fun ruled the night air in magical mystery. We would climb the little control tower that held a cable for crossing winter canyon floods, and wait for the special moment. We were never disappointed, as the bats would swarm on schedule and entertain us in a way that became the highlight of the day. I suppose that the myths about the little creatures clearly accelerated our teenage anxiety and fun. But it is sad, and yet liberating at the same time, to find out – as an adult – the real truth. (Revealed in Chapter IX)

Upon returning from our ghostly adventure, we would often lounge on the grass in the evening that had been warmed by the day's summer sun. It was fun to quietly swim to the little raft in the dark and lie there under the stars. The air was as warm as the water, quiet and peace was everywhere; well, that is until the trains would slowly clang through the canyon across from the park.

This soon became an expected event that we actually looked forward to. We would count the cars and fantasize as to what the letters on them meant: *Santa Fe, Cotton Belt,* etc., and how many cars there were or when the caboose was coming and so on. Well, boys are boys, and adolescent mischief was always in the air. Ken was long asleep and we knew that we would soon have to pack up and head back to our respective homes; but first ... [PG rated]

As time went on, we began to notice some attendants on the train at each visit peering out of lit windows; some trains were even passenger types, and all were within visual distance to our little beach. Needless to say, skinny-dipping and moonlight "mooning" was in order.

"OK; Bret, you be the chick tonight."

Soon we discovered that if one of us masked as a woman – towel around the head with equipment neatly tucked out of sight, and if an impersonator put an arm around the appointed one, when the train's headlight would scan across the park the fun would be simply irresistible. Heads would peer out of windows, yells would seek friends' attention, and the unsuspecting folks must have surely thought that there were naked lovers lounging about a nudist camp while sporting their independence just for personal entertainment. Ah, to get away with that now. Not likely, I'm sure. The pervert police would surely display "lights and sirens," and be speeding on the way to eradicate the misguided youths.

Richard E. Taesch

*Confirmation "QSL" cards for radio contact; upper right:
United States Admiral Byrd Antarctic Expedition; lower
left: Soviet Union; both contacts were confirmed during the
Cold War years*

National NC-183-R (rack mount) communications receiver

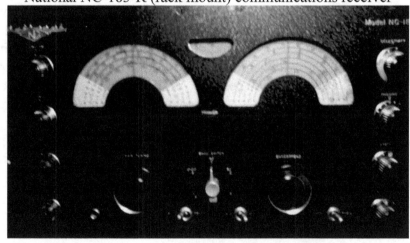

The "eyes" to my world then - and beyond

58

IX. Why is that?

My heart is often heavy as I retreat to contemplate the differences amongst us ...   What some know as beautiful, others will respond to in disgust ...

My youth was adequately filled with joys, and I was always grateful for the friends and family that helped my mother and me through our early and tragic loss. Mom braved it alone and went to work when dad's insurance money ran out; I was about 13 at that point. She made sure that I had a nice home with my own room for a radio shack, which also doubled as a bedroom and study. I never had less than wonderful Christmases there, and will always hold fond memories of that time.

But all throughout that growing period, with my early European roots, there was always a deep abiding sadness for the pains in the world: wars, starvation, and cruelty; there was also the increasing awareness of military service, which would soon change many of our lives. The Vietnam conflict, the ever-present air raid sirens, and schoolteachers making sure we were always aware of the threats that we faced, clearly could not be put aside for very long at any one time.

It was sometime during those years – somewhere before River's End and college – that I began to observe an unfortunate conflict within human nature; this, in spite of the fact that there were so many wonderful humans always around me. But it was those I could not see, the ones who seemed to represent in my mind the fears and insecurities carried by sensitive children and young adults. Even now, I see evidence everywhere that, *what man cannot control, he seems to destroy.* And I must admit that such an observation was not necessarily a result of the great tragedies such as Holocaust, famine, or even my own personal loss at age ten. Nor was it like today's ever-present environmental concerns – those with sobering ramifications, and solutions not yet known even unto many scientists. It was the little tragedies; that where truth is not likely to be set right in our lifetimes.

And just how does this all fit in with Richard's purpose for writing his own story? The answer is within who he became, and what personal views he must live with, right or wrong. My opinions on such things were formed by the fact that we, as humans, often spread myths through ignorance; myths that can cause tremendous harm to fellow creatures as well as to our own ecosystem, and which we then pass on to our children. Those behind the greater evils will sooner or later be reckoned with in some way. But the smaller victims' stories remain small, that is until the cause of their harm catches up with all of us.

For those who feel deeply for them that have little choice, or a voice in their fate, see the beautiful story told in the movie, *"Bless the Beasts and the Children"* filmed sometime in the 1970's.

Let us take for example our River's End bats. I learned that they are not evil and disease-spreading creatures as some would have us believe; and it is not true that they are blind. They are one example of the "little victims," and demonstrate many ecological losses to mankind itself as a result of their being so badly misunderstood.

I suppose that I could never find a shortage of illustrations to write about; but perhaps as my own education was advancing, so also was my sensitivity to such things, as many childhood fears based on ignorance were now gradually falling away. If one were to take the negative effects of bat myths and apply the equivalent of that which has been learned to more publicized subjects, the potential impact might analytically prove no less than catastrophic.

We need the little things, as we are too small of a creature ourselves to view the larger events in full focus without enjoying the ability to compare them to those that we can see in miniature. Simply compare the concept to the unimaginable vastness of outer space. It is then that we realize no living creature's story is a *little* thing at all; especially considering the affect it may have upon us.

So amazing to me are the differences between us as humans. Some have poisoned and exterminated the little creatures, others build "bat houses" in their yards to purposely attract and observe them. Kindly indulge me as I attempt to share a few enlightenments that have certainly contributed to my own life, and have become an inseparable part of this story. Once again, I must yield to the educator inside.

Dr. Denny Constantine is a public health veterinarian in California (taken from a 2005 publication; source credits to follow).

He is one of the world's leading authorities on health issues with respect to rabies in bats. He is quoted to say in a response to an inquiry: *"The public health problems posed by bats are relatively insignificant compared to the public health problems usually initiated by those who publicize bats as problematic, typically resulting in an exaggerated, inappropriate public response, damaging to the public health."* Dr. Constantine concluded his response with: *"Given this predisposition, the public generally will accept, if not embellish, any story or half-truth concerning bats that is suggested."* [1]

Bats pollinate and disperse seeds for many of the world's most ecologically and economically important plants. A good example from Dr. Merlin Tuttle's wonderful book, *America's Neighborhood Bats,* is the famous baobab tree on the eastern African savannas. This tree is so important to survival of other kinds of wildlife that it is often called the "Tree of Life." [2]

Tuttle recommends rabies vaccination for all those who regularly handle wildlife of any kind*. However, public health records indicate that very few people have actually died from bat-related diseases. [3]

Given such important and badly needed enlightenment, is there anyone who would still believe the myths of those who originated them? Perhaps then my view might someday become a hope in that:

What man cannot understand, may he always look upon in wonder as he seeks ongoing enlightenment.

Permission for this accounting has been given by the original book author, as well as the book publisher.

---

*See more on this subject in *"Bat Evolution, Ecology and Conservation"* (Springer); Dr. Tuttle's chapter in the book is titled: *Education Challenges in Bat Conservation, - See also* <u>Merlin Tuttle's Bat Conservation</u>.

RT and "Bro" Greg, at age 18

---

[1] *America's Neighborhood Bats,* by Merlin D. Tuttle Ph.D., Second Revised Edition – Copyright © 2005 by the University of Texas Press. All rights reserved [Page 19] [Used by permission.]

[2] Ibid, Page 14

[3] Ibid, Pages 21; 23-24

X. The adventures of my youth

Some playful embellishments may be included

About life before, and after River's End

Although one cannot quite compare our adventures to Tom Sawyer or Huckleberry Finn, at times the Hardy Boys might draw a few similarities. The pre-River's End explorations that were at hand for us during our teens included Regie, another of my young radio buddies, and a most unique character. While some of us took comfort in having our musical instruments and radio stations near us in our rooms, Regie's bedroom was complete with a large aquarium that contained (supposedly) a large man-eating fish. He reveled in watching visitors cringe when nearing the tank, and having *Jeffrey* whip his tail thereby splashing water defiantly over the top; ah well, to each his own.

Regie lived near an expanding airport where many of the homes at the north end of the runway were being abandoned in order to make way for new approach path clearance. Bicycle safaris to the "haunted" houses became quite frequent; soon they grew into more daring adventures. None were quite as exciting as a tour of the flood control tunnels under parts of the valley headed by *"B-wana,"* Regie.

It was rumored that he had mapped out many of the tunnels on his bike, and could come out at the large Sepulveda flood control basin several miles away. Well, we can't be completely sure of the accuracy of such tales, but one safari that we were present on ourselves did produce an interesting activity, one that Regie claimed full innovative invention for. (All names are fictionalized.)

Having freshened up with an application of his homebrew hair tonic (green stuff that always made his hair look like a Hollywood *piece* that no amount of wind could disturb), Regie biked himself out to mid valley where his buddy, John, myself, and Doug (a novice class radio ham) were to meet him. "YO! Onward to the wash," was the cry of the little band of outlaws. Neerbeer (a non-alcoholic beverage, tasting like real beer), a good supply of rock salt, candy in the pockets, and the journey began.

We were able to enter the huge tunnel at a point in the wash - a delightful and un-interrupted sand creek that ran much of the length of our San Fernando Valley at that time. Its purpose was that of controlling rising waters during the rainy season, as the area was prone to street flooding; it has been said that the valley was an ancient lakebed long ago. Our adventures through the wash often took us on miles of secret travels through the local communities, while never needing to cross a street. This particular day, *bwana* was to take us deep into a subway that ran somewhere under the main business section of our town.

Mission possible

Although Regie supplied each of us with flashlights, we were instructed that they were only to be used for emergencies; to become an official "swamp bunny," we were to adjust our vision to the darkness as part of the day's maneuvers. Before entering the tunnel, a briefing took place intended to familiarize us with the mission and what was ahead.

It seemed that by day's end, bwana and his men would succeed in introducing the rumor of an alien-type of Loch Ness monster being spotted in the drainage system of the city. We looked suspiciously at each other as he seriously explained the cause at hand; we had come to expect the unexpected from him, and were never disappointed. Rather than bore you by telling the plan, I will simply describe the un-describable.

As a caveat, however, do bear in mind that the time was 1958; innocent pranks generally did not bring out the S.W.A.T. team, and such things were never threatening, nor resulted in harm to anyone. For those impressionable young folks of today, be aware that gangs are serious business, and such an adventure only meant for fun would be best not even considered in this millennium.

We obediently complied with our training activities. Sometime after entering the dark tunnel, a small beam of light appeared in the distance ahead of us; Regie's hand went up in commando style and all *horses* promptly stopped. On the ceiling near the beginning of a curvature in the pipe, was a small iron ladder leading to a secondary opening; this in turn ascended upward to the street. If you have ever stood at a bus stop, you may have noticed the little horizontal drains in the curb. Such orifices are intended for water in the street to run into, and consequently drain down through the tunnels below and on to the flood control basin. Summer season was dry now, and the small amount of water from plants and such was not disruptive to bwana's itinerary.

As we gathered around to observe his climb up and through the pipe toward the light of the street above, one could clearly see the ankle of a well-dressed lady in stockings and high heel shoes; she was most likely waiting for the bus to come along with other passengers. Now for one moment, if you can place yourself on the street waiting for the metro, and unaware of the uninteresting hole in the curb near to which pairs of feet are gathered, you may have guessed at the pageant about to occur.

You are observing the folks anticipating their rides, or perhaps you may even be filming a *Candid Camera* episode in the fifties. Suddenly, a monstrous hand (hairy glove adorned) slowly appears from out of the sewer, gently wraps its fingers around the lady's ankle, and quickly releases it when the stomping and screaming begins. Chaos at the bus stop is in order; bwana retrieves the monster hand and slides down the pipe; on the bike he goes, giving the order: *"Get'em up; move'em out!"*

Well, even if the cops arrived, and even after the scarcely believable story was told, Regie's band of outlaws would probably have been nowhere to be found. Few knew the dank subway as well as bwana did; he quickly led us to the light of day, and a return to an anonymous and innocent-looking group of boys enjoying a bicycle ride. Oh no, that's not the end of this day, not quite yet.

On to the basin ... let the games begin!

The warm summer days were always right for adventure; after all, we had *wheels* (two each), and intrigue was always in the wind. The Sepulveda basin was a vast open preserve, with dirt roads and farmlands used for growing crops. It was completely surrounded by a retaining wall built by the Army Corps of Engineers; there was also a large dam spillway that led to a great flat concrete area often used by model airplane enthusiasts. At that time, access to the basin was open to everyone, and served as open space and flood control. The hundreds of acres somewhat resembled that of a miniature Midwestern plain.

Lovers would find their way into the concrete area in the darkness of weekend nights, and many hiding places were available and conducive to that which we were not quite ready for, but most interested in to observe and discuss.

Unfortunately, we were not likely to be present in the darkness for the good stuff, but in time, the remnants of many years of such carnal activities provided a fertile ground for *condom-ring-hunting.* This is an exclusive sport whereby one sees how many dried condoms he can find, and only those where the outer ring remains. One gathers as many as possible, and the ride back into civilization sporting dozens of the day's harvest of rings on the bike handle bars, is quite comparable to a broom placed at the top of a submarine conning tower returning to port. If the ship has been victorious in its mission, it might often display the military equivalent of "clean sweep"; thus the significance of the broom.

Mister Destructo™ *comes out of hiding*

The times before acquiring our first cars were perhaps the best times of our lives. Our world was smaller, and exploration of it was to us as exciting as traveling the world is for many of the more fortunate young people of today. As I observe my students at the same age as I was at certain points, I marvel at the fact that few do not have Smart Phones and new cars, and have seen and done it all before age 18. In many ways I pity them, as I truly believe that simple joys found in rites of passage have been denied them.

Greg and I did many things while attended perhaps one of the most prestigious high schools in Los Angeles; but never did we deny ourselves the joy of being children. Even when we were well beyond typical childhood, we found much fun in making a hobby of trips to a local toy store to purchase some kid's toy or new game for fun at each Christmas. Surely, we went roller-skating, bike riding, double dating, and all of the things that 17- and 18-year-olds enjoyed; but the fun of being a little kid again simply fascinated us, and provided hours of laughter and friendship.

One year, "Mister Destructo" was the *toy-de-année*. It was a very large, and yet quite intricate plastic robot for 1960; he stood nearly three feet tall, and a long cable with remote control could be used to eject rockets from a launcher in his head. The arms would also rotate, projecting small cannon balls across the room, while tractor devices in the feet would allow it to walk. The purchase was made, and Mr. D was to be housed in secret somewhere in my radio room to await commands from either of us.

After I graduated high school, my mother re-married to my stepfather, Lloyd. They had just retired to sleep one evening when a strange whirring sound began to echo down the hallway from their bedroom.

"What the hell ..." came a voice from my mom.

"Jesus Christ!" said a man's voice, while bolting straight up in bed staring at the shadow of a mysterious creature slowly pushing the door ajar and entering the room: Grind, buzz, creak, it went; rocket launcher opened; rockets shot forth, and eyes flashed with weird space-like appearances. Well, having become quite familiar with our antics, mom and Lloyd soon burst into hysterical laughter, completely spoiling the fun but relieving pressure of the scolding that could have otherwise been. Mr. D was put back into quiet quarters, and time went on: time for us to become fascinated with other things, and for dust to gather upon his mechanical being. However, a resurrection was looming in the future ...

Can Lloyd come out to play?

My new stepfather, recently retired from his job, now had more time to chat with neighbors, make house repairs, and other activities of interest. The little boy next door would come to see him while he sat on the porch enjoying the new retirement quiet. Mark would bring little games, and Lloyd became a kind of big brother, as his parents often worked late. My own life at that time became quite busy teaching music and traveling here and there to play band engagements. I was not home as much then, but I did enjoy the times with mom and Lloyd when I was there.

Sitting and studying in my radio room one Sunday, I could hear that Mark had come to visit, and overheard him showing Lloyd his new toy; guess what? It was none other than a Mister Destructo just like Greg's and mine. Ours had been resting for many months, and though I wasn't certain if it still had battery power, I just couldn't resist this opportunity. Mark was quite unaware that we also housed the same one.

A short time went by while I covertly listened to him demonstrating to Lloyd his wonderful robot; Mark didn't know that I was lurking in the radio shack as he continued to march the toy around our living room proudly. Suddenly, he became aware that a similar sound was coming from somewhere, but where, he thought. He stopped, looking confused in his nine-year-old countenance, and when Mr. D emerged from the dark hall, a camera could not have begun to capture the surprise, the fright, and beautiful child-like joy that this gave to him. A full-blown confrontation commenced, and the two robots battled it out for supremacy near an hour at least. Trivia? Of course! But as said before, it's the little things: the light on a child's face, and the laughter that clearly mattered on that day.

Ya mean I gotta' work, and give money into the household too?

The economic side of growing up began to chew at our naive heels, but only led to little jobs and even more adventures to tell. In the years before mom re-married, my first job was that of what was known as "pulling targets" at the local rifle range in the hills nearby. Our friend, Doc, in addition to my radio mentor and surrogate dad, was an avid rifleman (target shooting only). He taught me to shoot quite well, help reload ammo, and would occasionally take me along to his competition matches at the range. He suggested that I might like to earn some money by pulling targets for the matches, and that it might be fun as well. I contacted our friend John, bwana Regie, and Doug (my ham friend); the four of us then marched off to be trained for the tasks at hand.

We were informed that the pay rate would be that of fifty cents per hour. All were elated, as none of us had ever earned that much money returning pop bottles or trading bubble gum cards, and we liked adventure and the unique title (pit boys) that was given to us. There were several categories of chores; the most risky one was called "running deer." Doug was assigned to that one.

A cable on a pulley ran across the target area of perhaps thirty feet wide. A wooden deer would be slowly drawn by hand along the path as a moving target for the shooters to practice. The cable would occasionally hang up, and Doug would have to wave a white flag and yell "Time" in order to run into the field safely to retrieve the deer. However, sometimes a rifleman would not hear the yell, and bullets would still be flying before Doug could run out. There was little risk, as the men were quite aware of the kids and their safety, and we were fairly convinced that they made a jovial sport out of watching us freak out.

Back in the trenches behind the fixed targets, Regie, John, and I would each man a large steel frame. The structure held a target that could be raised above the concrete bunker over our heads, then lowered down to calculate hits for scoring. The frames, when fully raised above the top of the bunker, stood at least fifteen feet above our heads, and were equipped with concrete counterbalances as weight to hold them up. Once the target had been hit, our job was to grab the steel pipe at the bottom then swing the weight of our bodies in order to lower it for re-patching. After hits were calculated, the unit was raised, and special long paddles of different colors called *Maggie's Drawers* were flagged in combinations that would send the score to the rifleman. Well, it wasn't uncommon for one of us to mess up the tally; well knowing this possibility, the shooters always kept their own telescopes in order to confirm the signals that the pit boys would send.

An old-time Army field phone hung on the concrete wall behind us, and if it rang, we knew that one of us was in trouble for sure. But no chastising coming in from the phone could quite compare to the spray of dirt that would come down upon your head when your rifleman would somehow manage to shoot low enough to send a dust storm into the bunker. They always said that it was not deliberate, but now give me a break! These guys were award-

69

winning marksmen; no one could convince us that it was even remotely possible for them to miss anything that they did not intend to. We knew their scores, and they knew we knew that too.

On one occasion, the rapid-fire matches were moving so quickly that we were unable to lower and raise the targets fast enough. This particular day, Regie's target didn't quite settle into its steel frame completely, and began to wobble as he raised it in a usual panic. As I glanced over to him, there he was looking up at the wavering monster towering above, knowing that an inevitable disaster was about to occur.

The paper target was mounted on canvas stretched over a large, but lightweight wooden frame; down it came with Regie directly under it. An "eeehoooee" (otherwise known as a swamp-call) was heard, and next thing that we saw was only Regie's head sticking through the canvas contraption. He simply looked ahead while checking to see if his green hair-tonic brew was still in working order. It was, and the only thing that was not destroyed other than his cranium was his hairdo. The field phone began to ring off the hook and even if it hadn't been there, one could easily hear the cursing from hundreds of feet away in the direction of the marksmen, followed promptly with the expected dust and gravel shower intended to get our attention; it most definitely did!

The thousand-yard large-bore range was much more fun for us. Even though none of us were old enough to drive, an old truck was available for us to make the trek back and forth from the benches to the bunker. We would take turns driving it over the rocks and dirt – doors flapping open and shut, as the latches did not work. Once settled into the pit, the usual raising, lowering, and scoring would commence. It was a little too dangerous for the riflemen to shoot dust down onto us, as they were firing large bore guns of early military type known as M1, 30-06 (excuse my terminology, but big loud things they were). The only thing that seemed to entertain the shooters when we messed up a score was to see that a bullet whizzed around the bunker on both sides. From 1,000 yards, the sound of the projectile was no less than unsettling; one could hear it coming as it zinged alongside the concrete wall like a rocket; I suppose that this was the equivalent to "hey guys straighten up and fly right; OK?"

Proms & girls require more income; on to a new profession: Newspaper "stuffing" in Louie's garage!*

As we began to acquire our first automobiles, entertain girlfriends, and for those of us who had expensive hobbies like radio, our need for pocket money increased considerably. My school friend, David, was with me in classes throughout grade school, and for a short time after high school began; he was the youngest of seven brothers and a sister, and from a very Italian family. Dad was the local distributor for the L.A. Times newspaper, and owned a large home in the valley where the family had been raised on the income from the home-based distribution center. All of the children worked for the business while growing up, and others were often hired at $15 per week to work with the papers for the Sunday and daily editions. Sections of the Sunday paper were prepared throughout the week as various parts would be delivered by the *Times* truck. (*Stuffing means assembling parts into sections.)

Generations of young men had been given work at the site over many years; at one time, the facility handled over 35,000 papers per week. A large garage was specially equipped to process the different stages. Work would often begin at 3am on weekends, and after school on weekday afternoons, we would gather faithfully to man our posts. Mr. V was a hard boss, but with a heart as big as his voice. Over the door of the back entrance to the house was the sign in Italian: *"Chi non lavora non mangia."* Loosely translated, I believe it means: "He who does not work does not eat." Greg soon joined me at the workplace, and we began to earn enough money to maintain our old cars and afford nice outings with our girlfriends.

Our high school Junior Prom was approaching, so several of us decided that we would attend together in a group of couples. The activity that followed the dances at local restaurants was always fun; this prom year, it was to be remembered all our lives long. The *Crescendo* jazz club on Sunset Boulevard in Hollywood was known to be a very exclusive spot where many famous artists appeared weekly. One of our friends in the group suggested that we go there after the prom, as the great Ella Fitzgerald was appearing that night. Our friend Mitch's mother's boyfriend had apparently acquired tickets for all of us. However, upon arriving at the club, even with reservations, we were disappointed to see that the line waiting to get in was nearly a block long. This was not good, as we were hoping to impress our dates while formally attired in our *rented* tuxedos. We waited in the line patiently, but anticipated the worst.

Suddenly a gentleman came down the line outside of the club with his clipboard, and called our party of six. What? Who? How? These were all questions that the puzzled group was thinking at the same time. Well, apparently Mitch's mother and her boyfriend were also inside, completely unknown to us. Being a man of apparent means, he had tipped the waiter very handsomely and asked to have special reservations made immediately for us. It was almost embarrassing to step out of the long line and into the club while passing others still waiting in hopes of being seated. As if that was not enough, our reserved tables were all on the front row close to the stage; Ella's toes were less than a yard away from us. She had recently completed a tour in Berlin, and was singing a performance that night from the album, *Ella in Berlin - Mack the Knife*. It was a night to remember and a very rare privilege. However, one unexpected incident stands out for me. Having subsequently spent my life as a musician and teacher, I so well understand how a performer might feel when patrons would rather chat than to listen.

Ella's accompanist was none other than the great jazz pianist, Oscar Peterson! Before Ella came out to do her show, Oscar was quietly playing alone to entertain those that were dining. Somehow the chatter gradually became so loud that one had to strain to hear the intricate jazz lines that were being offered to his fans. I will never forget the silence that fell over the dining area when he stopped playing and walked up to the microphone; very politely and respectfully he asked [paraphrased] *if his playing was disturbing their visiting and pleasant dining, that he would be very happy to play softer, or take an intermission if they would prefer.*

If you can't stuff faster, we'll banish you to Patty's garage!

Work at the Times garage brought many long days, but left most of us with fond memories, not to mention great stories to share with

72

our dates at dances or sock hops (uh, well, not all discussions could be shared, however).

Uncle Patty was the boss's brother-in-law, and Louie had set him up in the paper business as a part of the family. Patty (short for Patrick) was a red-faced, pleasant and jovial Irishman. His garage was nothing on the grandeur of Louie's where I worked, and occasionally his operation would get behind in the weekend production. Reinforcements would then be sent from "headquarters" in Van Nuys to help get the lead out, so to speak. Without help, the news would be late in arriving at venues to go on sale for Sunday morning.

Now at 4am, most of us moved a little faster than Patty, but not too much. Patty had an old 50's Ford pickup truck that papers would be loaded into, and one of us would be appointed to take the huge bundles to the liquor stores and markets on the route; this would take place on Sunday morning somewhere before sunup. Most of us who were exiled to Patty's on any given day would always wonder why the run would take so long. The truck would leave with a load at about 4:30 am, and sometimes return well after sunrise.

One morning Patty received a call from one of the customers telling him that his truck was seen sitting against the curb on Ventura Boulevard, but on the wrong side of the street! Well, apparently our driver – sleepy as we all were – had fallen asleep as was typical during deliveries. The old truck was probably a little faster than I can walk, but not much, so not a lot of danger was imminent, especially in 1959 traffic at 5 am on a Sunday morning.

As the story was circulated throughout the garage, *truck* apparently found its own way to the opposite side of the street while its pilot in command caught up on some beauty sleep. He finally made it back for a second load, eyes looking somewhat like a cross between those of a bloodhound and two urine holes in the snow.

Back at the ranch (garage), Louie's boys would continue to stuff, stack, and work feverishly to meet the delivery times. Trucks would roll in and out throughout the morning to be refilled with bundles for delivery to markets and such. Once in a while (viewed from the outside in total darkness), the windows of the large work building (blocked so light from inside would not disturb neighbors in wee hours) would come bursting open; heads would poke out in desperate attempts to breathe fresh air, as apparently Louie's coffee and doughnuts supplied for the sleepy crew were beginning to work.

But not all times at the place was toil and sweat. Often jokes and camaraderie would fill the air, and on lazy warm afternoons while waiting for the Times truck to deliver our work, great plans would be discussed such as drag races to prove one's supremacy. Yes, the *California Penis Enlargement* was quite alive, even in the late fifties. The faster one's car would go, the bigger one's member was believed to be. Today it seems that the more noise or presence that one makes – boom boxes on wheels, loud motors, blinding blue headlights, and such – the longer it becomes; that is, if you catch the reverse analogy. Perhaps this phenomenon could be analytically compared to the significance of *Pinocchio's* nose.

Not all of us high school seniors had to work ...
The race happens tomorrow!

Joe had just acquired a brand new 1959 Chevy Impala convertible as a gift from his dad for upcoming graduation. It was shining white in color, with lush red and white leather inside. David was the youngest of Louie's sons who worked with us at the Times garage, and like myself, only had an old car, but proud of it he was: a 1940 Desoto four-door sedan with paint peeling off. David was somewhat popular in school, but Joe's shiny new car was beginning to move in on his territory.

Following school one afternoon, he was waiting at a stoplight; Joe pulled up next to him – new car complete with girls – and began laughing at the shabby old Desoto. Now what Joe didn't know, was that the old car was no slouch in the speed department; but he would enjoy making fun of David while jokingly challenging him to a drag race whenever they met. The old Desoto had a stick shift on the column, and it interestingly curved upward. This was not by design, and we would muse that it was perhaps from repeated speed shifting occurring over the car's long life. It was a sight to behold: rickety, faded paint, and very old high top design.

Having become quite annoyed at the constant badgering and "better than you" attitude that Joe was so good at, David challenged him to a scheduled race on Ranchito Street; the time and day was to be set, and friends would be there to flag them off and to declare the winner. Well, the laughter from Joe and female friends was heard all through Notre Dame as the challenge was accepted.

The day came, and neighbors helped to safely close off the area. There they both were on one end of the street, side by side, waiting like two snorting horses at Santa Anita Race Track. Girlfriends were there, and many from both sides gathered to see the event. Sadly for Joe, only David and those of us who knew a little about cars were aware of the so-called "handicap."

Although the Impala was an eight-cylinder engine, it was also a two speed automatic – slower than molasses in January! The flag went down, the cars began to move. Before Joe could wipe the laugh off of his face, the old Desoto was nearly halfway down the block even before Joe could get very far off the line. There he was proudly wearing his Notre Dame senior jacket, girls and all, car accelerating like a metro bus pulling away from a stop while his competitor watched him far back in the rear-view mirror that was only taped to the windshield of the old car, and at a blinding speed of about 30 mph (just slightly more than the speed limit).

In today's world and more dense cities, such nonsense would certainly be dealt with severely, and so it should. Even then, to drag race in such a way on a residential street was truly pushing one's luck. But that was then; somehow we miraculously seemed to survive such things, and fortunately no one was ever hurt.

Alas, David soon moved up to his brother's '56 Chevy; it was a beauty to behold: shiny black and a real Corvette engine. That car was perhaps one of the fastest that I knew at that time, and today would be a priceless classic.

(Grin!)

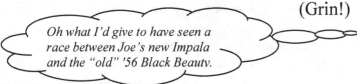

Oh what I'd give to have seen a race between Joe's new Impala and the "old" '56 Black Beauty.

Outtake

Many months following the writing of this chapter, David walked back into my life (July, 2011). It will take us perhaps the rest of our lives to catch up on the many things that we have both lived since our last meeting forty years ago. He worked and worked to find me, and once we connected, he expressed things that I never knew – things about our friendship and how they influenced his future. He felt compelled to tell me that music and radio had become a significant part of his life, and waited long for the chance to express it.

Completely unknown to me, David had become a Morse code *intercept* operator in the Army. He had also sustained serious injuries on active duty while serving our country. After returning from service he became a competent and busy performer in the music industry. All but one of his brothers is still living, although his father and mom are gone now. His family was like my own, and I was treated like one of them. I told David that he was like having a brother then, as I never had one of my own. Needless to say, this reunion had to come to pass; without it, my own remembrance would not be complete

Tom moves up to a hot rod Ford [PG rated - with smiles]

As time went on we began to upgrade our wheels considerably. Anyone who has enjoyed movies about teens growing up, their cars and love adventures, would surely know about the drive-in hotspots. *Bob's Big Boy* was the spot in Van Nuys at the time, and we would drive around and around, in and out of the parking lot to show off our cars to potential female admirers; in and out over and over again, until finally settling into a drive-in parking space to order a Coke and fries, not unlike a fly finally landing on a discarded sandwich.

Tom, one of our more affluent school friends, had just moved up to a '55 Ford Thunderbird – beautiful teal blue and quite *quick*, indeed.

A drive up to the ridge-top road above the valley to park with one's girl was quite a common sport in the fifties, and perhaps even now. Tom was well known for his ventures with different ladies who admired him, er, his car, er, his, uh well, whichever. One

76

particular trip was perhaps the one that finally brought him down a notch or two, at least to some amount of humility.

As the story goes, he had carelessly tossed the contraceptive device of the evening (sometimes called a "raincoat") out the window of the car upon completion of the activities at hand. Following the mountain indulgence, he and girl decided to cruise through Bob's Big Boy to top off the evening's pleasures. As they proudly circled through the parking lot in traditional style, they noticed folks looking out of cars while laughing hysterically. Beginning to feel a bit conspicuous but not knowing why, they decided to call it a night and leave for home.

Tom, gentleman that he was, drove up to the girl's home, stepped out of his door to open the other door for her, and spotted the unspeakable: there was the used condom merrily swinging from his door handle in much the same manner that had entertained the onlookers while cruising through Bob's earlier. Perhaps the analogous "Clean Sweep" could have been applied in order to maintain one's dignity, but then ...

Uh ... no, ma; Tom's was teal blue; besides...
This one is a '56 anyway

MID SPRING
XI. Obstacles are those terrifying things …

1961 brought many interesting changes into Richard's life: graduation from high school, the beginning of a career, and plans for college were all brewing. *Gigs* (music performing engagements) were becoming a new way to earn money; as such, music friends and I were able to work together in small dance bands quite often. At ages 18-20, we were not yet allowed to perform in clubs where alcohol was served, but numerous school dances, weddings, and parties kept us quite busy. After passing age 21, the frat houses (fraternities), clubs, and hotel parties provided not only income, but the stories of things that we saw and experienced could fill a novel guaranteed never to be boring. Some of those adventures lie ahead for you as we travel on through springtime.

I lived at home with my folks up until my marriage at age 24, and worked every weekend playing in various groups while booking agents kept us busy. But no one was more surprised than I when, in June of 1961, the owner of the academy at which I was still taking lessons approached me and said: "Richard, would you consider giving some guitar lessons for us?" And now after fifty years of working as a full-time music teacher, ne'er a month passes without a student or a parent asking, "Just how did you get into this work?" My answer is generally the short version:

"Well, I was only 18, but had been involved at the academy since age 7. I was now studying along with a friend while also continuing private lessons. Mr. Adler came up to me one day and asked if I would consider being a student teacher; they put a coat and tie on me, and said that I was now to become *Mr.* Taesch!" I took to teaching music very naturally; as time went on, my friend Greg was asked if he would give lessons there as well.

It is quite amusing how a costume, uniform, or a prop can create an image. Put a policeman's uniform on a young man that you once gave a scolding to for not practicing, and later if he stops you for a traffic violation, you respond to him with "… yes, officer." Here I was barely out of high school, yet the suit and tie encouraged parents of students to ask me for advice on child rearing.

Similarly, my colleague at the conservatory where I have now taught for many years (peeking ahead into summer season) recently took an official president appointment for a state organization. While walking through a hotel during a conference, he needed access to certain areas of the facility in order to evaluate accommodations for meeting rooms. He stopped an official-looking gentleman and asked how to proceed. The man, aware of the circumstances and my friend's position, told him that the best way to walk into any restricted areas of the hotel is simply to carry a clipboard. It didn't matter what was on the board, or whether you had any official identification. We had quite a laugh later at the fact that it truly did work.

It seems that if one walks with confidence, well dressed and appearing as though one knows what one is doing, as long as you have a clipboard in hand, no one stops to question why you are entering any area that you desire to. After all, you must be official, otherwise why would you be carrying a clipboard? And to complete the analogy, as long as I came into the school with my briefcase, my coat and tie and carrying my musical instrument, voila! I was Mr. Taesch: the college graduate; the learned one; a wise guru in mankind's quest for musical advancement; amazing indeed! Good grief, I didn't even know yet whether I would go on to college as an electronics engineer or as a music education major, but *Mr. Taesch* I was, nonetheless. Conversely, imagine walking into your dentist's office for the first visit. If he appeared dressed in sneakers and shorts, and carrying a drill in his hip pocket, what would be your reaction? Yes, *image* is definitely *imaginary*.

Side bar: Acme Carpet Cleaning

It is said that if you look like you are supposed to be doing something official, whether or not you are up to mischief, you can sometimes succeed without notice. It was during the time that I was being Mr. Taesch that the following story was told to me (loosely remembered facsimile; names and place changed to protect the forgetful; some creative imagination may be included).

It was early on Sunday morning, and Catholic mass was just under way. Father was facing the altar with his back to the congregation, raising and lowering fervent praying hands while chanting in Latin and carrying out the beautiful drama of the mass. Congregation was piously assembled in pews, and the smell of incense and candles brought a spiritual and religious air to the morning. Lent had just begun, and many attendees were probably contemplating as to whether they should make a pit stop at the confessional before receiving the sacraments; lovely organ music and serenity was typical of the season.

Suddenly, two gentlemen dressed in workman's clothes and shirts with *"Acme Carpet Cleaning Service"* written on their backs, walked boldly down the aisle towards the back. Although without clipboards, they looked quite official; many of the people in the church stirred some, as this did seem quite unusual. Father noticed, but quietly thought that perhaps the men were called by someone in the office and may have just gotten the appointment date confused; or maybe Sunday was the only day they could pick up the carpeting. Oh well, on with mass, and best to not allow the short intrusion to disrupt God's time. The church was a very old and beautiful one, well appointed with the usual lush decorum conducive to praise and glory. A very old and expensive antique wool carpet spanned about a hundred feet as a runner that extended directly down the center aisle.

The two workmen proceeded to quietly and carefully begin rolling the item up from the back of the church, while working their way to the front not far from the little gate to the sanctuary. They then hoisted the heavy roll upon their shoulders while the priest prepared for the morning's sermon. The church filled with praying congregation looked on, trying not to be distracted at the work being quietly carried out before them. The Acme workers marched their cargo down the aisle then disappeared into a panel truck bearing the same company lettering. The carpet was never seen again, nor did *Acme Carpet Cleaning* ever turn up listed in the Yellow Pages.

Obstacles be damned

Even though some of us now held the distinguished title of music instructors, the mere idea that we might be heading towards a life as musicians was more than a few of our respective families could handle. All night gigs, liquor, and a decadent life without financial security were all that some could envision for their sons.

The father of one of our musician friends worked for a government contract electronics business that was doing well in the newly emerging technology industry at that time. The family finally convinced him to abandon music other than as an avocation and hobby, and to take advantage of an employment opportunity for young family members of workers. He would begin a simple job in the "stable" and promising electronics field.

Although we all continued to gig together and make our retreats to River's End quite regularly, Ron was now wearing a shirt and tie (with token name-tag), and working on electronic assembly projects. Security, respect, and promise for his future were traded for the uncertainty of being a musician. Mom was happy, dad had a ride to work, and family was quite relieved that sensibility had prevailed for the young man.

Meanwhile, Richard was still somewhat confused as to what his future would bring, but somehow family pressure was not as intense as with some of his peers. Having been actively interested in electronics, radio, and such, music seemed to remain an ever-present, but illusive associate for me. I promptly registered at a community college in preparation for what I thought would make family happy in the study of *electronic engineering.* I willingly put music aside pretending that it wasn't really important to me, and off to college I went. I measured capacitance, resistance, and learned to use test instruments, that which I should have known more about in ham radio. But the luxury of Doc's mentoring helped me through the back door, and directly to the fun of operating equipment rather than knowing how to repair it.

A few months into the courses I was failing miserably, particularly at math. Grades were very poor, and I had no idea as to what I was doing. Truth to tell, the only way that I made it through high school geometry was the fact that my aunt knew the teacher! I failed algebra, and although I hated the mandatory summer school, I did manage to proudly pass the course with a D!

At the same time, the draft was looming and Vietnam was ever closer as the conflict accelerated. Would I be called? Would I be able to continue in some kind of work? Would I be able to pursue my dreams (whatever that meant) were all questions and confusion quite common to many young men during that time. Militant people would wonder why we just didn't enlist at a time when "our country needed us." Others had serious misgivings about the morality of the Vietnam involvement; nonetheless, we now waited for our fate to be decided by someone and something completely out of our control.

I then decided to switch my major to that of *electronic technology.* For some reason it seemed more doable, and at least I could still consider some kind of job security since I was feeling the pressure of believing that music was not the way to go. And yet, no matter how much I loved my radio hobby, I still could not completely embrace the idea of a career in technology. Even as a musician, I disliked working in recording studio sessions although I had little choice at times. I seemed to remain hopelessly disinterested in the developing recording industry that was a passion for many of my peers. I struggled in school, and ended up dropping all classes with a deplorable grade average and much humiliation.

One early morning, I awoke in my little bed that was only a few feet from the radio station that had always been my friend and companion – not my career, however. I just stared at the ceiling, and to this day I will never forget the vision that I experienced: "Ta' hell wid' em' all!" I said to myself. "I'm going to stay in music, and I don't care what anyone thinks."

That same day, I wrote to a local university to try and register as a Music Major. My grades from the junior college were so bad that I could not enter the university, so they suggested that *Mr. Taesch* might attend another community college until he made up some of the deficits. I then went back to the same college as before in electronics, registered, and was accepted into a music program, but on academic probation the entire time that I was there. The distinguished *Mr.* Taesch kept that to himself, and not a word was spoken to students or their parents. Off to music school I happily went, and never looked back. Mom and Lloyd just smiled at me, and a little twinkle in Lloyd's eye told me all that I needed to know.

"Obstacles are those frightful things you see when you take your eyes off your goal."

– Henry Ford

Suddenly the electronics industry began to fail, which came as a surprise to everyone at that time. Factories closed, and the bottom nearly dropped out of the space and technology field leaving numerous workers unemployed. Many of my friends had gone into "secure" jobs, and most had lost those positions. Richard was the only one that simply would not follow advice to abandon the *unstable* music profession; He was left, however, as the only one who still had a job, but in the music industry. I now think that my students somehow sensed that I had finally come home.

Along with a circle of special friends, I continued to share adventures both on bandstands and with many other interests typical of young men entering the *twenty-something* age group. I was now firmly entrenched in music as an unquestionable career. I often feel that I was not unlike Marc in our eighth grade story about Mahoney '58. Like him, I was never much of a scholar, and at times I've been able to imagine what it might have been like for him. Music and teaching was the only thing that came easy for me, and I sometimes wonder if my decision to pursue it as a life's work was some kind of divine intervention – that which one is *supposed* to do; or perhaps it was simply the easy way out, as it seemed to be the only thing that I could do somewhat well as opposed to a normal vocational choice.

I must ponder, however, that after enduring three certifications from The Library of Congress, perhaps I am doing what I am supposed to do after all. But I will most likely never completely know the answer to the question, and frankly, I have no interest in finding out at this point in time. The future was not for me to know then, and it is not for me to know now.

A dear friend and mentor, who you will soon again meet, often expressed a thought: Richard, just do the work, and the rest will take care of itself. Now all I had to do was, "do the work." That seemed easy enough; at least much easier than spending one's time trying to figure it all out when one grows up.

The lesson here was clearly: *keep your eyes on your goals at all times, and obstacles be dammed.* A very applicable analogy is one that is often in the form of advice for music sight-reading: *"Keep your eye on the eighth note."* In music braille, the eighth note never changes appearance, and all other values are mere additions of a dot 3 or 6 to the braille cell; in print music, use the eighth note as the focal rhythmic point. Since there are rather few primary note values in the entire spectrum of music with all others being only variations of those, keeping one's eye (or braille reading finger) on the mighty eighth note is essential; translation: take your eye or finger off of the goal, and you will surely lose your place and stumble.

Christmas shopping in our wetsuits

Water skiing soon took hold of both Greg and me with a firm grip. The son of the owner of Adler Music Academy where we taught offered to take us with him on his skiing days. He had a nice little ski boat, and we would sometimes volunteer to use our cars for towing it to lakes nearby. He taught us to water ski on short morning trips to the nearby Hansen Dam reservoir; we would often make it back barely in time to transfer from swimsuits into coat and tie to begin the afternoon's lessons. At that time, very few lakes for water sports were close enough to enjoy without major trips and long hours on the road. Hansen Dam was within minutes of our academy and homes, and was a perfect place to learn to ski.

The lake was very small, however, and clearly an inspiration for learning not to fall off of one's ski on a busy day. You see, the ski area was so small that the pattern of a circle was required for boats to travel around the outside perimeter of the lake; if one fell off of the ski, there was no choice but to wait for the boat to make a complete circle before coming back to pick you up. Boaters were accustomed to this arrangement; the most challenging part was keeping one's head clearly above water with hand raised in the air, while boats and skiers under tow would whiz close by you on both sides yelling something to the effect of our aforementioned swamp call - "*eeehooeeee!*" Strange as it may seem, more accidents have been known to happen where there is much more water surface to use. Skiing at the dam could be adequately compared to the "boys only" speed races at the Rainbow Roller Rink on a Friday night – trial by fire, er, water, that is.

We soon tired of depending on friends for our new passion, and decided that we should own our own boat. Neither of us had credit nor cash to accomplish such a thing, so Greg's brother offered to finance the purchase of a 14-foot ski boat, and we would then pay him monthly. Of course top secret was essential; if our parents had found out that we had taken on such a responsibility without their permission, we'd have been in much trouble. Time went by, and the secret was let out. By that time, the folks had already guessed by our strange habits that we had done exactly what we did. We celebrated by taking my mom and stepdad with us on a ski outing to Lake Elsinore on the historic first day of its re-opening after many years of being dry.

During the winter months, we would make the three-hour drive to the great Salton Sea in the Coachella Valley. Water temperatures in the eighties were not unusual even in December, and with nearly four-hundred square miles of water surface, one need not worry about falling off of skis, except whether your boat could find you and your wayward ski. Many trips to the sea followed, and later would find me performing there at yacht clubs and enjoying winter sunshine with my new wife after 1968. Then I did not know that Salton Sea Beach might one day be considered as my potential home.

Meanwhile, we were aware that we were not supposed to take the boat out ourselves without brother Don on weekends. But this particular day was Christmas Eve and a weekday. So we decided that no one would be the wiser if we could bag a few laps at Hansen Dam before getting back to do a bit of Christmas shopping. The water at the dam was colder than imaginable, so with wetsuits upon us, we were the only two skiers on the lake. It was wonderful, and a great time was had. However, time got away from us and little was left to return the boat home, change, and do the shopping that we had planned.

No choice was left but to haul ourselves still dressed in swimsuits and wetsuit tops, boat and trailer behind car, and try to find a place to park both units at the posh Broadway department store in Panorama City. It was approaching dark, and what I would give to have photos of folks watching us park that rig, exit the car in wetsuits and bare feet, then enter the department store with straight faces as though everyone else was dressed as we were. After all, it's California; doesn't everybody go water skiing on Christmas Eve?

* * *

Although living in uncertain times, we continued to work in music, doing gigs, teaching, and the like. Some friends in our circle seemed quite focused on their future in a more conventional way; others were taming obstacles and managing goals fairly well.

Meanwhile, the war was becoming worse by the day; although the air raid sirens rarely sounded now, anxiety was everywhere. We remained ever aware of how or whether we might be affected, continuing with our lives as best that we could.

Suddenly, Greg and I were both called for military service. After the pre-induction physicals and other procedures, we received our classifications. Even though now married, Greg was still called to active duty, and I was somehow passed over. *There but for you, go I.* Essentially as I saw it, he sacrificed his future so that others like me might not have to. And so the wonderful song, *"My Old Friend"** sung by Gregory Hines, will always occupy a very special place in my life. (*Composer: Jimmy Cobb)

All things do change ... 1953 revisited

We met one last time while he was on leave in uniform. We both enjoyed a lunch together at the familiar hangout, Lido Pizza in Van Nuys. Greg went off to his new duty, and no more than a few weeks passed when I received a call from his brother's wife.

"Richard, I don't know where to begin, but Greg is in a hospital in South Vietnam; he stepped on an enemy land mine, and both of his legs are severely shredded; we don't know if he will lose them, or what."

What was there to do now? Absolutely nothing could be done but to wait for the results of numerous surgeries and procedures, and uncertain news to come. Strangely, the knock on the door in 1953 at age ten seemed to pound again in my brain, returning with a fearful presence.

I began to imagine our times together, along with others in "Rivers Six" as we called ourselves, while trying to relive moments from a state of mind then, and how to deal with them now. Time healed some things, but so much of his body was still yet to heal.

He began to recover slowly with the help of his lovely wife, Barbara. I married in 1968, and although clearly stealing ahead into late spring, I am happy to speak of the wonderful visits that my young wife and I had when we traveled to see them.

The family moved from place to place, state to state, while working to settle into some kind of job situation. Children were growing, and what a lovely family they were! His spirit was good, as he never lost a sense of humor or his warm attitude. One visit in late spring found us enjoying a dinner together; my wife suddenly said to him: "Greg, if it's ok, can I ask you a question?"

"Sure!"

"What is it like to receive a *Purple Heart*?" [1]

A Little Vignette for My Story
Contributed by Gregory Febbo

My medical treatment was initiated on the USS Sanctuary, followed by transfers to Tripler Army Hospital, Fort Ord Hospital, and eventually to the VA Hospital in Los Angeles to complete rehabilitation, and where I could reside with my wife Barbara and daughter, Maria.

Dr. Burgess was a very well known Orthopedic Surgeon, and was in charge of our Amputee Clinic. I am sure he was responsible for other clinics and medical areas but that was too long ago for me to remember. He was also responsible for the creation of the *Seattle Foot* which jump-started interest throughout the prosthetic field. He was the founder of the private Prosthetic Research Center in Seattle where ex Boeing engineers helped to create the Seattle Foot.

* * *

Long after many years had passed, and following my marriage in late spring, Greg and I were still able to remain in communication. I was later pleased to hear that he was now serving as assistant to the Chief of Prosthetics at the VA hospital facility in Seattle.

Prior to that time, I had never heard of Dr. Ernest Burgess* or his sister, Lurrine Burgess. My teaching work at Southern California Conservatory of Music in 1976 was still nearly seven years into the future. Moreover, the founding of the school itself by Lurrine in 1971 had not yet come to pass. I joined the SCCM guitar faculty in 1976, and continued occasional visits with Greg and his family; for many years, I was still completely unaware that his boss at the Seattle VA was our Ernie, or that he was our conservatory director's brother.

*See *Prosthetics Outreach Foundation* at: www.pof.com

---

[1] The Korean War had just ended. Sara's father was en-route home to his wife and unborn daughter after serving in the Air Force. Apparently, an enemy plane was unaware of the declaration and fired upon his aircraft. All were lost, and Sara was born without ever knowing him.

"Spend time with me in the green quiet places ..."

(The above photo was taken looking directly across the hills towards *34ᵗʰ Street*)*

explained in Mid Summer

XII.
A Story Yet to Be Told

My next chapter will wander into late spring then venture into the early years of my new life as a very happily married man. It will introduce a number of fun stories that only working musicians ever seem to experience. The earliest of my adventures in the wilds as a hiker will also describe some rather unusual encounters with wildlife.

With St. Francis of Assisi (the patron saint of the animals), I cannot compare, nor would I *ever* encourage complacency to potential danger; but hiking in solitude for many years has taken me close to unusual situations and animal communication that surely will be fun for me to tell in this work; hopefully it will prove entertaining for you. I also hope that the opportunity I have had to shed many myths and fears about the darkness and animal encounters might also help others to enjoy a different view about some of their own fears. My wish for others – if only for a while as a book adventure – is to experience some similar liberation from old demons – common fears that we all share prior to enlightenment. Look forward to many animal encounters come summer.

Before we segue into Late Spring, let's relax a bit and read a little short story that brings some things into better focus, adding a finishing touch to Mid Spring. It is called *A Story Yet to Be Told,* and was written to bring attention to SCCM for the purpose of fund-raising. Its implications tend to span seasons, therefore seemed appropriate here. The chronology covers about 1971 to 2005, and might serve as a kind of isolated microcosm and digest for spring through summer. So, if you desire, take a side trip now before going into *Late Spring;* peek ahead through time along with me, and when we return, perhaps the coming seasons might have more meaning. Although out of date with many later events, the story is only slightly edited for our book; it appears in the general form that it was originally written. Please take a little time to enjoy it. When you arrive at the end of Page 245, you may better see why I chose to include this little microcosm within my story.

Richard E. Taesch

[Reprinted here with permission of "Late Spring" and "Early Summer"]

A STORY YET TO BE TOLD

By Richard Taesch

A story about courage and music;
About ideals, adversity, and success

Born in 1971 in about eight hundred square feet of store-front space, the Southern California Conservatory of Music set out on an incredible and impossible voyage. This voyage would take the little school and all whom it has touched through a thirty-five year journey - a journey from the storefront to the grandeur of a five-acre campus, back again to the store-front, and on to West Hills California where the magic still lived.

This is not a story of that ever-elusive endowment needed to secure the right environment to teach the art of music. It is a story of the people whose lives are different because a few folks still believe that music is just as important as oil, and like all precious resources, it must be shared. Come laugh a little, cry a little and most of all, share in the riches of the little school that never should have been.

Being born into the Burgess family of successful doctors and businessmen, Lurrine Burgess began an uphill struggle to become a musician. Impractical, insolvent, unstable; nevertheless, she finally obtained her degree in music. Feeling lost in a rational world, she awoke one morning with a flash of inspiration that her destiny was to establish a school of music.

The initial struggle immediately progressed from uphill, to a vertical cliff hanging ascent. In 1971 and of all places, Southern California, the idea of a European-type of classical conservatory would never be accepted. Just ask the governing bodies who must define the school's function and academic classification - now you have a challenge!

Miss Burgess opened the school in a shabby, vacant machine shop. She went to potential grant-makers asking for such absurd items as pianos for her faculty (non-existent), and for her students of which there were four. Their question: "How do you expect to run a school?"

Such went the general gist in the early days. Told that her crazy idea would never fly, the tenacious Director and future President of what was to become a first-rate California non-profit, public benefit corporation imitated the bumblebee, which – according to the laws of physics - should not be capable of flight. According to one SCCM faculty member of 30 years whose biography would later appear in *Who's Who in America*: "Well, Lurrine, look at it this way... if it was not for the dreamers, the practical people of the world would have nothing to do."

The little venture gained full non-profit 501(c) (3) corporate status in 1972, and expanded into a whopping 1,700 square feet of storefront campus. Soon the Conservatory became a California Private Postsecondary, degree-granting institution. This authorization remained in effect until 1995 when a re-organization of state education administration no longer allowed for degrees to be given by the school.

Students began coming from everywhere in the 1970's. Through a belief in the school and where it wanted to go, major foundations such as Weingart, Irvine, Jones, and Disney made possible four beautiful studio upright Baldwin pianos and three soundproof teaching modules.

Impractical, humble, shabby - all of the worst descriptions were quite applicable. But pride and a strong purpose of destiny ignored such things. Some of the finest teaching faculty would be attracted to the Southern California Observatory ... er, Southern California Conservancy ... er - oh well, "The Conservatory" as many have come to know it.

Hal Johnson, founder of the SCCM Composition Department, was once awarded a certificate of appreciation personally by actress Bette Davis for his contributions to the Hollywood Canteen - a special center for entertainment of military soldiers during World War II. Among many of Hal's accomplishments was the organization and implementation of the former SCCM Degree Program structure.

All of the nine degree-grantees in the school's history studied composition with Hal, and his graduates still stand tall in the music industry. Among them is the musical director for one of the largest video game producers in the world. Another is a major music industry arranger and composer. All of them studied from Hal's unique textbooks titled, *"Practical Composition,"* a set of texts for which he willed the copyrights to SCCM upon his death in 1997. Hal's books are still awaiting publication - another project the lean SCCM administrative staff has not the time, nor the funds to complete.

Hal's works ranged from chamber music to documentaries, from symphonies to pop songs, and several beautiful chamber operas, which have been performed by SCCM students. He wrote for many early television shows, and through his association with band-leader Martin Denny, SCCM was offered the donation of Mr. Denny's exotic and authentic musical instruments used in a popular series of recordings for which Hal arranged and produced. Unfortunately, there was not room in the school archive for this precious donation, therefore, it was never acquired.

Hal's career was tragically cut short by the onset of Parkinson's disease which made it impossible to continue sharing his vast knowledge with students. His manuscripts of many years of musical success remain in the SCCM archive today - buried in storage, along with many other treasures. [Relocated with his family, ca. 2014]

Even Miss Burgess, a registered librettist of children's operas, found time to teach as well as serve as director, office manager, bookkeeper, etc., etc. Her "Children's Musical Theatre" (later called *Young Musical Theatre*) program performed original children's operas every quarter for nearly all the years since the school's inception. Sadly, upon her death in 2005, the widely loved Musical Theatre died at SCCM along with her.

In addition to a teacher of voice, conducting, musicology, and music theory, Miss B also performed miracles with children's singing, molding them into serious performers each quarter. A large costume wardrobe was created in-house over the years, and a small, well-equipped theatre became an icon in the well-known storefront. Because the children's shows became so loved and respected, several national opera companies even borrowed the scores to produce their own children's operas. Publication of the many productions originating at the conservatory is only a glimmer of hope for the *someday* department.

It is impossible to describe the many ways that Musical Theatre touched the lives of so many children: the deaf child who learned to sing on pitch by sensing vibration; the blind child who learned stage blocking and theatre techniques from his sighted peers; several generations of children in the same families returning quarter after quarter as their young voices and self-confidence grew.

Early on, audiences would come unannounced and without reservations. On one occasion, the fire department raided a performance just as it began. After watching the entire show from various locations about the stage (no, they did not pay the admission fee), the eight firemen then ordered everyone out into the parking lot and counted 111 heads. The theatre was supposed to hold no more than 49. Since then, reservations were strongly advised.

As if the school had not achieved enough significant heights for its short existence, in the 1980's Mr. Grant Horrocks joined the SCCM piano faculty. He later became head of the piano department, and soon became Conservatory Division chair. He joined Richard Taesch in the new Braille Music Division in 1993.

Grant brought much pride to SCCM when he became Los Angeles Representative for Royal Conservatory of Music Examination Center. The center was based in Toronto, Canada, where he earned his diploma in piano performance. At one point, his program at SCCM conducted the examinations of twelve blind SCCM students along with all of the candidates in Southern California. Moreover, the second highest grade in the state that year was a blind SCCM student! Among many duties at the school, Grant watched over the prestigious scholarship recitals held on Sunday evenings each quarter. Strings, flutes, guitars, pianos, all performers of award winning competitions and orchestras, graced the small recital room of the original building, and later at the new campus, for nearly six years. Music filled the air, and the word "practical" was rarely spoken.

The Braille Music Division clearly brought a new world into the little school; by 1999, SCCM became the only school of music in the world to host a fully functional facility for blind students wishing to study music. In the program's early development, it was often difficult to maintain the necessary dignity to posture the BMD at large. In one humorous incident while the venture was struggling for survival, it was scheduled to present students at a local Kiwanis club dinner. Upon meeting with the Kiwanis officials on an afternoon before the event, Richard and a colleague rushed to the country club to meet the committee - late as usual - not yet in dress clothes.

Driving up a mountainous road to the country club, they stopped the car (which had no reverse gear) and proceeded to duck behind a tree for a change into white shirts and ties. With dressing not yet complete, along passed the committee members in their car glaring at the strange-looking individuals who appeared out-of-place in such an environment. After the meeting as the group said their goodbyes in the parking lot, the two *executives* found a way to delay their departure so as not to bring attention to the get-away-car seen earlier. It was always up to discussion as to whether they did not want the committee to recognize the car from the costume change, or whether it might be undesirable for them to witness the *successful* department heads pushing their ailing car out of a parking space.

By the year 2000, the SCCM Braille Music Division enrollment grew to well over thirty blind students. At a new 5-acre campus, the school would often house resident blind students. Some would come from such prestigious schools as Yale or Eastman School of Music, in order to study braille music, piano, and Computer Music Arts at SCCM.

The worldwide network, MENVI - *Music Education Network for The Visually Impaired*, was founded at, and continued to maintain its headquarters at SCCM. MENVI is a free service, [then] sponsored and funded by the conservatory. The network provides a committee of specialists who remain available to blind music students and their families worldwide. Advisors are all blind musicians and students. A fine website was constructed and is currently maintained by a young blind man - a former student of SCCM. (www.menvi.org)

Conservatory success stories are many, but particularly noteworthy is that of a blind child whose name is Sean. His special education resources felt that he was too learning-disabled to ever read braille. He would remain illiterate, as his disability was considered far too challenging. In the mid-nineties, SCCM began an outreach program at a district school for visually impaired children. The music teacher felt that he might have a musical gift, and asked if the program would take close notice of him. It was discovered that he had what is known as "perfect pitch," otherwise defined as tonal frequency recognition.

The boy was given a full need-scholarship at SCCM, and in two lessons he was reading braille music while singing all pitches from the dots under his fingers. Within two months, he was reading literary braille at his school. He has since passed RCM examinations and learns his vocal repertoire completely from the contracted braille text. The music teacher, who introduced him to SCCM, would later retire from the school district and join the SCCM Braille Music Division faculty.

No story would be complete without the search for a new home. And so SCCM has searched for a larger facility since its inception. Funding, location, administration, support, all seemed to be out of reach for the little school that never should have happened. Property after property was investigated. Everything was always out of reach; always beyond the means of the school that survived on love, contributions, and yes, tenacity.

Dr. Ernest Burgess, the brother of SCCM's founder, became quite intrigued with Lurrine's vision in the early eighties. Dr. Burgess was a world-renowned orthopedic surgeon, and was also founder of the Prosthetics Outreach Foundation based in Seattle, Washington. Dr. Burgess was the inventor of an artificial foot for Vietnam veteran amputees. He began to pledge scholarship support to the school, and encouraged the search for a new campus. At one unexpected meeting, faculty member, Richard Taesch, discovered that Dr. Burgess and he shared a common bond. Unknown to him then, Richard's long-time school friend had come to work for Dr. Burgess in the Amputee Clinic, and worked as an Assistant to the Chief of Prosthetics at the VA hospital in

Seattle. It is indeed a small world (?). Dr. Burgess's Prosthetics Outreach Foundation still exists today.

In 1995, plans were made to obtain a beautiful 93-acre parcel in the Angeles National Forest. A building had been planned for the future, but through strange quirks of events a large estate became the preferred choice of the SCCM Board of Directors. After negotiating the purchase of the property through a deed in lieu, the school failed to obtain a conditional use permit.

The remainder of our story brings us full circle. After six years of unsuccessful attempts to obtain the conditional use permit, SCCM exhausted all of its funds, and the beautiful campus had to be sold with little left over. Dr. Burgess died unexpectedly, leaving the conservatory without his dedicated support. Once again, the school was back to only the magical place at which it began. The cost was high in the loss of the campus, as precious funds had been spent on maintenance and on legal services that were ineffective.

Along with many problems, the venture briefly took a severe toll on the spirit of the little conservatory. The flourishing Braille Music Division now had no home, and the resident blind students once housed there had no place to come study. On Saturdays, the satellite campus would once come alive with the energy and music of enthusiastic blind students. A brave faculty of eight professionals and volunteers worked continually with risk that the school's presence could be terminated at any time, as city permits were still not fully secured. Braille Music Division ceased its services for nearly two years. Exhausting nearly all left over funds from the sale, a leased building was found and renovated in West Hills California. Once again, the school hangs [hung] on the precipice of extinction. Funds are exhausted, and the struggle continues.

The story doesn't end here. Yes, the students who once graced the beautiful estate campus now have [had] a new home. The funds realized by the sale were not adequate to re-invest in real property for the school, but were carefully measured in order to obtain the leased building in which to re-open. With the passing of Miss Burgess, West Hills became the primary location for SCCM. [All facilities closed, March 2013]

The prestigious Fritz Burns Foundation continued to contribute substantially until Miss Burgess's passing. Having lost the support of foundations, operating funds are [were] now exhausted. Lurrine Burgess, Dr. Burgess, and many others - along with all the students and teachers - made an impractical dream a reality. There is no one who can take that dream from them. SCCM is [was] no less than a place of wonder, and yet the journey has [had] only begun.*

The Beginning…

*Revised again on 6-5-2020 (for this remembrance)

LATE SPRING
XIII. Ports in the storms

Circa 1964 to 1968 – a chronological kaleidoscope

Webster's applies *kaleidoscopic* (adj.) to "anything that constantly changes." The years following my high school graduation, my mother's re-marriage, and events from recent chapters – up until my own marriage in 1968 – seem to blend into a myriad of changing new adventures. Life and future goals were not yet completely defined, and now earning his own way, Richard was able to enjoy a fairly carefree existence spending money on cars, hobbies, and having fun.

It was rather unusual for a young man of *twenty-something* to be content living at home with his parents, but I was away many days of the week traveling to music gigs, teaching, practicing, and going to school; so it was more like renting a private room in a boarding house but with your family nearby. That home was to me a warm shelter and remained as such even after divorce.

Some of the escapades in this chapter may be slightly out of order kaleidoscopically at times, but all include familiar *ports* – those that provide refuge for one during the post-adolescent growing years. Perhaps we might think of our late spring as another microcosm, that is a kind of season within a season.

No, we won't be hearing much about *Casanova's* loves, at least not yet. Being rather withdrawn at that time, I preferred to observe my friends' heartaches as opposed to creating those of my own. I did, however, make up for some lost time after divorce (… to be confessed in summer); my wife was clearly my first love and my first real romance. Like my friends the coyotes, perhaps many of us are much like them in some ways. I once learned in a nature talk that – contrary to popular belief – they do not run in packs, only in families, and that they mate only once – and for life. Nonetheless, 1968 brought a new order and a more diligent timeframe, but for now some weightlessness was still to be enjoyed.

Early adventures on the bandstand:
UCLA Fraternity Row, et al

Several of my musical friends and I formed a kind of society band called *The Rhythmaires,* which doubled for top-forty as well. Now today, a name like *The Eclectic Scrotum* might be more appropriate; however, a combined dance band and top-forty theme was well received within the social club and hotel wedding circles in the sixties; and believe it or not, even in the college frat houses. A very busy booking agent soon began contracting the little unit for weekly jobs, and we were seldom without work. We would mount the bandstand with uniform coats and bow ties; but as soon as the rock energy began to rise, we could easily duck behind amps and come out with phony wigs for anything from Beatles to Stones, James Brown to Little Richard, Big Dick, or whatever your preference.

Upon arriving at our job site on one particular week, we became aware that it was a large estate ranch with much acreage around it, guarded at the front entrance by a tall and tough-looking Indian man (as in American-type: hair-band, feathers, tomahawk, and all). Next to him was a small bar equipped with beer keg and cups intended to lubricate the guests as they arrived. Tickets had been sold, and admittance required proof of purchase and included consumption of at least one large container poured skillfully from the contents of the keg.

The fraternity decided to hold their homecoming party at the ranch in Chatsworth California, instead of the Gayley Street frat house in West L.A. For most of the gigs that we played, we were able to control and pass over alcohol while we worked; but following the initial requirement for admission, we had decided to make an exception this time. The band was graciously welcomed, and many helped us to lug equipment from cars and to place it in the selected performance area.

As the evening (and morning) progressed, our somewhat virgin bodies had consumed more beer than any of us thought could be produced in any one brewery. To this day, I have no idea how I arrived home, who drove my car back, or how I found my way into bed without my parents waking up. For years thereafter, simply driving by the brewery located near a freeway that I often used, and while smelling the hops and grains in the air, would send me into a state of near-terminal nausea.

After a few similar episodes with the same miserable results, I would find myself far more skillful at sneaking into our house late in the night; and when ejection of such toxins became imminent, I would simply open the back window in my room, hang sinful head out into the night and covertly proceed. However, I did often wonder – at 2 or 3am in the morning – just what the gagging sounded like to the little convent of nuns directly across the street. Perhaps they thought that a neighbor had acquired a special breed of dog, and it was just barking to be let out.

As time went on, there was not one of the UCLA frat houses on *fraternity row* that we did not play for parties every weekend. The band was quite popular, and even as the rock scene began to overshadow us, we continued to work. Sororities, military bases, hotels, and beauty pageants were venues that kept us busy continuously. Every altercation imaginable was experienced during those times, including beer being poured down the bell of our saxophone player's horn, stale bread rolls being thrown at a country club maitre d' by a very angry best man at a wedding, raids, fights, and much more that would surely amuse the reader. But do take heed younger readers; as from a dedicated observer and occasional participant, alcohol abuse is simply not worth the risks in any *season!*

And yet no story would be complete without the journey to a distinguished presidential campaign dinner that required a $1,000 per plate contribution.

Upon driving up to unload our gear at the rear entrance of the auditorium (yes, musicians were still required to use the back door), I noticed a large truck unloading what appeared to be hundreds of foam covered plates that looked like take-out dinners. The truck was lettered with: *Lone Fried Chicken.* Workers as busy as a two-way freeway of ants proceeded to roll handcart stacks of the curious items into the kitchen facility. Hundreds of very well dressed political guests sat visiting and sipping, while distinguished waiters did what distinguished waiters do. Cocktail music was in the air while the dance band quietly brought equipment through the kitchen heading for the bandstand inside.

As I passed Tom the bass player while carting his gear on a hand-truck, I said: "Tom, is it my imagination, or did I actually see what I just saw?"

"Nope, you got it; bigger n' stink, they're serving take out chicken and passing it off for a grand a plate!"

The tact de jour was to open each two-dollar dinner, plop it on a fancy plate, add a little parsley, and voila! We now have a thousand-dollar dinner – bon appetite!

Now I could say that I had seen it all, but wait; it does get better. You see, seldom do planners of such events consider that anyone outside of their cloistered circle will notice "inside track" activities. Musicians are not unlike servants or waiters; they look straight ahead, do their job, and oh, the things that they see and hear could create scandals unlimited. But everyone knows that you can't trust a musician not to exaggerate a good story; this one just happens to be true. (Sorry, garage band rock groups; if these stories don't seem real, your time will come.)

On another occasion while arriving at an installation banquet for the _blank_ Company, we were asked to wait in the restaurant until the speeches were finished. Well, rather long-winded speakers took from 9pm until near midnight to wrap up their installation ceremonies. Meanwhile, the band sat patiently dressed in tuxedos while waiting in a booth that was only separated from the guests by a thin screen. Talks went on, and on, but soon the speeches somehow caught the attention of our naive – not yet wise-to-the-world – young group (text paraphrased):

Well, folks, I know that we are not too popular with our customers these days, as the shortages are causing much increased costs for them. But the truth is that we have more products than we know what to do with, and the only way that we can bring prices into reality is to create a shortage.

Now the exact verbiage of that recollection is loosely remembered here, but in 2011 one should easily recognize the concept, I'm sure. Sipping tonic water as was customary then, we all stopped our conversation, stared at each other, dropped mouths open and froze in disbelief as to what we had just heard, quite aware that this was a major company event. *"Too soon auld; too late schmart"* was a wonderful caption that I once saw hanging in a popular German restaurant. How true it is.

Later in an entrepreneurial advertising attempt, I decided that I would sit down to my mechanical typewriter and make a little flyer. The purpose was aimed at soliciting some work for our band, including some clubs and resorts that were out of town. The flyers were mailed, and as expected, no results - that is until a phone call came from the manager of the then known Holly House motel and restaurant in Salton City California. I was overjoyed, as not only would we be paid, but we would also be given a complimentary room for the duration of the gig with all food to be included. It was during the winter months, and while everyone in L.A. was dealing with cold weather, just three hours of driving distance away we were spending the days lounging by the pool, or water skiing on the sea whenever we were able to hitch a free tow from a boater.

For those unfamiliar with such a place (and many people are, it seems), the Salton Sea is a strange anomaly within an ancient sea sink thought once to be part of the Gulf of California. It reformed in 1906 from flooding due to an engineering failure, resulting in the largest body of water in California, and perhaps the only inland sea in the country. It is about 400 square miles of water surface. At 235 feet below sea level, the winter temperatures are quite warm. Water sports were at one time very popular there, and the *Salton City 500* speed boat races were once known the world over. Its appearance is not unlike the Dead Sea, or the Sea of Galilee in the old world. Current times have brought many problems to the once called "*California Rivera*" in the form of flooding and excessive salinity.

Early one morning as the sleepy musicians waltzed through the coffee shop for breakfast, the drummer (beard and hair not unlike a large shaggy dog whose hair left only his eyes and the tip of his nose visible) attracted the attention of several conservative-looking folks. Keep in mind that in the sixties, such an appearance was a statement of protest, and not at all typical of a musician who knew how to play the foxtrot. One gentleman made a comment about what kind of *crap* this band must be playing in the dining room. I overheard the comment and politely said to him:

"No, truly we play Glen Miller, Dorsey, and Goodman swing and dance music."

He responded, "I'll bet it's more like Glen Campbell." At that time even GC was considered to be rock music by some conservative types.

The first evening that we took to the bandstand, I think no one must have ever seen a bearded dog walking upright in a suit and tie before. Chris, the drummer, quietly took his place as the offended gentleman watched in disbelief while dining; our first set opened with a medley from the Cole Porter Songbook. Needless to say, much crow was to be eaten along with the man's first entrée that evening. A good ending: he danced to nearly every number, including Glen Miller and Glen Campbell tunes.

Many engagements at the Holly House followed over a period of a year or two. One such trip required that we play on the back of a truck in an open-air festival. My first influence for jazz guitar was the late Barney Kessel, a prominent jazz player at the time as well as a busy studio musician. After the truck bed gig was finished, a kindly gentleman came up to me and (temporarily) made my day with the compliment that I sounded a little like Barney at times. I was overjoyed, for to me this was the ultimate identity since I had little or no interest in rock players at that time.

Fearing that he might have given a false sense of confidence, he added: "I didn't mean that you are as good as him; I said that you sound *a little* like him – in spots." I was disappointed, but thanked him nevertheless.

Such things are not unusual for young ambitious players in the early days of their careers, as youthful ego seeks to impress listeners and fellow musicians. Perhaps one of the best lines that I heard a more experienced musician say to a neophyte sharing the same bandstand was: "Man, you really sounded good – *in places.*" Or perhaps upon parting at the end of a gig while shaking hands: "It was a great *pressure* playing *against* you." Yes, I do suppose that we all have our day putting down those who have not yet risen to our own particular level of incompetence. Ah, to be twenty-something again. Not me; no way, no how!

A time for other things: looking back at a memory or two

Musical engagements and performance continued in my life until at least 1998, but during the pre-nuptial years before 1968, radio remained my port from which to depart into warm familiar places. As a young ham I would admire and envy the large towers and powerful radio stations that the old-timers could afford, especially since they often owned large lots on which magnificent tall antenna structures could be placed. Worldwide communication was easy for them; there were no satellites, no Internet, no cable – only point to point *free* global communication.

Families of soldiers in foreign war theaters were kept in touch routinely through Amateur Radio by such services as "MARS," then meaning Military Amateur (or Affiliate) Radio Service. Major world disasters resulted in licensed hams pulling emergency communications together, while saving lives every year. That which we call *wireless* today seems to serve mostly as a visual marketing strategy as compared to "cordless."

One afternoon, a few novice ham friends and I decided to bicycle for a visit to a fellow whose antenna tower seemed to span half a city block right in the center of town. He owned the entire property facing two streets back to back, and we would often see him climbing that coveted structure while doing repairs. Such arrays were quite commonplace then and even welcomed by some knowledgeable neighbors; during power outages or natural disasters such as earthquakes, amateur operators often became a communication lifeline to many. Towers could extend as high as 60-100 feet in the air with guy lines spanning a half-acre or more.

This particular day our hero just happened to be working outside, and when we rolled up to his fence we began to chat with him. He was quite friendly, and invited us in to see his rig. An entire outside screened-in room was dedicated to the power transformer alone; it had been bought as surplus from an old AM broadcast station, and was probably capable of running a transmitter of 50,000 watts or more.

The power limit for amateur stations at that time was 1,000 watts input; more than that may have been used, but was strictly against

FCC rules. However, no rule said one could not possess a station of higher capabilities, only that excessive power was never to be used for licensed amateur transmitting. FCC also reserved the right to take control of any station at any time, and designate it to emergency communication if needed. Thus the capitalized title, *Amateur Radio Service,* obligates licensed hams to remain available if ever called upon; in concept, this arrangement is not unlike a radio equivalent that might be compared to the National Guard.

As we entered the man's operating room, often called a *hamshack,* racks and racks of radio gear towered above our heads – some homebrew, some state of the art commercial gear of the day. Today, large heavy vintage antique radios are often affectionately termed as "boat anchors." His desk held microphones and telegraph keys, as well as what is known as semi-automatic keys – those where weights allow the repetitive action of the Morse code dot characters. It was quite obvious, even to us, that this station could perhaps rival one of the local rock and roll broadcast facilities in the power department, but knowing the legality of such a thing, we were a bit hesitant to ask him just how much it could run.

As the conversation warmed up it slipped out that, if needed, he could push up to about 10 kilowatts, which is 10,000 watts of radio frequency input power. If ever convicted of such a violation, an amateur could face severe fines and prison sentences, so it is not to be taken lightly. Sometime after that exciting visit, we had read in the paper that a number of radio hams had been caught running illegal power levels during special contest events in order to gain a winner's edge. Sometime thereafter, several hams' call signs appeared in the news to be among a list of culprits. Oops!

Now typically, one might ask how an FCC agent could possibly know such a thing without being physically at the station itself to log its transmitter settings. No, informants were not among those who are now urged to snitch on their fellow drivers for what they might *suspect* as drunk driving; and most anyone who had seen a violator's radio room would not know how to read those settings anyway (perhaps like some informants). However, during contest periods, a very clever system was said to catch the "big guns" in the act, so to speak. This account may be based somewhat on hearsay, but seemed to be well known gossip to many at the time.

Apparently, the agents – equipped with a panel truck and rotating antenna on the roof – would set up in an open area so as to draw a signal reading on a station; they would record what is known as a *field-strength* indication from a distance away. An FCC rep would then knock on the door and officially ask if he might be able to take a power reading as routine practice. If the operator became aware that an agent was about to ring his doorbell, he most likely reduced power to the legal limit; not unlike when you drop your speed suddenly on the freeway as you spot a policeman ahead.

Readings were taken, and once compliance was verified, the agent politely apologized for the interruption and assured the ham that this was only a routine check randomly carried out during some contests. He then thanked the operator and headed back to the monitoring station. At that point, comparing the reading to the original one would show a dramatic decrease of power; it was then quite easy to prove that there was a violation of federal communications law. Gotcha!

Some of my favorite radio stories with a few heroes too

During World War II, letters would find their way to families of captured soldiers from folks who stood by listening to short-wave radio broadcasts. They would collect information from propaganda stations describing the capture of loved ones as prisoners of war. Such broadcasts were said to be common during wartime, as the information of captured individuals by name was believed to weaken the morale of the Allied forces. The listeners would seek out, and write letters to families of the soldiers, letting them know that they were at least alive and well. Thus they became *ports* in wartime storms for many very worried families.

There are many intriguing stories of underground radio operations during wartimes that have appeared in books, radio, and movies for generations. I once gave the gift of a recently published true story in a book called *"World War II Radio Heroes: Letters of Compassion."* Author: Lisa Spahr (*Copyright 2008*). (The author's grandfather had been captured as a POW.)

107

An article called *"Treachery in the Air"* (*"Fighting the Radio Fifth Column"*), appeared in a September 1940 issue of *The American Magazine*. The opening description of the article was about American efforts to track down radio spies hiding themselves amongst U.S. Amateur Radio operators. Such was an effort to undermine America's defenses in World War II.[1] Romance and adventure on the magic of the radio waves was quite common in days of old, and remains quite a contrast to what today is known as "spam" and some unfortunate online activities.

One part of the article describes a worsening situation that lead to severe FCC limiting of ham radio operations. At that time, there were in excess of 50,000 licensed amateur stations. Radio pirates would bootleg their assigned call letters, which made it extremely difficult to hunt spies down.[2]

During that time, it was prohibited for American amateurs to communicate with foreign operators, whether or not they were in neutral countries.*

Another intriguing story that was popular gossip in our own neighborhood was with respect to a tract house situated in the center of the San Fernando Valley. As kids, we always noticed the tall radio tower in the back yard of the house, but knew very little about the owners. Perhaps the story was a tale spread by the neighborhood kids, or perhaps it was true.

It seemed that neighbors would report that no one ever saw the occupants of that house come out of doors during a period of World War II, other than to pick up milk delivered to their doorstep or for the morning paper. Strangers could be seen coming and going, but never the family itself. Once the war was over, it was rumored that spies had taken over the home, keeping the family captive in order to facilitate secret messages by means of the very powerful Amateur Radio station there. Recorded facts may or may not be written somewhere, but how fun it was to consider the possibility that it just could have been the truth. The antenna was certainly a familiar icon to many, even well into the seventies.

No direct quotes appear in this description, other than the article title.

The lighthouse

I do hope, dear reader, that I have not bored you with technical stories that may be of no interest to you; but my adventures are my memoirs as well, and remain a part of me. I would like to think that such things might even be similar circumstantially to some of your own, even though we surely must have different points of reference. For example, each of us has reached for some lifeline at one time or another; a familiar street when you may be lost; the comfort of waking up in your own bed after a dream of being alone and confused; a friend, spouse, or parent when stricken with grief, all become "beacons" at times of stress. The little red light on the water tower back in winter – the one in my first trailer park at about age four – was my first non-human beacon. It was the one that told me when I was to return home to safety.

My own radio tower story, although not life-threatening, was also a beacon that I remember as a very young man while driving my first car.

My friend and I decided to take my little 1951 Chevy coupe for a trip to Ventura. We carried no money for gas, any food or water, and there were no cell phones then to call for help. Whether there was adequate tread on the old tires, I don't remember, but a car was a car, and as far as we were concerned it was supposed to take us somewhere, somehow.

Off we drove some ninety miles up the California coast on *El Camino Real*, the romantic Ventura Highway – happy and carefree. Arriving on the outskirts of the town, there was suddenly a strange sound coming from under the hood of the car soon to be followed by the engine stopping. We pulled over to the side of the road which just happened to be a parking area; we stopped safely out of the way and proceeded to look at each other: now what? I opened the hood of the car as though I knew what I was looking for, and was disappointed to see nothing that I could recognize.

"Well Mitch, I guess we best call for help. Have you got any change?"

"Nope."

There we sat; no phone, no money to make a call, and clearly up that old creek without a paddle. "Our parents are just gonna love this dumb ass caper; that is if we can ever find a way to get in touch with one of them."

I then remembered a story that I had once read about a lost child who recognized a familiar structure like the one she lived in. She walked up to the door and knocked. When the door opened, she asked:

"Do you know of anyone who lives in a house that looks just like yours?"

"Why yes," said the man; "I saw one just like it in the next village."

"Could you tell me where that is?" asked the girl.

"It's just down that road and a few kilometers to the right." With that information she was able to find her home, as the description was familiar to her and no doubt the right one.

"Mitch, our problems are over." I said. "Let's start walking toward the town; when we see a ham radio tower, we'll ask the owner to radio someone in our hometown and have the operator there make a phone call for us."

We walked for what seemed to be hours and saw nothing that resembled the familiar structure that we sought. Suddenly there it was: a sixty-foot tower with a three-element beam antenna on top of it, gloriously gracing the afternoon sky just like a lighthouse beacon for a lost ship.

We shyly walked up to the door and knocked just like the lost child in the story. A kind-looking man answered, and curiously asked if there was something that we wanted to sell. I said "no sir, but my call letters are Kn6TOB; my friend and I have broken down and have no way to contact help. Can you run a phone patch into Van Nuys to my mom for us, and ask her to send someone to tow us back?"

At that time radio relays were common, and the man knew just what he had to do. Although we were just kids, my novice call letters immediately created a bond, and the camaraderie associated with being a fellow Amateur Radio operator simply kicked into play. He asked us to wait outside, and what my mother's phone number was. Within a few minutes he returned and said: "Someone is on the way." He had contacted another amateur who in turn made the local call for us. No toll costs were incurred, and the rescue was now underway. A *port in the storm* and another beacon had been successfully located.

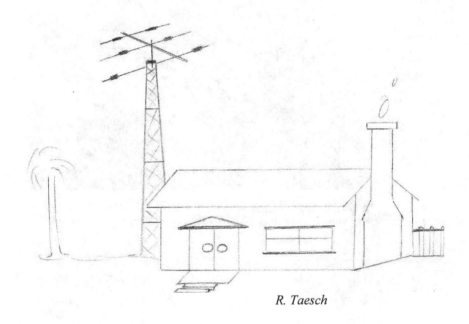

R. Taesch

[1] *The American Magazine,* September 1940, Page 44; Article by: Donald E. Keyhoe and John J. Daly;   Copyright, 1940, by the Crowell-Collier Publishing Company

[2] Ibid, Page 45

RHYTHMAIRES played at the Holly House for the Women's Club In stallation Dinner-Dance held in February. They will return April 6.

(Photo, circa 1967; a newsletter now out of print)

XIV. Prelude to 1968

Some pre-marital flashbacks

Memorable adventures, a desire to share them, and the lessons learned from them seem to supply much inspiration for many books and autobiographies. Even at a very young age, I was never in short supply of such times, and the joy of re-telling them to my new wife during our marriage was always very rewarding as it has become here. We would often sit for hours sipping hot cocoa in the winter or cool lemonade in the summer, and trade fun stories of our own childhoods.

We were not much more than children ourselves when we married in 1968; I was only 24, and Sara was 18. But when she and I had the opportunity of visiting my friends, it was as though she knew them. And so it was, as my little stories of our escapades had entertained her many times before actually meeting. Her and my stories were always interesting, as they were a tangible part of both our growing up.

Many of the places that I had frequented during bachelorhood or in my early youth were re-visited again after becoming married. They provided me with familiar places to share with my new spouse, and helped to retain a certain amount of freshness in the early days of our courtship and marriage. Conversely, many of the memorable places that we visited together then became those that I would share with others after our parting in 1980.

As to our *chronological kaleidoscope,* I have again chosen to visit some adventures of late spring out of sequence. Many just seem to be emerging unexpectedly, as though by some unexplainable subconscious thread – a kind of spirit crying out to be remembered at that pertinent moment so as not to become forgotten in time. Others are seen in my mind suddenly springing to life while writing of new episodes chronologically within the seasons. Nevertheless, the overall sequence of events provides the milestones of remembrance, while flashbacks and projections serve like musical ornamentation enhancing a current motif within the variations on a theme.

* * *

During the years from 1964 to about 1987, no trip to Palm Springs seemed complete without a trip to the famous Italian restaurant, *Georgio's*. As I understand the history, Georgio's was an integral part in the early development of the desert oasis. Indian Avenue was the main street leading into the picturesque hideaway village, known then mostly to movie stars and romantic storytellers. The little bistro was on the right side of the road as one drove into town, quite hard to miss, and known to all as an icon even though very simplistic compared with many found today.

How does one write about Georgio's? Where does one begin? I suppose if you have never seen the real thing – the red tablecloths, the candle wax melted down over the basket-cloaked Chianti bottles – then you may as well skip to the next chapter. However, it is best described within the little caption that Mr. Georgio himself professed; loosely remembered: *In Roma, itsa Alfredo's; in Palma Springa, itsa Georgio's.* Many a trip to Georgio's was made with my wife and me, and a few with new friends followed after 1980.

A couple would enter the modest but warm facility, and after being seated, a bottle of red wine was placed upon the table; there was no label and no plastic seal on the spout. The cork was simply placed in the bottle as though the wine was homemade – and *home-*made it was! One would naturally plan to not drive home immediately (if at all) following the feast, as this wine was like none other I have ever tasted – my French and Italian heritage notwithstanding. It seemed to roll down your throat like a velvet spirit straight from heaven. Upon entering the place, Mr. Georgio himself would sit in your booth and welcome you while treating you and your date as though royalty, even though photos of celebrity patrons covered the walls. Gifts and souvenir menus were provided complimentarily.

One couldn't help but to notice that when a lady entered the powder room, after a fashion there would sometimes be a musical fanfare played throughout the entire restaurant; a bell would ring, and a resounding applause among the regulars would commence. Well, it seemed that inside of the ladies room there was a very artistic painting of a gentleman high up on the wall; he had no clothing except that of a cloth over his privates. The cloth was within reach of anyone who came close to the painting, and needless to say, it was an open invitation to consider lifting it to see what was under. After all, if one glanced around first, a girl could be assured that no self-respecting lady would be the wiser. Naturally, curiosity usually won.

However, if the distinguished and respectable patron did lift that cloth to see what was under it, the fanfare and bells would toll outside in the restaurant while making it quite clear to all just who lifted the kilt when exiting the restroom. Busted! And of course there was the hardcore regular, the lady who would proudly exit then take a full bow while joyfully accepting credit for the peek.

Ah, but humiliation was not reserved just for the ladies. In the gentlemen's room was the lovely portrait of a beautiful Italian woman directly over the urinal. When one would admiringly look up to her while tending to business, the smiling eyes would gradually peer down on target to one's member in hand.

And so the fun went; but oh the food was wonderful, and the wine, like no other. Only my mother (and Greg's) could make Italian food that tasteful. Georgio's was one of those pleasures that I described earlier – discovered well before I was married, and quite by accident as a result of an earlier adventure worth telling here.

Sadly, upon visiting Palm Springs years later, Georgio's was gone; only the high-tech so-called *Italian* clones were left – those with pink décor, chrome table legs, and glass tops with pale red cloths under them so that what you spilled can be scooped easily up after you've tipped and are happily gone. Yes, "virtual reality" certainly does exist in places other than the Internet.

Greg and I made regular trips to the Salton Sea before his marriage, and well before mine. He had recently bought a new 1963 Chevrolet Impala, and loved to travel whenever possible. During our water skiing ventures earlier, we remembered that it was often warm there even in the winter months, and the nights brought tropical water temperatures that invited night swimming and skinny-dipping in warm phosphor-lit salt water. A three-hour drive was well worth the reward, and a return home before 2am would leave no one of our parents the wiser – uh, so we thought. One must pass through the Palm Springs area while traveling to Salton. One particular night returning from a routine moonlight swim, his car stopped and we were hopelessly stranded.

We were just outside of the city limits on Interstate 10; the winds were blowing so strongly that, when we decided the only alternative was to hike into Palm Springs, we actually had to lock arms to avoid being blown off of the bridge that crossed over the freeway. Into town several miles we walked, arriving many hours later. We were able to make a phone call to the Auto Club and have the car towed to a garage in town. We slept in the car, and upon waking at daylight began to contemplate what chaos would be going on back home as a result of our obvious absence.

We did made a call before sleeping, so they had not contacted the missing persons bureau yet. Our excuse was quite creative, but I must admit that I cannot recall the exact verbiage; let's just say that whatever it was, it did provide us with a little more time to make up a few more alibis. Even though into our twenties, we both still lived at our parents' homes, and such a caper was highly frowned upon no matter.

Greg was able to withdraw some cash from a bank that he used at home. We rented a new car, checked into the Palm Springs Riviera, and as though there would never be consequences to face upon our return, we proceeded to have one bloody great time for several days while the car's engine was being rebuilt. Now imagine this scenario: here we are lounging by the pool in the PS sun, sipping margaritas and puffing rum-soaked cigars; the server suddenly brings a phone to one of the sunbathing guests. "You have a call sir!" The conversation goes something like ...

Are you two OK; should we wire you money? Do you need us to come there and bring you home? Damn it! Get your post-adolescent butts back here right now, or we'll call the police for sure.

Response: Uh, no Uncle Marty; we're understandably a little stressed sitting in this tiny motel room, but OK overall. We'll let you know if we need help and keep you posted. Please don't worry.

We then discovered Georgio's where the waiters soon knew us by name. All we needed now was to worry about was what this whole thing was going to cost. Well, after a few days of it, Uncle Marty having been pestered by one's mother, decided to simply assure her that he would pick up the tab and to just "chill out" in

1960's terms. A few G's was nothing compared to the aggravation that mom was providing to him. My stepdad fortunately found the whole thing the most amusing event since Mr. Destructo.

XV. Married life with an expanding vocation

June 15, 1968 – a memorial to Wes

Denis was a musician friend that I met while teaching at the Adler Music Academy. He was primarily a five-string banjo picker, and performed in a very good folk-singing group, occasionally tinkering with the bass. My own band, *Rhythmaires*, was suddenly in dire need of a bass player for a gig that weekend at the famed Ambassador Hotel in Los Angeles. The event that we were booked to play was for the *Alumni Club,* a singles social group that we often worked for.

I asked Den if he knew a bass player; he hesitated, changed the subject, and just reminded me that the room was the popular *Embassy* ballroom within the hotel, and that it was the same room in which Senator Robert Kennedy was later assassinated. For a moment, we both quietly recalled that the podium he was standing near appeared to be the same familiar one that bandleaders sometimes used for announcements, as it was visible on the news coverage.

Alas, I persisted in my question; knowing that a bass player was not to be found in time, and aware that Denny sometimes doubled on electric bass in his group even though he did not think of himself as a bassist, I asked him if he'd consider a rehearsal to try some of our charts for the gig Friday night.

"You've gotta be kidding," he responded.

"No, I'm stuck, and I'll bet you can do it."

Den was primarily a folk and pop player, and rarely played a standard or a swing tune; but he was familiar with the style to some degree, and of course the rock tunes were easy for him. The rehearsal went fine, as did the gig.

He became so fascinated with playing the electric bass, that his very celebrated career thereafter was now completely dedicated to the instrument. After outgrowing the Rhythmaires, he went on to tour with some of the top names of the time, and to be among the busiest recording bassists in the business. But before his success took hold, we had played many dance band gigs together.

During the time of our many adventures on and off of the bandstand, was when I met Den's cousin, Sara; we were married on June 15, 1968. Denny and I each stood up to be best man in our respective weddings. The outcome of both is no more than history, and the demise of my ten-year marriage was later to become the beginning of my *summer*.

Sara and I met through my work as a jazz and commercial guitarist. How sobering to find out later that one of my guitar idols, Wes Montgomery, died in his wife's arms on June 15, 1968. My new life was just beginning that day; *for all too soon,* his life had just ended.

Some stories and highlights of late spring
The growing of a music teacher

Now having "family" responsibilities, Mr. Adler, the academy's director where I taught, approached me (and my clipboard) to consider teaching piano classes. Oh yes, I was indeed a guitarist, and such was my primary instrument. However, in 1963 during my probationary stint in college (shame, shame), I began the serious study of piano under the tutelage of the recognized pedagogue, the late Charles Lewis. I was truly fortunate to be accepted into his studio, and that was only because of another employee of the academy who just happened to know Charles. I studied with him for over six years from 1963 to 1969.

My purpose for learning piano was only that it seemed the mysterious "foot in my back" was telling me that I must do so. I asked no questions and complied. Unbeknownst to me, this would become one of the most important decisions that I made during my career; had I not done such, the study of music braille some twenty years later – including my current status as a state organization's music specialist – would have never been possible.

Charles was a very tolerant teacher, especially considering that he was accustomed to artist-level students; here I was a guitar player doing commercial gigs in hotels. I never rose to become a virtuoso pianist, but somehow he seemed to know (in his own crystal ball) that one day I would need the precious knowledge that he was giving to me, and that I would continue to pass the gift on to others.

I often played my recitals with deep circles under my eyes from 3am gigs the night before. My last performance was the complex Schubert Impromptu No. 3 in G-flat Major. I can remember sitting at the concert grand piano at a Music Teachers' Association program; my pedaling foot was shaking as though afflicted, and even through the fright of the experience, a few notes of the familiar black-key descending arpeggios did in fact come through somehow. Mr. Lewis gifted me with a photograph of that performance; the shaking didn't show, but the bags under my eyes from a gig the night before told everything. Perhaps that same frat house Indian was taking tickets at the ballroom door in the Beverly Hilton, but alas my memory has (conveniently) lost track of that one just in time.

My shining moment was earned, however, when I had submitted (by Charles' request) a composition for a special festival of the Music Teachers' Association of California. It was called *How the Sun Rose*, composed on the poem, *"I'll tell you How the Sun Rose"* by Emily Dickinson, when I was in college. The entry took first place, and was performed at a San Francisco MTAC conference by a Japanese soprano who was later awarded an appointment with the Metropolitan Opera. Few knew that I had composed the piece on an electric guitar then later scored it for piano and voice (we *jazzers* do learn to fake quite early).

Mr. Lewis was patient beyond belief; for example, I would call at times following a hard week and many dance gigs, explaining that I just couldn't practice and that I wanted to cancel. His response: "Dick [he called me then], if you did not practice, that's all the more reason you need to come in as you can practice here with me!" (Now don't think that I have not used that line many times within my own responses to similar situations with students.) At other times, I would express much worry as to why I could not seem to play some passage in perhaps a Chopin Prelude; he would smile and say: "Now you must stop worrying so much; let me do the worrying, after all that's what you pay me for. If I think you need to worry, rest assured that I'd be the first to tell you."

Thus I had somehow become qualified to accept an appointment to become the official class piano teacher for the music academy, conducting up to thirteen separate classes of six students each, every week.

And if it should seem that the cost of living represents logical yearly increments do consider that my lessons with a recognized pedagogue cost all of seven dollars at that time in the early to late sixties. In 2011, a private lesson with a celebrated teacher could cost anywhere from $100 per hour to more than $275.

I enjoyed teaching the piano, but never desired to be a working performer at it. The classes were very well attended, and yet this chronicle would not be complete without telling how such a venture led to my association with the infamous *billiard ball* family.

There were four children altogether, although the only girl, Leah – adopted at birth – was just an infant when her three brothers enrolled in my classes. They ranged upward in ages from Mike (age 7), to Steven, then to Jerome the oldest. Years later my newest friend and colleague, Robb, would observe the boys still coming in for private piano lessons and one for guitar. They would come running in the front door of the music store with at least one sporting a freshly shaved head, bouncing like billiard balls on a pool table, all resounding: "Mr. Tish, Mr. Tish!" Robb called them "the billiard ball family." The butch haircuts, however, were not at all stylish for young boys at the time; rest assured there is a story in the works here.

Mom was a nurse at the same high school that Mrs. Mahoney (I) lived near many years before in winter. All of the children, however, attended a strict religious school in another part of the valley.

Jen was a great mom (a little like the prefect of discipline at Notre Dame), but a ramrod for sure. It was alleged that in the kitchen of the family home, hung a list of offenses and correlating punishments, clearly indicated as warnings for all kids to read daily. The warnings must have been like the distracting signs on the freeway that tell you what horrible things will happen should you forget your seatbelt; or perhaps the severe consequences of ditching jury duty printed in red on the dreaded envelope – all designed to strike fear into the hearts of potential law breakers. A misdemeanor (such as not practicing) was dealt with a specific number of lashes; a felony (such as a failing grade) was given social restrictions of a more severe nature along with a specific probationary period; a capital offense (such as ditching school) was punished by what is known as a "Buzz." A buzz was no less than a complete butch haircut – not to be taken lightly when longer hair and Elton John was a trend of the times. After all, a man's ego and macho image with the ladies was now at stake. Well, when all three boys came bouncing in one day – all three with buzzes – one can clearly see just how the *billiard balls* stigma came to be.

One afternoon, Steven came to his lesson sporting the evidence of a serious offense. Apparently, while walking daily by the closed practice room door, his mother noticed that he seemed to be making the same errors in the same passages while drilling the *Arabesque* by Burgmuller (Opus 100). She decided to peek in at his progress only to find a tape recorder sitting on the bench in his absence, an open window, and the boy merrily riding his little pony in the back forty. Now that's original! (Actually, I once thought of a variation on that myself, but lacked the billiard *balls* to pull it off.)

Young Leah – many years later as a teen – came back to study guitar with me. I couldn't help but marvel at the time warp, and how this teen – a once adopted infant – was now telling me about her boyfriends as a college kid. Yikes! Plug my ears, and let's try to get back to how to play a G7 chord.

Outtake: Nothing is new under the sun

Perhaps there is no teaching situation that spans generations of growing children more than that of private music instruction. Although many private music teachers also work in district schools, conservatories, or colleges, generally in classrooms, peers are either of the same approximate age group or are working in the same academic area. Those who have mostly taught in class venues may often feel unprepared to work a full schedule one-on-one, even where formal curriculum is in place.

When expanding the Braille Music Division of SCCM into a new campus, we had the honor of hiring very experienced colleagues who were either retired, or working part time as disabilities resource teachers. Most would adjust to individual lesson schedules rather quickly; but the freedom (and dire necessity) of flexible adjustments less common in class situations, could pose some challenges for one who has not taught or tutored privately before.

Classroom music teachers often adhere to what is known as the *"National Standards"* for music education; those guidelines are specific, and tend to guide newer instructors in most routine challenges and spontaneous problem solving. Conversely, in private and some conservatory work, unexpected issues occur often, and unconventional accommodations become quite commonplace.

A family may raise one or many children, watching them only once through each growth period to adulthood. A private music teacher in perhaps a fifty-year career, has not only seen students that attend for extended periods through thousands of such changes, but in addition, has had an enhanced vista of every different personality imaginable, as well as many family ethnic and economic backgrounds to compare them to. As a result, there has never been a shortage of entertaining and creative devices developed by music students (and their teachers) to draw upon. Please enjoy a few of the following quotes that I often had hanging on the walls of my studio:

ATTENTION STUDENTS:

Due to increased complexity of explanations caused by a sincere effort of students to develop more originality for excuses in being unprepared for lessons, kindly refer to excuses by number. Guidelines for excuse offerings, along with coinciding numbers, can be found in the publication: "Student Handbook for Required Standards in Procrastination." *Your cooperation is greatly appreciated. - R.T.*

Following is a notice found on a frustrated music teacher's bulletin board:

NOTICE TO STUDENTS:

You really can help prevent your teacher from falling asleep during your lesson by coming prepared.

If this is not possible, kindly make arrangements with other students scheduled before or after your lesson time to come somewhat prepared on alternate weeks. In this way, your teacher need only remain conscious for every other lesson.

Your cooperation is greatly appreciated. Thank you! - R.T.

The only problem with having nothing to do is that you never know when you are through! - R.T.

A landscape rich with heads buried in the sand may soon become a wasteland littered with posteriors. - R.T.

XVI. The early days of my career
And some colorful stories to go along

In 1970, just two years following my marriage, Adler Music Academy closed its doors after 30 years of business in Van Nuys (including a satellite in Canoga Park). Although my work there (and beyond) was always divided between performing in commercial groups and daily music lessons, I was mostly dedicated to teaching as my occupation. Fortunately, Mr. Adler had much loyalty to his faculty, and made arrangements for a new music store in the making to take over the teaching portion of his business. Equipment and classes were transferred very smoothly into the new "Center of Music," and few losses were encountered. Some of the office staff migrated to the new store, and a reasonably balanced transition was possible.

During those many years at Adler's, I had acquired a kind of second mom in one of the office people who also taught lessons there. Freddie (Winifred) was a very dear friend, and remained so to my wife and me beyond the transition, and long after retiring from her career in music. During the year prior to my marriage, she and some of her friends would make trips to the Salton Sea to hear our band at the Holly House. It was then that she decided that her *adopted son* (she also had two grown boys of her own) should own a little piece of real estate for his future.

She picked a realtor that she met over martinis while dining and listening, and put up the purchase money for me. I was then to pay her back when I could. I did so, and on a regular basis until the residential lot in Salton City was mine. It was later to become an asset to share with my wife. To this day some forty years later, the little security that I gained would never have been possible were it not for Freddie.

The seventies were good to me in the private music lesson business. Having worked diligently and steadily with the "Mr. Taesch" shirt and tie (notice that the coat was now gone), I had developed a reputation for training guitarists who were either in need of reading skills for session work, or for younger students in school jazz band and orchestras. My piano teacher, Charles Lewis, was a very close friend of Duke Miller. Duke was the first to establish a degree program in jazz and studio guitar at University of Southern California, Los Angeles – USC. Inspired, I became obsessed with developing curriculum for training guitarists in basic commercial reading techniques, and hoped to work with Duke one day. He passed before that was possible, but I continued working on my methodology nonetheless.

At that time, guitarists new to the business were often noted for being rather weak sight-readers; serious ones who were confronted with a need to survive in the demo-recording arena would seek teachers who could train them as quickly as possible. A sensitivity to my own early struggles with competent reading skills remained with me, and I was determined to find a way to help other guitarists avoid the humiliation that I had endured as a youth.

My reputation soon grew, and players came to me on a regular basis; many went on to very successful careers doing that which I generally avoided. There is a wonderful anecdote that goes something like: *How do you get a guitar player to turn his volume down?* Answer: *Put a chart* [written music] *in front of him.* My mission was to help turn the tide, and perhaps in my own small way, I may have made some contributions.

Under Hal Johnson's guidance (Chair of SCCM composition department), I later orchestrated the degree program in commercial guitar studies at the Southern California Conservatory of Music, a then well-rated California degree-granting institution. At that time, USC and the tiny SCCM were among the very few authorized schools permitted to grant college credit for jazz & commercial guitar studies; prior to that, mostly classic guitar programs were recognized. Some widely celebrated schools of Music, to my knowledge, still did not yet recognize even that. My syllabus for SCCM, *"Guitar Study for the College Commercial-Studio Guitar Student,"* enjoyed published status for a short time in the 1980's. Several books authored together with my colleague, Robb Navrides, were also published in a series called *The Commercial Guitarist,* and can still be viewed on Internet with a search on that title.

Valley Institute of Musical Theater

A young man who was a wonderful and talented student, opened a door for me in the more academic and formal world of musical theater productions. (At the time of his lessons, I was unaware that Larry was a victim of leukemia, and may have had only a short time to live.)

At that juncture, the prominent conductor, Dr. Tom Osborne, heard one of my student groups perform at a recital; he called early one morning and asked if I had anyone who could try out for a very important production of *West Side Story*. Apparently, his new organization would pull together full Broadway productions of musicals, going to the extreme of bringing the original consultants in to assist in authenticity for some of the programs. The shows would run for two full weeks, and were divided between two local college auditoriums. There were full costume departments, original music scores sometimes rented from New York, and a large student orchestra brought into the projects.

My young man auditioned for the guitar seat in the orchestra, and was accepted. He then brought the charts for West Side Story to me for help in training. The only chart that they could provide for the electric guitar part was on the conductor's score. "Larry," I said to him upon first seeing the mass of black dots on the score, "I'm glad it's you working from this chart, and not me." Well, we laughed together, but prepare him I did; but so glad that I didn't have to muster up the mental fortitude myself. It has once been said that an educator should be capable of teaching that which he or she may not prefer to do him or herself. Well, I could have done it perhaps, but Larry, there but for I go you this time.

The second year brought the production, *Damn Yankees*. Everyone had to audition for parts in those prestigious productions, and when director Tom again woke me up one morning asking if I had anyone to play the part, I told him that I'd see if I could find someone for the auditions.

"Richard, never mind; just send anyone that you know can do it. No need to audition, as I know your work and I trust your judgment." I was quite honored to say the least! One of my older students was the pick, and no questions were asked.

During one of the scheduled performances, the young man came down sick and could not make the rehearsal or the show that night. I sent our man Larry from West Side Story in his place, hoping that he could handle the gig. With only one rehearsal, he read the chart down and did the performance.

The following year, the institute chose to do *Oklahoma*. However, that year so many youngsters were trying out for the part from various studios around L.A., auditions were again necessary; I sent three of my best students, hoping that at least one would make it among the others. Once decisions were made, three young guitarists were picked to share alternate parts; all three were my students.

Now it might appear that I'm attempting to blow a pedagogical horn; but first consider that this was not at all about me. Guitarists at that time were simply not conditioned to reading orchestral parts; my students all read, and simply had that advantage. There was no magic, no superior talent, just basic musicianship as a priority along with a youthful competitive edge (a bit like those football players in high school who got all the attention instead of the musicians).

Perhaps you may find it interesting to note that, in musical theater productions where full orchestrations are required, electric guitar is very often written to play unison lines with the violin section. One does not audibly hear the guitar, but the purpose of the orchestrator is that of making the string lines more clear and defined; the electric guitar does this, but is strategically hidden. For Oklahoma, each of the three guitars filled different roles: that of two lead parts for violins I and II; the third was assigned to the rhythm section.

Music in braille? I've never heard of such a thing!

While still at Adler Music Academy, I was teaching a student whose mother was a certified literary braillist. She would bring the young man to his lessons then quietly wait in the room and study. She seemed to be reading from a piece of print music, while making notes from a braille instructional training manual. After a fashion, my curiosity became more than I could stand; I asked her: "Eileen, what kind of course is it that you're working on?"

She said that she had a credential in literary transcribing, and was now working on pursuing one in music braille. "You must be kidding. You mean that blind people can read music with braille?" She assured me that they could indeed, and that she was trying to expand her knowledge of the codes by learning music transcription. Up until that day, I had no idea that the boy's mother had a music background to begin with, or that music in braille even existed.

At that same time, I was in one of those slumps that comes periodically when our students are not productive, and we begin to ask ourselves just what is it all about. I began to think that it could be interesting to work toward developing a special program for blind guitar students – a kind of new spark for a waning energy. After doing some research, I found "Sounds of Music for the Blind," a foundation in Los Angeles headed by the wonderful Leonard Berling, blind himself. I attended classes for several months, and began the study of music and literary braille using a simple slate and stylus. Sometime later, the horrors of divorce descended upon my wife's and my life, and all efforts and progress stopped. They did not resume until well over five years later.

My marriage (of then eight years – ten years total) was beginning to crumble in very late spring. I began sensing that mom-in-law may have felt I was not productive in our marriage, and that learning braille might have appeared somewhat philanthropic. During one of our family motor home trips, I remember working quietly on my studies from Mr. Berling's class; I noticed that she was curiously watching me.

She then asked what I was doing.

"Oh, I'm just catching up on some assignments for when I get back."

Paraphrased: *No, I don't mean that; why are you wasting time on learning something like this?*

I said in an almost programmed response: "Mom; it's kinda' like something I once heard that a famous old jazz musician expressed to a king while on a good will tour. When asked *'what is jazz?'*, as I understand the story, he supposedly said something like: *Your Excellency sir, if you hasta ask, you ain't ever gonna know."*

She turned away, and never asked again.

It's almost Mother's Day 2011 ...
Time out for a thank you – May 6, 2011

Today while writing portions of this remembrance, I took some time out to visit my own mother's grave nearby. She passed away about this time on April 27, 1987 during my late spring. The old jazz musician I spoke of is also gone.

All had their own part in what has been contributed to our world. Old jazzers gave priceless inspiration to musicians, jazz fans, and the art of American music; my wife's mother contributed to humanity as a dedicated surgical nurse, as well as bringing my then best friend into the world; my own mom selflessly stepped aside even when she was very ill, never asking why I needed to do what I now do. Somehow she knew that I was not yet supposed to know that answer – no more than I could give one to mom-in-law at the time she asked the same question. Today's lesson, yesterday's and tomorrow's should always be:

Just do the work, and the rest will take care of itself.
– Dr. Ernest Burgess

This Mother's Day, thanks to my mom, and to all the moms who first taught us as children – in each of their own different way – that:

"Were it not for the dreamers, the practical folks of the world would have nothing to do."
- Richard Taesch

Dedicated to the memory of my mother, and composed for my blind students*:

And ... to Marie Navrides, October 6, 1929 - April 27, 2015

APRIL 27, 1987

Very slowly

Richard Taesch

(Left Hand)

L.H

From: "Introduction to Piano for the Blind Student," Repertoire, Book 1; Used here by permission of the publisher, www.dancingdots.com

Richard E. Taesch

Pacific Crest Trail in springtime, west of Oakdale Canyon Road

XVII. Spring:
"... for all too soon I will be gone."

Prelude

For me, the close of spring and the beginning of summer brought one heartache after another; but in other ways, it also brought an awakening of sorts – a rediscovery of some lost youth, new friends, and an almost refreshing letting-go of material things.

My wife and I owned a manufactured home in the hills well above the valley, and enjoyed a somewhat rural lifestyle for nearly six years up until our separation in ca. 1978. It was high in the open space hills that surrounded the mobile home community that I first experienced hiking. We would walk together in the *green quiet places,* discovering adventures never before possible in the urban towns that I grew up in.

During our last few years in that home, I continued to work as a commercial musician and music teacher. More and more I grew into my work and, unknowingly, further away from my little family. Amongst futile efforts to redeem some credibility about my professional endeavors, I engaged in several faculty positions simultaneously: 1976 began SCCM; a year later in 1977, I took on an independent music teaching and chapel music director job at the prestigious Harvard School for boys; it was sometime thereafter that I added my first college position at Los Angeles City College into the mix, and yet maintained a full roster of students at the music store where the *billiard balls* remained regulars.

In addition, I accepted officer duties with my branch of the Music Teachers' Association as well. All of this was an effort to become that which some family members felt I was not, that is to be – *successful.* All that resulted was complete failure, loss of my home, my wife, and all we had worked for.

I once overheard a friend tell her very unhappy husband: "... please don't ask me to change into your perfect mate; you won't like me any longer if I do." And so it was: go against your inner voices becoming someone else in order to please, you will surely lose each other, and that which could have been.

Richard E. Taesch

You ain't ever gonna' know
Looking ahead at what might <u>not</u> have been

There was no way to know where the study of music braille might go in Richard's future. Even if I had been able to give an intelligent response to a question of … *why are you doing that*, there were no demographics or precedents at the time that would have justified a business strategy – one that might satisfy a practical question from a business-minded in-law who is understandably looking out for her daughter's financial welfare. Just as in today's arena, there were no degrees or teaching credentials for music educators of blind students to specialize in music braille pedagogy; as a result, the possibility of career ramifications was not even an available rationale. Certainly a crystal ball might have been somewhat helpful, but then would I have recognized that which I saw in it?

Among the many things that came to pass some fifteen years following the question of … *why are you wasting time on something like this*, a little boy was to be lifted out of what was certain to become complete institutional dependency; how?: only through the enabling magic of music, braille literacy, his discovered gift of perfect pitch, and our belief in Ernie's words, "just do the work."

Sean was only nine years old when my partner Grant and I found him at a special school for visually impaired children. We were experimenting with an outreach program in music, and my part of the partnership was to introduce music reading to those students who did read literary braille. Sean was born prematurely at a hospital in Switzerland while his parents were en-route from Iran to America. His mother was a biochemist in her country, and felt that the hospital was giving him too much oxygen. They resisted, but she was proven to be right; the boy became blind as a result, and with the possibility of brain damage.

When we first met him at the school program during our outreach, he was terribly withdrawn, and appeared unable to relate to learning or any kind of social interaction. We began to speak to Sean, and decided that we would try to introduce him to music. He seemed to love listening to recordings that my partner would play

136

for him. I asked the music teacher if he read braille, and she informed me that the braille instructor considered him far too learning disabled to ever be taught to read. His mother felt, however, that if given a chance to read, he could.

I spoke to a school official, and knowing that we were both new in the business of disabilities, he felt the need to counsel us in some way. He told me that the boy's mother is not being realistic, and that she just cannot face the fact that he is simply not able to abstract in ways that are required to recognize the tactile characters of the braille cell.

The music teacher came to us covertly, explaining that he might have perfect pitch. She then asked if we could work with him outside of school, but that it would be best if we kept it to ourselves, as she could be in danger of stepping outside of protocol. We contacted Sean's mother and asked her if she would bring him to SCCM for a private musical evaluation; she agreed, but said she could not afford lessons for him. We told her that if this worked out, we would provide him with full scholarship, and there would be no cost to the family. In the early days of trying to build our program, a scholarship meant that we just taught for free – simple funding, indeed!

During the year prior to the first lesson with Sean, I had helped a prominent company design a music version of what is known as "*Tacktiles*™." The product is a set of large plastic tiles with various braille characters; they can be placed on a special surface designed so as to be re-arranged in any way necessary. My work with the company, and help from braille music specialist, Bettye Krolick, resulted in the first music version of that product.

Sean was able to recognize the dot positions on the large tiles in his first lesson, thereby immediately disproving the belief that he could not abstract a braille cell for tactile recognition. However, this did not happen on the first try. But as soon as he was told that the dots 145 represented the music note C, or *do,* he would sing the pitch exactly, and continue to do so each and every time that the same character was placed in front of him. A special pathway to his brain had apparently been opened through his perfect pitch, otherwise described by some as tonal frequency recognition.

By the end of his first lesson, Sean could recognize and sing ALL of the braille notes of the C scale *do re mi fa sol la ti do*, and perfectly in tune. By the end of the second lesson, he was able to add the value dots 3 and 6, thereby creating note values and rhythmic meter. Soon after, we introduced him to conventional braille on paper. By the end of his first quarter with us, the reading teacher at school was successful in teaching him literary braille; this was completely contrary to some specialists' evaluations, and to the belief that music reading should only be taught after learning literary braille. If that had been adhered to, the boy might have never learned to read braille at all; he would most likely have remained illiterate for the rest of his life. He went on to become a fine literary and music reader. He then studied voice with the director of SCCM, and learned to perform his repertoire in several languages – all from music braille scores, which included the words in their respective tongues.

...if you hasta ask, you ain't never gonna know.

The braille C scale in eighth notes

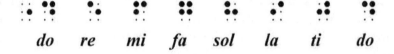

do   re   mi   fa   sol   la   ti   do

The braille C scale in quarter notes

"Professor Tish" trying out a new axe (Adler Music Academy, circa 1965)
(Photographer is unknown.)

*Robb's and my first book in the Commercial Guitarist series - Copyright © 1979
(Shown here by Robb's permission)*

XVIII. Spring's last days

Lessons at the new Center of Music (Adler Music Academy's descendant) were well under way in the 1970s, and many students came from many places. As said before, I continued to build a reputation for training session players of demo recording work and for touring gigs as well. I was always pleased to hear when well known celebrity groups made tours with students that I had trained for their rhythm sections at one time or another. Meanwhile, ideas were coming of age, and a guitar curriculum for the degree program at SCCM was beginning to stir in my mind after 1976.

Special friends and some rediscovered youth

Our little studios in the music store were not well sound proofed, and when two electric guitar teachers would work back to back, a cacophony was sure to result.

I was quite suspicious of the longhaired stranger working directly next to my room. His massive hair and beard was curly and bushy, yet seemed to enhance a friendly and musical countenance. The black-rimmed glasses complimented his pleasant smile but, nonetheless, *Richard the geezer* must have assumed that he was not to be trusted. After all, how can anyone ten years younger than I who looks like that be up to anything but drugs and rock n' roll? But all along, somehow I knew that Robb was someone that I would become very special friends with.

At times, I would hear him tuning up through the wall behind me while making adjustments to his, and his student's guitar. *Ha*, I thought; *now's my chance to mess with him*. I would playfully tune each string of my own guitar slightly flat or sharp, sounding it at exactly the same time that he did. He would keep plunking the string over and over in a futile attempt to find out why the note would never seem to settle into pitch. Through the wall of the room, he could not tell that there was an evil culprit on the other side generating the resulting dissonance.

We soon became life-long friends; we laughed until we cried at the antics of this jealous old fool of about thirty-four. Robb became one of the most loyal friends that I have, and his sister and family accepted me as though we were brothers.

We both began going through marital difficulties at about the same time. With no cooking activities at home any longer, we would join each other for café dinners late after our students were gone. Before going to eat, we would often play jazz tunes together, and I would offer what instruction I could in the way of the ten more years that I had on the planet (*Mr. Taesch* had not yet shed his skin).

Our friendship and adventures picked up much momentum once summer arrived. And such a good thing it was, as my summer began both of our single lives. Commiserating – which included other new peers with broken hearts and lady-chasing hormones that I met through Robb – was necessary therapy, without any doubt. Summer will be here soon enough; hopefully, my readers, you will not be disappointed. The good news is that I shed my dress shirt and tie, got rid of my own black-rimmed glasses, got my first permanent so that my hair would look like Robb's, and voila! I was no longer Mr. Taesch; now I was only *"Mr. Tish,"* as he still calls me to this day.

Robb opened doors for me that I had not peeked into for many years. His younger generation influence somewhat jarred me from the *old man* effects of my troubled times, and a new me was even becoming attractive to Richard himself.

A new and fresh musical awareness was emerging, and opened up much growth that had been suppressed for some time. We would dine together, spend days on the beach, and wonderful times were spent with him and his family as they treated me like their own. Robb was perhaps not aware of his influence, but were it not for him and a new awakening Richard would probably never have been inspired to write his own story, even though it would still be 33 years into the future.

The Circle "Oh" Ranch

The journey from late spring into becoming a divorcee without my spouse in summer was relatively short; but it does seem that several different lifetimes were lived within that span. It was almost as though the universe was preparing for me to confront a very different season – one that was to be filled with an enormous emotional struggle, but would be endured with the help of new friends and experiences. It was then I realized that keeping one's eyes on goals was of little use without fully experiencing the journey towards them.

Sara and I worked hard to make a good life for ourselves; we owned a home, two cars, and had some investments well before age thirty, and yet it seemed to be not enough. In early summer I can remember the feeling of letting it all go – walking on the beach for hours, kicking the sand and realizing there was no longer a house or loving wife to come home to. What happened; what did I do wrong, and what were the goals anyway? These were all questions that I asked myself over and over. While the answers continued to elude me, a new journey had just begun.

During our earlier years together, we had made good friends with a neighbor whose name was Ben. His own story was almost like a preview into my own future, as he had gone through a devastating divorce – a situation that I could not even begin relating to at that time. Ben lived next door to our apartment before we moved to our country home in 1973. Our garages faced a back alley, and when the garage doors were up, it was time to play. I would be working on my car, and Ben would often wander over and offer help and friendship.

We would sometimes sit and visit in his garage sipping a soda, while it seemed that I was providing a kind of therapy for him; he would talk of his divorce, his children, and how he managed the pain of loneliness. How lucky I thought: "I have such a wonderful life, and I'm so glad that we have such good friends." Later, the therapy roles would become strangely reversed.

Ben and his wife had purchased a five-acre spread in the high desert before their divorce. Although he gave up his house and most belongings so as to provide some security for his wife and children, he managed to keep that desert property for himself through the settlement.

Sara and I ventured out many times to Ben's place in the desert; he called it the *Circle Oh Ranch*. He slowly and carefully built a wonderful hideaway stick by stick. Friends donated many items to help in the process – furniture, materials, etc., and would spend many fun weekends there. I did not know then that the little place would later serve as a refuge for me in that very short dimension between spring and summer; oddly enough, it would then be re-visited twenty years after that time, abandoned and ravaged by vandals well after Ben's passing in 1994. Stay tuned for early summer.

Meanwhile, some late spring adventures on the bandstand

Music gigs continued throughout the remainder of spring and for a time, well into summer. But allow me to share a few fun stories now; as for me, this period during my spring could surely use some leggero (light, airy) notation.

Country club weddings and society dances were a common part of the work I was doing for a new group called *"The Con-Sorts."* Jay Conner was the bandleader and booking agent for the band. Jay was a policeman, but now working primarily in directing a police band, was semi-retired from normal work duties. His band consisted of not only small combo groups that he would send out to different engagements, but also a model big band that played mini versions of swing band charts of the forties. The group would perform for anything from weddings to beauty pageants, and many American Legion and other service club dances.

One particular weekend we were booked into the Palos Verdes Country Club for a very high society wedding party. The festivities went for most of the day, and the formal ballroom dance began at about 9pm. The band consisted of a four-horn front line – tenor and alto sax, trombone, and trumpet. The rhythm section was guitar (yours truly), piano, electric bass, and Jay on drums. Folks would often offer to buy the band a round of drinks in appreciation, and sometimes for honoring special requests.

A pleasantly sloshed lady came up to the band and asked what we would all like, as she was going to bring us a *round.* Six of us piped up that we would all like beers. She then staggered off to the bar to comply. A bit later she came back with six open bottles lined up on a tray that she was holding with one hand upward, not unlike a skilled cocktail waitress. Being unfamiliar with the fact that we could not respond properly because we were all playing at that moment, she asked: "Where should I put this?" None of us could do anything but look and nod at her as though trying to communicate "please wait." She looked desperately for some direction, but there was none to be found quite yet.

The lid of the grand piano was propped up, and the only flat spot was the harp upon which the strings and such are stretched. Our benefactor spotted it as an *island*, and began to approach the stand by trying to navigate a small stair-step up to the piano. While I tried to continue reading my chart, the entire scenario about to unfold became so clear that I could barely play, as my sides began to ache with laughter. One did not need a crystal ball to know what was about to happen.

The poor lady came up the stairs, spied the open lid then tried to lower the teetering platter down onto the flat piano harp. She tripped on a stair, and while the bottles started falling one by one like bowling pins into the open piano, beer began running through it as though down the Fire Falls at Yosemite. It was no doubt ruining the soundboard, and continued to flow down upon the drummer's canvas cases stored below. The more pissed Jay became while still trying to play, the more those of us who did not have horns in our mouths laughed convulsively looking straight ahead at our music, while notes and phrases from the horns squeaked and quivered hopelessly. Understand that this was not cruelty, nor meant in any way to negate our appreciation for her kindness; it was years and years of accumulated experiences watching folks make fools out of themselves during parties. It is a humor-conditioned state-of-mind that dance band musicians sometimes take on in order to maintain some sense of sanity.

Uncensored:

It is unfortunate that musicians are sometimes subjected to abuse while performing at intimate parties. At another gig, the president of the social club approached our fearless leader and informed him that an important guest always sat in with the hired bands, and that we were expected to make a place for him. He enjoyed sitting in so as to impress friends with his virtuosity. Jay asked: "but can he really play?" The spokesman insisted that since he was paying the bill, the band must accommodate the situation. Jay reluctantly agreed, and the gentleman soon approached the stand. Now he did not have his own horn, but did carry his own saxophone mouthpiece in his coat pocket.

Our own sax player somehow seemed to have a plan, and Jay knew never to question Bob's wisdom. He mysteriously rendered his horn after removing his own mouthpiece. Bob was the band's arranger, and one of the familiar musicians amongst the regulars. The man walked up, and in an expected cocky and obnoxious way, said: "Well dudes, what tunes d'ya you know?" What *he* didn't know was that we were working from band charts that required real musicians and professional experience to sight-read. He apparently expected to pick a tune and fake it, while the rest of us made him look good. Not to be!

Jay picked up Bob's energy, and when the man stepped up – all fans watching to see him show off – he again asked: "What are we going to play?" At this point it was too late for him to slip under the rug.

Jay smiled sweetly, pointed to the band charts and said: "Well you can read music, can't you?"

The man looked down at the fly spots on the music paper, and not wanting to lose face with his friends, said: "… uh, yeah, sure."

Well, he hadn't read a chart in perhaps years, but after a few drinks thought that he probably could still do it. He turned beet red, sat down behind the stand gazing blurry-eyed at the music in front of him, sweat pouring down while Jay counted the tune off. Admirers gazed lovingly while their maestro proceeded to step all over his virtual proboscis. Again, trying to contain one's laughter and play at the same time proved to be wonderful training, perhaps becoming useful for learning martial arts disciplines in my old age.

A little censored:

As we all know, it has always been a serious no-no to drink and drive an automobile; and well it should be. Many years of performing for service clubs, police, sheriff, and various kinds of parties and dances sometimes revealed those "inside" things that only we musicians were privileged to see. Some of the players in our band were also policeman, and I must say that over time, we observed more drinking and driving home than most folks ever do.

The gig was in an upstairs American Legion hall somewhere in Los Angeles; we were playing for some kind of state employees' office party. The band consisted of only four players that night, and the drinking and partying was in full force. This particular time, the grand chairman approached the stand demanding that we accommodate a lady who always sang with the band. We complied happily, and when she staggered up to the bandstand we asked her what she wanted to sing. She replied with a slurred tongue: "Baba, Backturd," a drunk's version of *Bye, Bye, Blackbird.* She proceeded to demand in an authoritative tone, that we play it in the key of D-flat.

Well, that tune is usually in F even for good singers; but our mischievous sax player, once again, winks and says "sure!" Meanwhile he leans over to us and says "do it in F, and when she gets to the high note, drop out and watch her try to reach it."

The grand moment came, and there she was screeching for a note that she couldn't reach in that key, standing out like a loud fart in a quiet church. After looking like a fool and well knowing why, she finished the tune. She then glared angrily at us while waiting for someone to help her off of the stage, as she was far too drunk to step down by herself. She was clearly quite humiliated, and pissed! Following that, we found out that she was a Superior Court judge. Three friends proceeded to help her down the stairs in order to get into her Lincoln Continental car so as to "drive" home, which of course she could not. Our bandleader just looked over at Bob and said: "Bobby, I sure as hell wouldn't want to be you going up in front of her tomorrow morning!"

September and the old "Schnozzle"

During my career I had the opportunity to perform with numerous celebrities, but none such an honor as that of the late Jimmy Durante, affectionately nicknamed the *Schnoz* due to his distinctive nose. Perhaps the most compelling performance of "*September Song*" that I have ever heard by any artist was his. It was in the late years of his life, and as the lyrics go, was truly the September of his own years. No version of that very meaningful song has ever been able to bring tears to my eyes in such a way.

We were performing for a special event at the L.A. Police Academy, and Mr. Durante was the featured guest. Our band had prepared some arrangements to back him with, and he would do his standup comedy as well. My music stand was at the end of the band lineup, and Jimmy was performing on my immediate left, slightly in front. I can't begin to express the excitement that I felt working next to this legend that I could remember in movies as a very small child.

He would often do things on gigs that were specifically meant for the musicians behind him to see, and while he was facing forward entertaining the audience at the same time. He proceeded to tip his derby hat to acknowledge the applause. Only we could see clearly that his toupee was attached to the back of his derby, and would lift away from his head when he tipped the hat. Funny is an understatement, and I laughed while everyone else was through laughing at the last joke. The audience apparently could not see his toupee lift, as it was intended for the musicians behind him. He suddenly turned around to me hearing my chuckle then said something like: *I had better laugh, as my job was hanging by a tread* [thread]! For those of you who never saw him perform, the spelling in that word, *thread*, was how he often spoke. At the same time, he took a few of the charts off of my stand and scattered them on the floor while exiting, audience in total laughter and applauding loudly. No more than a few seconds after he bows and exits the stage area, his assistant gathers up my music and immediately places it back – in order – and not a beat in the exit music was missed.

Oh no!

One of the last and most memorable gigs that I can remember from late spring was that of a special appearance by a guest performer at a national convention. Such gigs would happen often for the Con-Sorts little-big band, as the bandleader was still quite involved in public service groups, and had become an official in a service organization.

This particular event was held at a prestigious hotel with at least a thousand people attending. Jay was not there himself, but our arranger was leading the band in his place. Bobby was often a bit distracted, and details sometimes slipped his attention – uh, like will the grand piano be on stage when the band plays the walk-on theme from one of the guest's shows? Arrangements had been made, and by the time the show was supposed to begin, the hotel crew was to see that the large grand piano was shipped up to the grand ballroom, and placed with the orchestra waiting behind closed curtains while chatting and visiting.

The musicians often brought their wives or girlfriends to the gigs, as they all knew each other and enjoyed being together. For some reason, we were unaware that there was a change made in the time that our guest was scheduled to make his entrance. Much time went by, and with curtains drawn closed for an hour or two, we all sat on stage continuing to visit with wives and ladies sitting on the side with us. The band was set up, stands and charts in place, but still no piano. We were not worried yet, as the scheduled time was still quite later – so we thought.

Now you must first be made aware of some things about certain people before being fully able to appreciate the scenario that is about to unfold. All of us were dressed in black tuxedos, and this included Frank the alto sax player. Frank is a piece of work to behold – tall, and always seems to be relaxed. He is a long-time schoolteacher, and well conditioned to taking his time to do most things. Perhaps an Ichabod Crane might be a good visual image for you. Frank towered over most of us, and although a very fine musician, he never seemed to respond frantically to anything, much less an impending curtain call with an empty bandstand. Suddenly we became starkly aware that something was terribly wrong.

Scene 1: None of us were in our places, the piano was not yet brought to the stage, and all of us were scattered about the area conversing. Over the din of the crowd from out in front, comes the loud announcement: *"And now friends – Presenting: ..."* Apparently, the schedule had again been changed, and everyone seemed to be informed except for the orchestra that was supposed to play the celebrity onto the stage with his theme song while audience clapped and cheered. Curtain was supposed to slowly roll up while the music and fanfare was underway. Guess What?

Scene 2: I saw the curtain beginning to rise, and exclaimed: Yikes! Everyone scattered like crows feasting on a carcass when you drive by; Frank was caught completely across the large stage area, and was the last one to comprehend the situation. The curtain rises slowly, revealing black trousers and high heels running hither and yon toward sweet refuge in the wings – that is everyone except Frank! The curtain now rises to knee-level, then beyond; there are Frank's long legs walking very slowly past the empty bandstands in what could have been the quietest loud moment that I've ever heard in a gathering of so many people.

The performer enthusiastically trots onto the stage waiting for the theme song, suddenly realizing that there is no music and no orchestra waiting to play; he wheels around only to find the stage empty except for *Ichabod* slowly walking across with hands in pockets, head down resembling that of a pall bearer in a funeral procession, eyes occasionally darting sideways at the celebrity, and then towards the wings where he would soon disappear in complete silence.

Now I have heard of similar rare things before, and some comedians could have had a field day with this one. But this poor fellow was so taken off guard, that all he could do was to turn around and stare at the empty stage while over a thousand folks looked on with confused anticipation. Some momentary details have slipped away, but somehow while he was recovering from the shock, the curtain was dropped and he went ahead with a planned monologue that had nothing to do with what had just happened.

Following the finish, the curtain went up, bandstands were occupied, and the planned theme song played him off with a resounding applause. (Whew!) We couldn't help but wonder if the audience might have thought that this was part of the act. For certain, had it been Durante, such a stunt would have been quite believable.

The winner is …

Oh yes, lest we forget! We were performing again on the Queen Mary, this time for an organization of professional gardeners. We were to await the bandleader's cue to play a fanfare once an award was announced (Jay was the drummer, but at this moment was at the head table acting as the announcer).

It was a small band – drums, Fred on alto, I on guitar, and Tom on electric bass. Much time elapsed, and I could see poor Fred seated on his stool, saxophone poised in his hands, and sleepy eyes beginning to become apparent. Finally the big moment came. With perfect timing right at the downbeat for the fanfare, I missed the cue completely while watching Fred's head drop with a resounding snore – ZZZzzzz! The glorious and long-anticipated fanfare – Ta-Ta! –, now resulted in only that of one deep thud coming from an electric bass. Jay was understandably pissed, and right over the microphone he states in presence of everyone: "Thanks Guys!"

XIX. Epilogue for spring

In 1976, my cousin Evelyne from France came to spend two weeks with my wife and me. This was the very first time that I had ever met anyone from my own family living in the old country. To my knowledge, I was the only *Taesch* that lived in America, and had never met any other of my father's family in person.

Evelyne was only eighteen when she began writing to me with hopes to come to America. She and her boyfriend, Benoit, then flew from Paris to New York and proceeded to hitchhike across the country until they reached us in Los Angeles. Yes, risky it does sound; but they related the most wonderful experiences that anyone could imagine; *good old* American hospitality was there for them. They would tell of being picked up by folks who would take them in, and in return they would make French cooking for them – a refreshing change from the normal reports that some prefer us to remain stirred up over.

This was to be one of two last experiences that Sara and I would share. The first was a wonderful trip to the tip of Baja California in November of 1975. The new frontier road had just opened, and Baja was greener than it had been in over 100 years. Our two-week motor home trip there was never to be forgotten; Sara's mother and her new fiancé, Jim, made that possible for us. Later in summer, I took three weeks off, and we planned the wonderful stay for Evelyne and Benoit: Disneyland, Hollywood, museums, and more.

About a week into their visit, mom and Jim offered to take the tour to a higher level. They graciously rolled out the red carpet with motor home trips to Sequoia, San Francisco, private plane flights to Mexico, and so forth. Although ever so grateful to them, I couldn't help but to sense a message from within that there was more to life than what I could offer.

After Evelyne and Benoit returned to France, mom and Jim, with Sara, planned another trip; however, I could not take more time off to go with them. The last thing I can remember was waving goodbye while they drove off alone, and on to Yellowstone National Park. Someone peered at me curiously out of a window, while I remained behind so as to make up the lost income from the *French connection* a month before. I was one to rarely shed tears, perhaps not since 1953; but my eyes were definitely full of them that night as I watched them drive away. There were a few moments together with all of us following that event, but not often.

Near the same time mom and Jim married, and were completing construction on their grand home in a prestigious new development called Shadow Canyon. Sara would spend time there after the house was built while the folks would travel. I became quite fond of Jim, and much admired his gentle nature and character. His career as a pilot often reminded me of my dad.

The heart of a coyote

As the end grew closer, I would sometimes walk out into the hills alone at night. At that time, I knew little about hiking, and was just lucky I suppose. With a moon overhead there was minimal problem seeing, but I was still fearful of the coyotes that roamed and howled near us. Little by little, I came to find that the creatures would appear very near to me while I walked in sadness late into the darkness.

One evening as I sat near an old oak tree with a very heavy heart, I looked up to a small rise with a moon directly behind what was clearly the silhouette of a coyote peering down – looking, and somehow seeming to understand that I was a fellow creature in need of company. I began to lose my fear of them, and gradually welcomed their proximity to my trail. Later I learned that when they would cross back and forth in front of me, it was because my footsteps on the trail would stir up the field mice. They would then be able to catch the mice for food. They became my friends then; and to this day, my respect for them remains and continues to grow.

On one of my last outings with the family, we had made a trip to the Los Angeles Zoo. By then I began feeling somewhat like an outsider, but nevertheless was included that day.

As we entered the beginning of the zoo tour, a caged animal caught my attention. It was a lone coyote – completely out of place as I'd come to know them. I stopped for a moment to sit by the cage, watching the neurotic animal across the far end of his unnatural confines. I was completely taken with the piercing look in his eyes. He immediately made eye contact with me, staring in a way that seemed to penetrate deep into the inner places of my soul. It seemed in one way unearthly; and yet in another, a reaching out.

Someone became impatient and said something like: Are you going to sit there all day with that mangy animal, or come with the rest of us?

I responded that they should just go ahead, and I would catch up with them shortly. Off they went, probably just as glad to be rid of me for a while, as my company was not pleasant at that juncture.

The time was near noon; a short while later they came back to where they left me, wondering what happened. There I was, still sitting with the caged coyote that had edged his way close to the screen that separated us. We clearly bonded during that time and somehow became one in spirit. Perhaps it was now my turn to understand his heartache, and to wonder why he was imprisoned as an object only for curiosity seekers to gaze upon.

Once again, I ask: "Why is that?"

It often seems to me that those who spend their lives with music somehow appreciate the harmony of nature best. To many, the cries of a coyote are frightening; to others, they are musical and warm. The animal is perhaps one of the most misunderstood creatures there is. Poisoned, trapped, and driven away from our few remaining open spaces, he continues to survive and to treat those who live near with his loving song. The Indians seemed to know that that brother coyote could lead them to water, or to even predict rain.

In the "*Origin Legend of the Navajo Flintway*", a Yebichi dance chanted by the Navajo Indians describes the "*dawn child's*" song:

"*Just when morning is coming on, I give my call. ... Right out of my mouth I call. By means of darkness I call. I call when it is quite dark. With the aid of my tail I call. At dawn, you know also, I call. At sunrise I call.*" [1]

The Seri Indians sing:
[Chant taken from: "*The Last of the Seris*"]

> *The coyote is happy in the moonlight.*
> *He sings a song to the moon –*
> *While he dances.*
> *And he jumps far away –*
> *While he dances.*" [2]

And once again, I ask: *Why is it that what we cannot understand, we so often destroy?*

---

[1] Haile, Father Berard, *Origin Legend of the Navajo Flintway,* University of Chicago Press, Chicago, 1943, 101. [Used here by permission of University of Chicago Press]

[2] *The Last of the Seris:* Copyright © by Dane Coolidge and Mary Robert Coolidge. Copyright © renewed 1967 by Nancy Collins. All Rights reserved. Reprinted by permission by Golden West Literary Agency. [Permission updated 2020]

Photo: Lone coyote in a stream bed; taken by R.T.

Spring

I am peace – I am your new life – spend time with me in the green quiet places, **for all too soon**, I will be gone ...

SPRING
Richard Taesch

Freedom is not free, especially when you're kept in a cage

Radio antennas like the one above once graced many an American neighborhood. Then they were a symbol of freedom, and stood as sentries when radio amateurs were called upon to assist in emergencies. Today, they are banned in most residential neighborhoods, and enthusiasts must resort to stealth, nearly invisible, and less efficient arrays. Another lost freedom, yet hams continue to provide communication during satellite and Internet failures even to those who resent their presence. Reading the [Hurricane] "Katrina Files," one becomes starkly aware of the amateur service, and of lives that were saved when conventional communication failed.

EARLY SUMMER
XX. The joy and the journey

Prelude

The Station

"The Station" by Robert J. Hastings, is a writing that I would sometimes read as an opening at student recitals. In essence, the words describe life as a train upon which we are passengers. While each on our own journey, we peer out of windows watching towns and countryside pass by with only one thing in mind: that of when we arrive at our *station.* At that point all of life's longings will be satisfied, and our hopes and needs will be fulfilled as we have always planned. But in the end, we find that there is no station – only a journey: *an endless track* that we have failed to experience while ever looking ahead for the train stop.

The reading goes on to express a thought that we must enjoy the moments now, as there is no station, no assurance that our dreams will be fulfilled as we have envisioned. So, " *...climb more mountains, watch more sunsets, laugh more and cry less, ...* "* Such is the admonishment to enjoy and cherish your time before it is over, as otherwise you may pass your earthly station many times but will have never noticed it; happiness must therefore be found in the journey itself. And so spring will also end, having beckoned you to *"… spend time with me in the green quiet places, for all too soon, I will be gone ..."*

And each year – as long as one season may last – is another chance before the green grasses turn to golden brown. Summer can only arrive by following spring, and how better it is to prepare for fall by carrying *"summer's memory"* into it. So the goals are important, but I think that it's often the definition of those goals that matters even more; does the definition include the journey? Or will we end up with only empty stations?

As always, life seems to be a musical composition with perfect comparisons: *"Keep your eye on the eighth note"* was the musical sight-reading analogy to goals in an earlier chapter; and musically speaking, the eighth note is never an island; its only purpose is that of one component in the journey towards the next phrase. As the music moves towards the final cadence, we must remember that not all cadences need to resolve in the original key.

Early summer journeys, challenges, and perhaps a few too many eighth notes

For me, the transition into summer included many interesting situations. Once I realized that the marital *Coda* was coming near, I made futile attempts to change keys, but at a complete loss of where to start. Reluctantly, I agreed to put our home in the hills up for sale and to pursue the purchase of a tract home in the west valley. Perhaps at least twenty-five percent of gray hairs that I now have were earned during that process.

The market was quite good at the time, and our mobile home sold on the first day that it was advertised. However, after opening escrow on the house, our buyers backed out leaving us with no way to follow through with the purchase; moreover, I had already used their deposit to open the escrow.

A family friend then offered to loan $1,000 to me in order to refund our buyer's deposit money, assuring that we could pay it back after a pending subsequent sale, and not to worry. Following that, the market suddenly dropped and we could not sell; the seller of the house threatened to sue, *friend* called the 1k loan immediately due, and things worsened by the day. We then listed with a broker to sell; when finding buyers on our own, they would not co-operate with the listing broker, so then he threatens to sue. Yikes!

At that point, I was feeling a bit like Indiana Jones (Movie: *Temple of Doom*) on the precarious suspended rope bridge, squeezed between the spear-throwing natives on one end, and the *bad* guys on the other!

A comedy of terrors: The Tarantella in six-eighth time

The two sales finally went through, and during that year in the new house several rather entertaining events occurred. *Summer* for me really begins when the year was over and I was then living elsewhere. But a few things that took place just before that time may prove to entertain even the most devout pessimist.

The Shadow Canyon home was now mostly complete, and Sara spent much of her time house sitting there while her folks were away. On occasion I would go there to visit; sometimes we would barbecue while a friend or her sister would come to join us.

One late afternoon we were enjoying the hot spa located in the Spanish courtyard in front of the home. I was sitting alone in the water basking in the healing bubbles when brother-in-law suddenly says to me:

"Dick, there's a big tarantula just behind you."

"Yes, I know Bob; I saw him earlier today. He won't hurt anyone; he's been up on that wall for hours."

"No, you don't understand; I mean he is right behind your arm."

With my elbows propped up on the coping of the spa, I slowly looked over my right shoulder. There he was, working his way around the hot pool in hairy curiosity. I had never been that close to one before, but Sara had actually allowed it to walk on her hand earlier that day, so I had a little pre-conditioning of sorts.

I exclaimed the usual *Oh great,* now what do I do? Well, I felt that the best thing to do was just sit still. The creature then proceeded to tap my arm with one of his hairy legs as if asking to pass. I decided that I would comply, and moved my arm to watch him slowly walk around the spa edge several times before crawling back up to the wall from whence he came. That experience proved to be one more reason to suspect the unfortunate propensity in human nature to kill anything that has been determined must be harmful – whether or not it is.

The tarantula spider is a very docile creature; and although a bite can be painful, it is rarely harmful – quite contrary to similar myths that have followed other animals for many centuries. In some countries, children even keep them for pets.

I am told that the Italian dance, *Tarantella*, was named after the spider; apparently if someone had been bitten, the village folk would simply gather and dance until a major sweat was worked up, thus supposedly driving any toxins out of the person's body. I have had some occasions to gently encourage one of the creatures off of a trail so that it would not be harmed by mountain bike wheels, or by a frightened hiker. I have never been bitten in return.

This photo was taken a moment before I tapped him or her on its bottom to "dance" out of harm's way; a mountain bike was fast approaching us. (Courtesy of the East Canyon Wilderness near to 34th Street)

Outtake

Lest I forget, one amusing little story must be shared: In the process of attempting to upgrade our new West Hills house with a modern private bath for the guest bedroom, Richard assumed the role of carpenter and plumber. I tore out the old sink and wallpaper, and installed a lovely marble top counter with artistic flower-inlaid patterns. Having engaged the assistance of the plumbing department at the local hardware store, I felt quite confident in my project. However, the plumbing *specialist* somehow forgot to educate me in the necessity of having the hot and cold water flex lines "flanged" before installing them.

It was such a lovely new bathroom, and in hopes that the effort might please, I surprised Sara with my project. We spent some time visiting later that week, and one evening went to dinner together.

While driving up to the house upon our return, I noticed water pouring out of the garage in a near deluge down the driveway. Well, apparently Richard's plumbing job gave way, and not only was water running out of the blown-out flex lines, but for several hours had run throughout the house flooding all rooms and carpeting.

I procured a rented machine to vacuum the water up, but carpeting now ruined, I was forced to make an insurance claim. Cousin Rick was in the carpet business, and was delighted to help out; insurance paid some, but at the cost of about $1,500 deductible. I slept in our front room for about two months, and oh such beautiful new deep pile carpeting was the result (sigh!).

XXI. Summer begins at the Circle Oh Ranch

Circa 1978 - summer now having arrived, it was just a matter of time before I planned to move away from West Hills, giving up my interest in the house on agreeable terms. Meanwhile, I continued to commute to schools and to the studio where I was teaching privately. However, while I was still in the new house, my friend Ben from the *Circle Oh* felt that it would be good for me to get away from the surroundings for a while. He suggested that I spend the Fourth of July weekend at his place in the desert along with some of his other friends. Ben offered to trek out west and pick me up himself – a kind of rescue mission of sorts. I agreed, and another *story yet to be told* would soon be in the making; but first...

But first, let's set the stage and the scenery

No saga about the "*Oh*" should take place without first a description of the setting, along with some of the characters that would often frequent it. My Fourth of July there was indeed one of a kind; however, it will be best if delayed slightly in curious anticipation, so as to be framed with several short tales believed to be inseparable parts of the island ranch in the desert.

The legend of Grandmother's bell

The cabin and surrounding shelters were constructed stick by stick from donations made by friends and much hard work from helpers. All took early shape while Sara and I still lived next door to Ben before our move to the hills. Newspaper, for example, was saved by his neighbors to be used for insulation and stuffing within the rough walls of the homemade cabin. It worked well, as during the cold winter snows the little dwelling remained quite warm, and in summer remarkably cool. Hot water was never a problem during the day. Hundreds of feet of garden hose were spread down slope that led from a water tank; in sunshine, the hoses would become heated, delivering luxurious warm water directly to the kitchen tap.

And yes, the outdoor facility was complete with a half-moon carved in its door just like in old movies.

Stories and tall tales about the ranch were always quite plentiful. One afternoon, a visit over a beer in Ben's garage yielded the most incredible saga about a friend named, *Woof.* [1] Perhaps it was only a yarn, perhaps it was true; but nonetheless, it certainly was entertaining. As best as I recall, it evolved somewhat as follows.

Woof's grandmother had supposedly donated the money to place a huge steel bell in front of an elementary school somewhere in the south bay area. It weighed several hundred pounds, and was to be mounted upon a concrete pedestal with a bronze dedication.

The school, now closed, was being torn down. Woof figured that the bell belonged in his family. After convincing the powers that be, he decided to acquire the bell and one day donate it to the Circle Oh; if an agreement could be reached, it would then be hung on a platform that they would build to hold it.

Well, he must have pulled it off, as soon Woof supposedly invites Ben over to see a curious item carefully covered with blankets in the back of his panel truck. He uncovers it as though top secret, and sure enough, behold a huge (*liberty?*) bell that stands perhaps three feet high per Ben's description. It was later said to have been transported out to the *Oh*, and proudly hung from the large wooden structure that was built in waiting for the special day. They would ring the bell daily, and one could have heard it down in the towns far below.

Apparently, however, it turned out to be a misunderstanding, and that the bell was not destined for demolition along with the school after all. Soon some kind of article was said to have appeared in the personals of the local paper [paraphrased]: *Whoever acquired our bell, would you consider donating it back to us; we will happily pay expenses. It was a special project donated long ago by a member of our Women's Club* [Grandma?]. Well, I suppose that Grandma was a woman all right, but the only club that she may have had was the one she probably would have gone after Ben's buddy with, were she still living.

The story may have had a fairytale ending, however. Now no one seemed to know just how the bell mysteriously turned up missing from the *Oh* one weekend, as it would have taken a very large effort to remove it. Well, one might muse that a generous deed and relocation project of some kind might have taken place. Who knows, perhaps even the good ladies of the Women's Club eventually saw their bell once again.

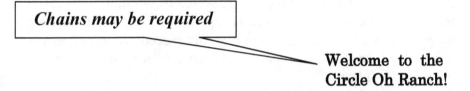

Chains may be required

Welcome to the Circle Oh Ranch!

The dirt roadway to the property circled around a ridge two or three times before structures came into view on the top. A number of interesting road signs and other anomalies had been collected over time, and not unlike the Burma Shave signs of yore, several lined the yellow brick (dirt) road going up to the site. Among some reproductions that I remember was a snow chain warning. It had been carefully altered to now say: "*Whips* and chains may be required." At times, rather unusual couples would be among the guests at Circle Oh, and perhaps the various signs were a way to make them feel at home on the way in.

Shenanigans of all imaginable kinds were part of visits, and Ben or cohorts would generally have one or two planned with which to entertain inebriated guests with. On this occasion, *friend,* Woof revealed to everyone that he had discovered a spring close by, and during the summer dry heat everyone was nagging him for a tour to see it. There were several old cars scattered about the place, all running, but none legal for anything except off road. Ben brought an old van up to the cabin and told the guests that the tour would begin as soon as they boarded. (RT was present on this one.)

Several folks gathered for the trip, decked out in shorts, floppies, and of course, towels with which to dry off after the refreshing dip in the cool *spring.* Marcy, a registered nurse, was among the

169

passengers. The trip began by circling around the property (about ten acres), then down a ravine, up the other side, round and round, and ends at the bottom of what seemed to be close to where we began; "Oh well; guess he has the route figured out."

"We've arrived at the spring!" clamors the pilot in command.

Everyone bails out of the van (which, by the way, had no doors or seats) and looks every which way for a spring. "Hey Woof, where is it?"

"Just follow me and Ben, we'll lead you to it."

They formed a caravan, marching through the blistering heat and dusty ravine, knowing that the reward would be worth it. After about five minutes, we came upon a rusty pipe in the ground with nothing wetter than an old automobile coil spring placed around it. Marcy quietly looks over to someone, then whispers: *"Just wait, I'll fix his ass good for this one."*

And fix it, she did! On a subsequent weekend, Marcy supposedly brought a large quantity of discarded bandage wrapping from the hospital that she worked in. Woof had a habit of becoming somewhat incapacitated on the weekend gatherings, while Ben and guests entertained themselves in various ways. He would often just pass out in the shade and hibernate for hours at a time, usually waking up unaware of any unusual behavior that may have preceded his long sleep. Marcy and several cohorts waited until he was definitely out for the afternoon; they then proceeded to wrap his entire body in the gauze, building plaster casts on his legs and arms with the materials that were smuggled in just for the occasion.

After several hours, Woof begins to stir and awaken in the evening coolness. Marcy and other guests are gathered around, sipping and chatting in what appeared to be typical relaxation. As he begins coming to, he gazes around blurry eyed at the casts and bandages within which he has been professionally wrapped.

"Oh jeez, don't tell me I've gone and done it – oh no!"

Marcy comes over to him with a straight face just as all have been rehearsing to use upon his awakening.

"Marcy, Marcy, what the hell happened to me?"

"Aw, Woof, don't you remember?"

"No, no, please help me" he grumbles.

"Well, you tried to jump off of the roof of the trailer; you were mumbling something like 'I'm going to dive right into that pool!' I guess you thought there was one, and ..."

"Oh my god, Marcy, how could I ..."

By this time, the perpetrators couldn't hold their laughter any longer. He then spotted a set of shoulders shaking behind a newspaper and slowly began to figure it out. I do believe that – although he didn't quite take the pledge – his drinking may have taken a more tempered direction at least, not to mention a few less pranks on Ben's guests thereafter.

A "streak" of genius! The Woof in cheap clothing

In about 1978 – the same time that the Circle Oh Ranch was entertaining its guests regularly – the *streaking* phase was in full force. For those who may not remember that time in our history, *streaking* was a practice whereby one would seek a place or an event where he or she was sure to be noticed by many. Unannounced, one would then run through a meeting, concert, or across a performance stage completely butt-naked then disappear. Streakers were seen dashing through passenger planes, across television cameras, through churches, and just about anywhere imaginable. And for the "tsk, tsk" folks' information, there are those of us who truly feel that the trend came at a time in American history when we desperately needed a national kind of humor to take our minds off of many grim events. Streaking certainly provided a unique form of light distraction, no matter what one's view of it may have been.

On some occasions, Ben, Woof, and a few of Ben's male friends would head out to a local old time café for early breakfast during a weekend at the ranch. This story came to me from an undisclosed source, but knowing about the culprits, I can feel quite comfortable reconstructing the event, if only for fun.

All of the players knew the waitresses in the café, but of course would never be recognized by same while dressed in their birthday suits (?). It was about 6am in the morning, and breakfast was being served to the regulars. The smell of fresh coffee, bacon, and country music playing on the jukebox filled the air. The "boys" gathered outside the back of the little café making sure that proper *un*-costumes were adorned, and the mission began.

They ran through the café, jumped up on the counter and across a table, jumped down then disappeared out the front door before anyone could gather his or her wits. Twenty minutes later, they appear as normal patrons in the front door – fully dressed – with straight faces and head for a booth. Greetings are exchanged with the regulars, and menus now hide what remains of anything familiar from the event of a short time before. Sober faces typical of any sleepy Sunday morning breakfast-seeking entourage are displayed.

Apparently, one of the shocked customers (or?) recognized some part of one of the earlier phantom's anatomy – namely his face and mustache. Quietly the sheriff was called, and the clock ticks. In he walks, clearly familiar with the innocent-looking group enjoying a hot cup of morning coffee.

"OK, what's this all about?"

All look up as if: What do you mean, officer?

Well, the deputy, trying to hold his laughter for the benefit of the outraged, pretends to order the bunch outside for a discussion. They gather quite seriously at the black and white while waiting for the lecture: "Now; [uncensored] which one of you weenie-waggers was the head of this caper?" Apparently, the incognito streakers fess up, and officer gives a stern admonition while trying everything possible to appear quite serious. Breakfast is served inside; so now let's get on with our Sunday.

* * *

Independence Day 1978

Now perhaps you see why the general setting needed to be provided before my own little story could be told. Although possibly only an anticlimax to what I have already described, Richard's memoirs would not be complete without it.

As planned, Ben made the trip to pick me up in West Hills, and off we headed to the desert island – sometimes known only as "the ranch." When we arrived, there were already some of his friends and guests gathered about playing with some fireworks. Upon climbing out of the car, the first thing that I saw was some kind of rocket being fired out of a homemade pipe launcher. The beer had already begun to flow, and apparently Independence Day had also been declared. The remainder of the evening proved to be a strange kind of surreal experience, one that even I sometimes find it hard to believe I witnessed. Having been a married man with responsibilities, and a respected shirt and tie "Mr. Tish," I probably didn't settle into the whole idea until it was just about over. But an experience that I will always cherish, it certainly turned out to be.

One or two cars and a pickup truck were in the process of being loaded up with ice chests and boxes of food. A short trip to an old wooden frame house on a dirt back road would lead us to where the party would take place. It was the hide-away home of an Indian family well known to the locals; Buck was the host, and his mother, whose husband was a flight instructor at a soaring school nearby, was there for the festivities. Barbecues smoked, and refreshments were everywhere. Upon arriving, the first things that I saw were several motorcycles complete with gang-looking riders pulling up. "Oh no," I thought to myself; "how did I get into this?"

Well, before going further, rest assured that I ended up meeting some of the most wonderful and gentle people that I had ever experienced. The bikers were fun, and as genuine as were all of Ben's friends. Ben places a glass in my one hand, and a bottle of white wine in the other, then says: "Go forth and multiply." Now, I've yet to know what he meant, but I did pretend to hold that glass throughout the evening in a way that enabled me to somewhat appear like one of the rest of them, whether or not there was always anything in it except ice.

Upon walking up to the old wooden house, the first thing that I observed was the back side of a rather stout fellow sitting on an open windowsill inside; behind him crept a culprit who planted a small firecracker into his rear jeans pocket, lit it, and ran. I stood speechless while the fuse burnt to activate the expected explosion, thinking that the gentleman's rear anatomy might become the "multiply" that Ben meant. Well, it did go off; the burly biker simply turned around, scratched the spot, declared some expletives then continued visiting his friend with beverage still firmly in hand. Such things went on all evening, and as dangerous as it sounds nothing more than fun-filled retaliations continued. No one was hurt, as the little firecrackers were startling though seemingly harmless when detonated.

Buck's mom was quite notorious, as when she would attend parties – to which she was always invited – she would bring her youngest son with her in order to drive the old *Sedan de Ville* back across the desert dirt road to their home after the party, as she would become quite unable to do so herself. The boy could barely see over the steering wheel so pillows were used, and he became a kind of "designated driver." Now here she was, very distinguished school teacher-looking, short gray-black hair, not unlike any of our own mothers or grandmothers, except for the fact that she was not seen without a beer can in her hand the entire night. Never have I seen anyone consume *suds* quite like that.

Everyone would try to catch a friend off guard with some kind of firecracker prank, and *mom*'s son was no exception. As I sat on a bench nearby watching her chatting away with someone, Buck sneaks up behind her. He plants a firecracker under her right shoe as she is standing up during the chat. The cracker goes off; her long matronly dress flies up momentarily from the impact; she gingerly looks around, then down at the shoe with raised eyebrows and continues to visit as if nothing had happened. I think that I laughed harder that night than I had in many months, especially considering the heavy heart that I was carrying with a divorce pending.

The little house was full of people; dancing, drinking, and firecrackers seemed to be going off all around me. But with all of that, the most memorable part was the tiny little kittens that ran hither and yon between dancing and shuffling feet with only the moonlight glowing through open windows; I was terrified for them, as it was inevitable that one would be crushed sooner or later by a drunk. Music played, and the song *"How Deep Is Your Love"* by Bee Gees will remain in my memory for as long as I live. To this day, I cannot hear that song without thinking of my friend, Ben; *for all too soon,* he passed away in 1994.

On the bright side, I'm sure that you're wondering about the kittens. Not one of the little guys or gals was hurt, and amongst all of the dancing and crowding, they probably had as much fun observing the strange festivities as I did.

As the sun was about to rise, Mom staggered into a back room to waken her little son. Off they drove into the dusty desert horizon from whence they came.

Outtake

As said, mom's husband was a pilot and flight instructor at a local soaring school where I later trained while becoming a sailplane pilot. Many special things were described to have taken place there long before I became involved: there were weddings on gliders in flight with reverend doing ceremonies from the ground over the aircraft radio. There was also a very sad funeral: ashes were dropped from an open cockpit while the sailplane circled quietly and mysteriously with friends and mourners gathered below.

Two very significant parallels resulted from that whole experience for me: (1) I became familiar with the place and the people that would help to lift my fear of flying; (2) Ben rescuing me from West Hills at that particular time, may have been the primary uplifting and therapeutic event that proved to me there could be life after divorce.

---

[1] I couldn't help but to wonder if "*Woof*" acquired his name by sounding like a special breed of dog barking too (see Page 101).

All that remained of the Circle Oh bunkhouse in 1998

XXII. *A new life and new adventures*

The period between 1980 and 1990 proved to be a significant turning point in my life and in my career – a new kaleidoscope with different colors. In 1990, ten years after becoming a renter again, I would move into my own home in another country environment. But this decade – from 1980 following the "letting go" and re-adjustments – was well packed with events, ranging from very special romantic friendships to my first experience as an author.

Certainly one's own struggle with separation changes is not unique. My partner's adjustment to how and why all became as it did must have been just as difficult as my own. I do believe that the unequalled joy and bonding that result in a human marriage relationship is a mere child of the pain when torn asunder.

I once read that there is a hierarchy of devastating events that plague humans. Number one is the loss of a child; number two is none other than divorce; following those is the death of a spouse, parent, and so on down the line. As long as I draw breath, I will never understand how so many friends I have known endured divorce more than once. Ours took place over thirty years ago, and as of the writing of this chapter in May of 2011, I am still a single man [and in 2020].

I began to rebuild hope, and met many wonderful women – some through caring friends and others just by chance. Feelings of lost love began to turn into sentimental themes describing a new love discovered. One pop song from the 1980s, tells the heartfelt story of meeting that "right one" finally, but after becoming devoted to a wonderful one; yet one that may not have been really right. Every man and woman in that never-ending search will experience it sooner or later. Should we then remind ourselves once again about that *journey*? I will write about some of my special friends and the very meaningful people that they were a bit later. But first ...

But first, Professor "Tish" goes back to college

When I joined the community services faculty at a local college, the school had perhaps the most significant jazz band program anywhere. There were five separate jazz ensembles at that time, and all were top notch. However, it soon became evident that one reason the bands were so extraordinary was the fact that many out-of-work jazz musicians would join them in order to keep in shape. The bands were beginning to take awards everywhere, as they were covertly loaded with professional musicians who would sign up for band classes. Soon, certain safeguards were put into place so that younger and less experienced players would then have a chance, as otherwise the groups would fill up with old pros, leaving no room for upcoming hopefuls.

The guitar has always challenged its players in mastering reading skills. Consequently, weak readers are common amongst us, and this was where I came in (having been there myself). Young men and women would try out for the jazz ensemble, and if they could not make the B, C, or D band, they would be recommended to take my class in order to improve musical weak spots. The classes lasted for about eight weeks, and in the beginning were sometimes filled with as many as thirty or more guitarists. The textbook that was required was the one that my colleague, Robb, and I co-wrote together. As mentioned earlier, *"The Commercial Guitarist"* can still be found on Internet as an out-of-print publication.

My curriculum was based on that book, and designed to bring players into a place of understanding fingerboard organization, improvisation, chord accompaniment charts, and the basics of position layouts that facilitated sight-reading for commercial applications. After a class series would finish, some of the students continued to study with me at Southern California Conservatory of Music in the guitar program; others went on to earn their music degrees there, and a few remain friends to this day.

Following a few months of ongoing classes at the college, I received a letter from a renowned publisher of music textbooks. The letter came to me personally from the editor. She expressed an awareness of the class that I had been teaching at CC, and asked if I would be interested in authoring a special book based upon the subject material therein. I was honored, indeed! At that time, publishers would work hand-in-hand with an author and gladly accept a rough manuscript.

A year passed before I woke up to the reality that I had put the project off too long, and began to work on a book that was clearly aligned with their guidelines. I created an extensive manuscript completely on a mechanical portable typewriter, adding drawn graphics and hand-copied music. Sadly, the same person was no longer in charge of the project, and the book never became a reality – at least not as yet, some thirty years later.

The search goes on

My career continued to grow during the eighties in spite of personal turbulence, and as 1990 drew closer, publications and specialist appointments became imminent. But "no man is an island" has many different meanings, and Richard's professional life was now more complex with the ever-growing awareness of an empty "station."

When first moving out on my own, it seemed that the only way to heal the pain of divorce was to seek a new relationship. I felt somewhat of a lost soul from that point, but as would most red-blooded males, I soon became re-awakened to lady-watching as many eligible single women came to and fro for lessons at the conservatory. As I began to take notice, our director seemed rather pleasantly amused when sadness appeared to be lifting some; she did remain cautious, however, as she regarded the faculty/student interaction very seriously.

One afternoon, I came into school for work carrying my heavy brief case in one hand, and two guitar cases – one under an arm and the other gripped in hand. Miss B exclaimed with a one-liner that she was so good at: "Richard, if you keep that up your arms will stretch down to the floor!"

I quickly responded: "... all the better to hug fat girls with." She rolled her eyes and smiled while trying to remain dignified in a somewhat puritanical manner.

Some family history

In early 1981, one of my adult students brought a friend along with her to a school where I was teaching. As time went on I began to ask the student about her friend. She carefully told me that she was interested in meeting, but was unable to quite yet.

A year went by, and one day Leanne stopped by the school seemingly just to say hello. She also brought her young daughter with her from a previous marriage. I was very glad to see her and asked how things were. I then sensed a message of some kind and asked her for a date. We soon became good friends with some very interesting things in common.

As strange as it might seem, she was from a family where the sport of professional boxing was a very strong part. I then found out that she was actually a lady referee for men's heavyweight semi-pro matches. Her father had apparently been a legendary boxer, and she was trying to make her own way in the field without relying on his fame. Her goal was to excel in women's sports, and to participate in the Olympic Games. Now mind you, this lady was not muscular and masculine as one might tend to imagine. She was a beautiful girl, petite and sweet natured as anyone could ever be. She simply knew her sport well; and yet it was interesting for me to imagine her in the ring, standing between two heavyweight contenders while pulling them apart during a skirmish.

In my own family there was also some boxing history. It is something that I sometimes tend to forget about, not being much of a sports fan. However, two of my mother's brothers were once recognized as *bantamweight* champs in the Chicago area long ago. I couldn't help but to ask her if she had ever heard of them.

"Leanne, do you think that anyone in your family has ever heard of Louie and Tommy Moran?"

"Of course; the Moran brothers were household names with my father when I was growing up."

"Wow! They were my uncles, and the one that's still living is my Godfather!" Well, needless to say, we were both fascinated with the coincidence.

Richard the Realtor

Gigs continued to supplement my teaching income during the eighties, and as in earlier times, they were never without the typical musician experiences. Our bookings were in many interesting places, such as on the ship *R.M.S. Queen Mary;* we also played charter cruises in the harbors, made flights to Catalina Island, not to mention weekly weddings and banquets for society groups in many hotels around California.

The most interesting of those engagements was for a celebrity who had written and recorded a hit song. We were honored to play for his wedding and enjoyed meeting the singer's musical director. Apparently, our rendition of the tune with the tiny quartet was just fine with him. We were aware, however, that the song was recorded with full orchestra and we could not come close to that quality; but no one seemed to be disappointed when we played it for the wedding dance. Now if one considers the words of songs about lost love, it might have been a kind of harbinger of things to come, seeing that soon after the marriage the couple broke up.

There seemed to us no reason that anyone was unhappy with our performance, except that the mother of the bride never sent a check for the bandleader; apparently, she had decided that she didn't like the band and proceeded to stiff the leader even after he had paid the sidemen in cash up front. Now to what this all has to do with, you will have to wade through my rather short experimental escapade in the real estate world first.

That was the worst band I've ever heard!

Not counting the days as a kid pulling targets at the shooting range, and the growing years in newspaper work, my occupation has always been that of a working musician and music teacher. Music

181

was, and still is, all that I've ever been employed as; that is, except for a five-year stint as a real estate agent when I actively led two lives.

I had gone through much self-doubt after my own marriage ended. Questions of regret plagued my thoughts: "perhaps her mother was right; maybe I should have tried to make more money; maybe I could now see if there is something other than music that I'm suited for; maybe I could have been more *of this, or more of that, ...*" and so on and on my mind would race.

During the process of the selling and buying venture with the new house in West Hills, I became acquainted with the agent that worked with us through that difficult time. I admired him, and did find his work fascinating. He approached me one day within the first year after my giving up the house, and offered to help train me for a part time job in real estate. He assured me that it would not be a change of career, only a second occupation just to help with money and to see how I liked it. Well, I decided that the only way that I would ever deal with the agony of now ever-present uncertainty, was to give this a try and find out once and for all – just who am I?

His office offered to sponsor me in the schooling, and I passed my real estate exam on the first try. The office was in a very prestigious part of the valley with a number of successful agents on board, including an obnoxious eighteen-year-old, Donald, who had already become a million-dollar seller. Just before I entered the field, the market was at a high that has never been equaled since. One needn't even know how to sell, as clients were coming in and begging to buy homes.

As with my usual luck, the interest rates began to climb, and the market went down, and down, until the office that I was working in had to close. Not being any kind of sales person, I was really out of luck. However, I had met an agent who held the listing on a mobile home that I had shown to a young lady client, and we somehow became acquaintances. When my office was closing, she suggested that I come to work in hers, and perhaps consider working with her as a partner in mobile home sales. She was a competent and honest salesperson, and we made a fairly effective team in spite of the worsening housing market. I would spend mornings when I wasn't teaching at Harvard School, SCCM, or privately, in the new office making calls and searching for clients.

This particular morning, one of the gentleman agents that I had come to know came in with his new friend; she looked incredibly familiar to me, but I just couldn't place from where or when. He introduced us and told her I was a musician, and that I played for weddings and such. As we began to chat, she revealed a most interesting story: Evidently she and her husband had separated soon after their marriage; she then began to chat about the location and events of their wedding, and she remembered the band that played for the reception *was the worst band that she had ever heard.*

On came the lights, and as soon as I was able to picture the girl outside of a veil and wedding dress – bingo! I maintained my composure, straightened my tie, and said: "Oh, I'm so sorry to hear that; what was the problem?" (Coincidence? Egad!) She didn't seem to have anything specific to comment on, but just said that her mother was *pissed* at the caterers, and got even by refusing to pay them and the bandleader. (I knew that I shouldn't have played those hip jazz chords in their wedding dance – drat!)

Oh, you'll just love this very quiet mobile home park

My real estate career ended after nearly five years, but while it lasted, I did learn much about myself as a salesman – I wasn't! I was good at the finance part and loved showing homes, but I doubt that I could have sold a blanket to an Eskimo if my life depended on it. My partner and I continued to sell homes as a team, and even in spite of the downtrend, mobiles of all sizes continued to draw buyers. We sold some in high mountain *eagles' roosts* that were larger than stick-built houses, and yet small ones in trailer parks for older folks on fixed incomes.

Now, I suppose that one must become comfortable with his or her personal set of ethics when it comes to the world of business. But for one who gives music lessons for a profession, bending facts around corners doesn't quite cut it.

In one humorous situation, another associate and I were in the process of showing a small home in a park to a retired elderly lady and her protective family. We were in separate cars, as Jim's was more suited for passengers; I followed behind them in my sports car. We were driving the buyers out of the park after showing the home, and apparently they felt confident that this was indeed a very quiet and peaceful place – a concern of theirs from the beginning. I was completely un-aware, however, that there was an active train track immediately behind the fence at the back of the park.

All of a sudden, I heard a train whistling in the distance, growing louder and louder. I could see Jim in the car ahead of me chatting away, and pointing out the lovely amenities of the little community, while he casually began rolling up the windows.

The lady did make the purchase, but later sued the realty company because she felt that she had not been adequately informed that the swamp cooler didn't work well. Speaking of swamps, and in learning to cope with such situations, it was about that time that I had posted a sign in my kitchen that stated: *"When you are up to your ass in alligators, it is difficult to remind yourself that your initial objective was to drain the swamp."** To this day when perplexing and precarious situations arise, I find it somewhat of a comfort to pass by and read that sign as a reminder. (**Source unknown*)

Gigs, new adventures, and very special people

As the search for that right one marched on, it seemed that each new friendship brought its own kind of adventure along with it. My musician friend, Chad, from high school days had also been through a divorce and had many bits of encouragement for me. He had been through all the usual new bachelor things to later finding a new wife, and was a good shoulder to lean upon when things became emotionally difficult.

His family had been longtime friends with another family that raised three very lovely daughters. He introduced me to one of them that he felt would make a nice friend. As time went on, Shelly and I

184

managed to spend much quality time together, listening to music, attending concerts, and such.

I always enjoyed taking my dates to nice places, and making sure that they were treated well and with respect. One particular evening, Shelly and I ventured out for dinner to an anchored merchant ship that was now serving as a maritime museum and restaurant. I had worked band gigs in the ship's banquet rooms many times, and it was always fun walking about the decks to see the historical items on board, and for me, particularly the radio room.

After dinner, we spent some time in the lounge having cocktails and listening to a great little combo that played older standards. At a nearby table there was a group of people who were quite jovial, and much laughter came from there. They somehow invited us to join them as we looked alone and in need of company (so they thought). We obliged, and they generously paid our tab.

The band was conducting a "name that tune" game with a free drink as a prize to the winner. No one knew that I was a musician, and I was able to beat everyone at the table by naming most of the selections very quickly – so much so, that for each new free drink, I would designate it to go to the fun folks near us in a kind of appreciation for their hospitality.

Soon we discovered that the man at the head of the group had his yacht tied up to the bow of the ship, and was inviting the couples to join him on a harbor cruise later that evening – drinks and cheer on him. We finished the evening, discussed the invitation, and decided why not. After being assured that our cars were safe in the parking lot, we went on the yacht with our newfound comrades. A few hours before, we were complete strangers; now we were all shipmates.

Up on the bridge with the captain, one only needed to pick up a microphone to order a drink, and up would come the attendant with platter in hand. As a result, by the time we were heading back to port at about 3am, everyone was much too tired to drive and not in a safe condition at that. The captain suggested that we all just sleep on the boat, as there were enough bunks and accommodations for all.

We awoke in the morning, and before being brought back to the ship where cars were parked from the night before, the gentleman bought all of us breakfast as if he had not done enough already. Having told friends about that experience, few actually believed something like that could happen in today's world; but indeed it can, and did for us. We all went our separate ways, and have never seen or heard of each other since. Shelly and I dated for about a year, and - *for all too soon* - my restlessness along with missing my ex, once again got the best of another very special friendship.

Uh; ... but you're on the air!

Dating seemed to slow down when 1990 grew closer and just as well, as life became more complicated with my stepdad passing and mom soon to follow; but there were many wonderful friends made during that decade, including Victoria, and each one is a life story unto itself. One was a popular radio announcer, and would sometimes call me from her program on a rock station during the day. She knew I liked a particular tune by "*Genesis*," and would call to let me know that she was about to play it. It was fun listening to the song while she would chat to me on the phone between plays.

One afternoon she became involved in our conversation; I suddenly noticed that there was a dead space on the radio following the last play. I said to her: "Uh, Jean, I think you're up."

"Oh no ..." and the phone went silent; but the radio then promptly came alive with her lovely voice in stereo. I can imagine that many curious listeners were looking about to see if the power in their homes had gone off, or if the car radio had failed.

For all too soon

R.T and singer on the job in Little Tokyo, Los Angeles

XXIII. Transitions

As early summer neared the second half of its decade (circa 1984), many things that would shape the rest of my earthly life had come to pass. For one, I resumed the study of braille transcription; but the creative days were shared with the regretful passing of my stepfather, followed a few years later by my dear mother in 1987. It seemed that everyone who was close as family goes was leaving our veil of tears during this time, and one after the other. Soon after my mom left us, I learned from a friend that Doc (who I've written about earlier) had passed away without my knowledge, or my ever seeing him again. That coupled with the loss of a wife a few years before, left quite a void – one that could only be filled by returning to creative projects that might benefit others; thus ideas for shaping what would one day become the SCCM *Braille Music Division* began to stir.

All of my mother's five brothers and sister are now passed, and I have no contact with my family in France any longer. I did hope to one day visit my Uncle Charles there. (I wrote about his WWII heroic deeds earlier in this remembrance.) He sent a rather strange letter to me in the mid eighties, the first since I was a child. I replied back to him, as it seemed that he needed to make contact with me in a very serious way. I wrote immediately, but only received a response from cousin Evelyne that he too had died before having received it. A few others remain, but most tend to be strangers amongst family who I have never met.

Doc's memory is perhaps one of the more durable in what I consider to be immediate family, next to my own mother, father, and stepfather. How fortunate are those of us who were blessed with such unconditional love, and everything that they could give in the way of emotional, material, and character support. As did our Ernie Burgess as a model, it is that which we give back in their honor that truly makes a difference – and, long after we are gone. Some thoughts about Doc follow.

A short flashback: ... what then is a "gentle-man?"

I've known many folks who consider fishing and hunting to be natural and normal sports, and I most clearly respect the man or woman who takes a deer or goes fishing in order to bring food to the table. After all, if those of us who are meat-eaters could see what goes on in a slaughterhouse, we could never resent the former. But it is the trophy hunter that is difficult for me to understand. Speaking only for myself, creating a pleasurable experience out of the fear or suffering of an animal for entertainment, is simply not OK – at least not in any way that I am able to comprehend.

One summer, Doc provided my mother and me with a fun little vacation trip to Lake Isabella on the Kern River. I was perhaps about fifteen years old at the time, and he felt that he would make an effort to do some "dad" things with me, such as recreational fishing on the lake. He knew my father loved to fish, and that when I was a small child, we would often go to nearby lakes where he would make a catch; we would then cook and eat a feast there at the campsite. Doc was never a father himself, much less a fisherman; our relationship was more like buddies rather than father and son. But as my dad's best friend, somehow he felt the need to fill a void for me at that particular time in his life.

We were fishing in a small boat on the lake, and I had caught some fish as did he. I somehow sensed his discomfort with something, but was too young to analyze it at the time. He was trying to be the mentor and do what good dads often do, that is to go fishing with their boy. I, on the other hand, crumbled inside at watching the live fish hauled into the boat struggling, while hooks were pulled from their bleeding mouths in what seemed to me as a child to be heartless cruelty. As I would watch the process, I could literally feel the pain that I am told they do not feel (I've often wondered if anyone has ever asked one if it hurts?). After all, I thought: "I guess this is what we're supposed to do for fun." However, I would not let on, as I did not want to hurt my friend's feelings; both of us disliked it, yet neither would let it show. I suddenly put my rod down and became rather silent for a while. Doc continued fishing, but noticed that I appeared sad.

He then said: "Hey Dick, what's the matter?"

"Doc, I'm kinda not into this for some reason; I just don't feel too good."

He looked over to me intuitively in what seemed to be sheer joy and said: "Am I glad to hear that! I've always hated leisure fishing; can't seem to get into sport killing for some reason."*

We grinned warmly at each other, put our fishing rods aside, returned the little creatures to the water then continued to just enjoy the boating while having a good laugh. Now this was a strong yet *gentle* man, one who took trophies of all kinds on the rifle ranges. He loaded his own ammo and loved guns, but he was never interested in hunting or fishing for entertainment, nor ever saw an animal through a rifle sight.

*After all of these years, it finally occurred to me a reason why he never liked to eat fish.

A Little Album of Personal Vignettes*

A picture paints a thousand words

One famous entertainer was also an artist. I've never been able to connect this particular work to him myself, so I have not included his name. The work, as I perceived the description, has always remained indelibly etched in my mind. Apparently, it is his personal response to an old sportsman picture that shows a man sitting before a warm fire in a log cabin. The man is wearing a hat of some kind with warmers on his ears. His feet are propped up on a little stool, pipe in mouth and reading a book. At his feet is a traditional bear rug with the mouth gaping open, front legs and claws outstretched; it is rather bizarre, yet meant as a kind of warm cozy scene that may have once adorned a typical sportsman's den in American homes.

Supposedly, the artist's painting is described somewhat as follows: The scene appears quite the same as above, except that it shows a bear sitting in the comfortable chair instead of a man, and with a human rug at his feet.

Vignette: A short, delicate literary sketch (Webster's New World Dictionary 1979 – Pocket-Size Edition)

I once read a story that told of the last grizzly bear to exist in California. A hunter was alleged to have tracked the animal down and killed it in the year 1917. The California state flag now *bears* the image of a lone bruin as an identifying moniker.

Even a fly knows when you're trying to kill it

I began the day's hike as usual on a trailhead near my home. I generally make every effort to avoid other hikers, as solitude is usually my preference. A stocky gentleman wearing what appeared to be a kind of scout uniform, climbed out of his truck; I couldn't help but notice that his license plate had the name of a nearby mountain on it. Having climbed to its peak in our national forest many times, I could not help but say to him how much I liked that plate, as I was familiar with its meaning. We began hiking together, and visited as though we had met before.

His name was Michael, and he explained to me that he was the primary force behind restoration of the trail leading up to the mountain from the wilderness side. Immediately we bonded, as I was not only impressed, but I made sure that he knew how much I appreciated his kind of contributions to our forest trails. We chatted about hikes and other trails that we both knew, and exchanged the many animal sightings that were fun to relate.

As we spoke about one of our favorite wild creatures, the mountain lion, he began to tell a story about something that had happened in his neighborhood recently. It was apparent that something was nagging at him, as there was definitely an emotional reaction of some kind in his voice.

His son had told him of a cougar that had wandered into a parking lot not far from the forest boundary. Shoppers panicked, and the authorities were called to deal with the *"problem."* The cat, sensing danger, ran up into a tall tree for safety. When the animal control officers finally arrived, somehow the lion had magically disappeared – to where, no one could tell.

Michael continued to relate the story, and said that his boy asked him: Dad, how did the lion know that anyone was after him?

"Son, even a fly knows when you're trying to kill it."

Damn it, they're eating my plants!

A friend's mom-in-law kept a small handgun on a windowsill directly over the sink in her luxurious kitchen. She would take much pleasure in shooting at the small animals that she felt were munching on her plants within view: squirrels, birds, rabbits, were all fair game to her. *Well, I got another one today*, was the gist of a comment now and then. Rick wouldn't say exactly what was going on inside of his mind upon hearing such things, but he did manage to reveal his guilt once and for all, and confess some thirty years later: "Yes, it was none other than I who was tripping her traps in the lower level garage."

As some of you may know, John Muir, celebrated American naturalist, and Gordon Pinchot, the founder of the U.S. Forest Service, were said to be friends. However, as I recall an old documentary, John's philosophy was that nature should be conserved, and not abused only to satisfy man's needs.* Mr. Pinchot evidently disagreed, and felt that resources and natural things should be freely consumed and used, as they are only meant for man's benefit rather than that of preservation. Now what this has to do with "Annie Oakley" of Hidden Canyon would be that of just what came first – her impressive house or the little creatures that she could not seem to co-exist with.

*"Climb the mountains and get their good tidings. Nature's peace will flow into you as sunshine flows into trees."
– John Muir

You keep that up, and that damn thing will surely kill you one day

When I first moved to my new home in 1990, there was a rather interesting lady who came to my door; she was kind enough to offer cooking and conversation. I wasn't sure whether she was just being neighborly (even though she lived way down the hill), or had romantic hopes. She was lovely, there was no doubt; but alas ...

She told me some interesting animal stories typical of the surroundings, as there are open hills and countryside all around us. Rattlesnakes are always a concern here, and a very young one had wandered into her yard to make his home. Well, not to hold prejudice, but rats and mice can create untold havoc on the underside of mobile homes, and rattlesnakes are quite effective in creating a kind of balance, as it were. Jenny decided that she would make a pet out of the little snake, and hopefully he would return the favor and go catch mice when he or she grew up. It was no longer than pet garter snake that one's child would keep in a cage for fun; this one just had a strange looking rattle on the tail, nothing really to be concerned about(?).

She would bring food to the young snake that she kept in a glass aquarium; often it would consist of small live creatures. One would simply open the top of the dwelling, wait for the token rattle then place food in for consumption.

Now boyfriend would visit several times a week, and one day exclaimed to her in an annoyed tone: "Jenny, I'm telling you that you are crazy! One day that damn thing is going to bite you for sure. Don't you know how dangerous they are?" Guess what? *Slim* never bit the hand that fed him (or her), and the only reason Jenny had to send it back into the hills on its own, was that she could not afford a tank that would hold a full grown California Diamondback! Besides, he probably outgrew the mice that he was originally hired to control anyway.

Anyone who has ever soared ...

One tow-pilot who I met when learning to fly sailplanes has remained my dearest friend and a kind of big brother to this day. I can still remember the words "Atta boy, Richard" echoing over the aircraft radio when I released after a tow, promptly catching a thermal that would take me up like an elevator – soaring on the power of nature just like a hawk.

He lives [lived] alone far out in the California desert, but does have some contact with his daughter at times. He tells of how his grandson has taken up the sport of being a *hawker*. The bird is kept in captivity, and training is a part of the sport. My friend talks of the fascinating and interesting work with the hawk, but said very quietly to me one day: "*Richard, no one who has ever soared in a sailplane would ever keep a bird like that in a cage.*" His glance towards me and the expression on his face tells me that he understands the heart of the captive bird; perhaps the boy - now a pilot himself - does as well. The man has hunted for food before, and believes in the constitutional right to bear arms; he knows that, whether animal or man, every living thing has a first right to be free; I believe that he believes, man must earn that right – animals inherit it. [Bob passed on February 3, 2016, and is now *free*.]

Return of the iris meadow

I think that most of us try to contribute to betterment of someone or something at one time or another in our lives. Some may contribute a million dollar endowment to a music conservatory or to cancer research; others simply pick up a piece of litter – a contribution quite significant on its own scale.

I've hiked for many years on the beautiful trails high up in the Mt. Pinos wilderness of Los Padres National Forest. At the 8,700-foot level, there is a cutoff path leading south to a beautiful trail camp. One passes a natural spring, often the only source of water for hikers in the summer. The little spring has flowed slowly down-slope into a lower meadow for perhaps hundreds of years, creating the most beautiful and brilliant field of wild iris flowers I have ever witnessed. Each spring season I would look forward to making that trek, if only to see that meadow in full bloom. Humans are rarely seen there, and the silence is cathartic.

One particular spring, I came within view of the meadow only to find it dried up and barren. "What could have possibly happened?" I thought to myself. It hadn't been a drought winter, as the spring was flowing as usual. However, I suddenly noticed that there were what appeared to be mountain bike tracks cutting deep into the mud now across the trail; mud that used to be only fresh spring water trickling across small stones, which then ran down into the lush grasses to where the iris meadow had been. It was apparent that some effects of civilization had found their way into nature's secret garden. The riders had piled rocks in the small creek so as to make a better and easier crossing. They must have certainly been unaware of the fact that that they had diverted the trickling creek, thereby destroying the meadow below that had been there long before they were born.

After recovering from the shock, I decided that I would try to see if I could repair the damage. I took off my daypack and started work in the complete solitude of that setting. I removed the rocks that diverted the creek then tried to re-create a shallow crossing over the trickling water that the bikes would find acceptable. Water began to slowly flow down toward the dry meadow once again. Feeling good about things, I saddled up and continued my hike.

I returned to the spot before the end of that season only to find that the bike riders had undone what I had done, and the meadow was dry as before. I again repaired it, and upon another return, and another, again found it destroyed.

OK, now it was time for war! In the past, I had made the minimal changes with what I was able to gather and hoped that it would be sufficient, or that the bike crossing was just a random occurrence. Not to be, as the trail that they had now discovered led down the backside of the mountain, and was a perfect return for a loop trip through another trail camp. This time I was angered and resented the people that I had never met; it was now time to get serious. I again took off my daypack and resigned myself to aborting the hike, working into darkness if necessary. I was no stranger to night hiking, and after all, duty called!

I began clearing the creek once again, but realized that if the effort was to result in anything permanent, I would need to somehow find a way to arrange some stumps and large rocks in such a way that no one could – or would want to make the effort to –

change it. It would require the rest of the afternoon and serious physical work. Thought needed to go into making the fix seem natural, and to simply restore what had been before.

I sweated and labored for hours, placing things in such a way so as to create an obvious but natural bypass for the bikes on their journey, but so that it would leave the creek in its original path to the dry meadow below. At the end of the day, I was so exhausted and bruised that I could not hike out yet. I lay down in the dry meadow and fell fast asleep. After hours of darkness, I awoke to see a lone coyote peering curiously down at me. Hiking back through the night, I arrived at my car at near 2am quite pleasantly exhausted and feeling very satisfied.

I didn't return to that site for the rest of the summer, as I just wasn't sure that I would be able to face another deformation of the beautiful meadow. Having no idea of what I might find, I wasn't sure that I would ever return there again.

The following spring I did return. Walking very cautiously into view of the once full meadow of wild iris flowers, I couldn't believe what I was seeing! The meadow was in the most beautiful state that I had ever seen it, and the little creek was still flowing exactly as I had left it the previous year. And if that wasn't enough, it was now apparent that either the bikers themselves, or perhaps other concerned folks had worked to improve what I had done, adding their own touch in order to help preserve nature's intentions. Yes, I suppose that little things do matter.

"To laugh often and much; to win the respect of intelligent people and the affection of children; to earn the appreciation of honest critics and endure the betrayal of false friends; to appreciate beauty; to find the best in others; to leave the world a bit better, whether by a healthy child, a garden patch or a redeemed social condition; to know even one life has breathed easier because you have lived. This is to have succeeded." *

– Ralph Waldo Emerson

*Discovered by Sara, circa 1975

Richard E. Taesch

A gentle man and his young friend

Photos courtesy of RT's mother, Ann Taesch (deceased)

198

XXIV. The eighties wind to a close

I resumed the study of braille transcription in about 1983, and was certified in the literary code by The Library of Congress in 1988. One must complete the literary training before being allowed to begin the music transcription program. Five years seems a long period for one course, as one could conceivably complete a full college degree in that time. However, then my only tools for completion of assignments were that of a manual slate and stylus, and later a mechanical braille-writing device which allowed six-key entry directly onto a sheet of special paper.

The course was demanding; strikeouts counted heavily against your assignments and were completely unacceptable in a trial manuscript. Many times I would arrive at the last cell of a page after some 25 lines of braille then find one miserable error. A curse word or two was customary, and back to the drawing slate I went. It became particularly interesting when I had completed several pages, only to find an error that I missed some three or four pages back, one that would cause subsequent pages to be off in spacing. Considering that it could take the better part of an hour to re-braille one page, it's amazing that transcribers ever completed courses at all. I did manage to somehow receive a letter of commendation indicating that the score on my test manuscript was 100. I had no computer assistance at that time, and yet somehow managed a perfect submission.

Our music library at SCCM contained many thousands of manuscripts completed long ago by transcribers who only used such mechanical means. It is amazing to me how they were able to do such fine work, and to produce vast numbers of large volumes without braille word-processing capabilities. My greatest respect and admiration goes to those who walked through that dotted labyrinth long before my time. My trial manuscript was approximately a thirty-page work in length; a hand-brailled textbook could be several hundred.

Once the literary credential was in place, music study began right away. On October 20 1992, I received my Library of Congress certificate for music braille itself. Active music transcribers are still somewhat few, but at that time, I did have the honor of becoming the only person in the United States to be certified in music braille that year.

Looking a little ahead, and in the rearview mirror: "this driver reads braille"

While my own story about that coveted certificate is still fresh, along with my attribution to those who have gone before, I must take a moment to tell you a little about Bettye Krolick, often called *The Godmother of Braille Music*. Bettye was a very special friend, and her help and guidance during my early years in the field inspired me to dedicate my series of *"An Introduction to Music for the Blind Student"* courses to her. The dedication reads:

"This work is dedicated to Bettye Krolick, whose love for her calling and her continual support has been a companion to me throughout this journey ..."

Bettye helped so many people in so very many ways. One day while browsing artifacts for sale at a conference for vision professionals, I spotted a perfect little gift to send to her as a token of appreciation. It was a frame for one's car license plate that read: *"Driver Reads Braille."* I sent the item, and received a thank you call from her. She began to laugh, and said that it was actually true; well, I knew her background as a world-known braille specialist and lecturer, but I didn't quite understand her yet. She explained to me that when she had been touring the southwestern United States while demonstrating the first computer braille word processing programs, she would drive for hours between universities and such, therefore becoming quite weary.

She went on to describe how she would place a braille novel on the car seat next to her to see if she could read by touch. (Even the most skilled of sighted braillists generally do not read by touch.) Soon she was able to read entire novels and books while she was driving as long as they were in braille. So, *Driver Reads Braille* was truly suited for Bettye. Now I wonder what the cell phone "hands-free" law would do with that one today. I can imagine the police report on a citation: *"Violation: Driver was seen reading braille while operating a motor vehicle."*

Among the many accomplishments in her life, Bettye Krolick also served as the North American delegate for Braille Authority of North America (BANA) in Switzerland, when music became the first braille code in the world to be internationally unified (1997). Bettye was also a fine violinist who (before retirement) played in professional symphonic orchestras. It was she who stood behind me 100% when first stepping into the role of advocate for young Natalie, the young blind violinist I spoke of in winter. Bettye supported the approach that I took, which then became Natalie's springboard into her future.

The last few years

Thanks to folks like Bettye and others, my new career was beginning to progress; fortunate it was, as were it not for that reason to throw my feet out of bed each morning, I may have ended up who knows where. Losses of close family, wife, friends, and a general state of heartache and poverty were relentlessly present every day. Life was growing increasingly more complex, as when my mother's time was nearing the end, she became somewhat of a stranger.

Friday nights became our time to visit and watch favorite TV shows. I would come to her home following my teaching work, and we would enjoy dinner with a glass of wine and spend the evening visiting. I would sometimes tell her a joke, and off color or not, she would roar with healthy laughter. Dinner visits and watching the *Rockford Files* became the best part of my week; it seemed that we had not treated ourselves to family conversations since I was a small boy. Little by little, however, she seemed to become disturbed more frequently, and I would find it increasingly more difficult to communicate with her in the present.

Reflecting back just a little

In earlier years before my own marriage, my stepfather and I would often be awakened by the sound of my mom sitting in our

201

kitchen smoking and drinking coffee in the wee hours, while having very heated conversations with her-self. It frightened me, but it would come and go, and oftentimes she was just her wonderful self. We learned to make light of it and would often find her laughing along with us about her innocent "nutty" moments.

She was the last child born into an Italian family of five brothers and a sister in Brooklyn New York. Her mother was from Naples Italy, and spoke very broken English. My mom never really got to know her, as by the time she was born, mama was growing old and unable to raise another child. My mother, as a result, spent most of her youth being raised in a Catholic convent – a boarding situation for their school dedicated mostly to orphaned children. The conversations with her own self would often be as though she was back in the convent, and living a kind of childhood in that past time. At other times, we would detect what appeared to be a kind of paranoia: she would sometimes cross the street, insisting that a person approaching her on the sidewalk was an enemy of some kind.

Lloyd, my stepdad, had such a good sense of humor, and so loved my mom. He lived with her growing changes every day and somehow managed to maintain as light an attitude as possible. I believe this helped her as well. At one visit, he would tell us both that the neighbor in the apartment next door told him: "Gee, Ann sure spends a lot of time on the phone." Well, we all knew that it was a good way to make the best of the fact that she spent many hours a day in self-reflecting conversations about much that we could never really understand. These days, whenever I see someone shopping and merrily talking to themselves, I think of her, and can't help but to think how unfortunate it is that we didn't have hands-free cell phones then; now folks can rant and rave on the streets or annoy fellow shoppers, and no one knows or cares if there is someone on the other end or not. Lonely? Just wear a phony earphone.

Oddly enough, as I now recall things that she was trying to express (those which I discounted then), I see much wisdom in certain things that came to pass – things that she seemed to know which I could not. I have since observed the so-called wackiest of folks even in some forms of approaching dementia, to have an uncanny and accurate view of the universe – one that we will never fully comprehend in our so called *normal* states of mind.

Those who feel they deserve it the least ...

My mother had an incredible understanding of one situation that inspires me to this day. A young music friend, with whom I played gigs in the sixties, later went on to become quite well known as a touring and recording session musician. He was heard on albums with some of the most celebrated pop and rock artists of our time.

My mom knew him, as all of my music friends sooner or later would spend time at our home. We would all come to know our respective friends' families at one time or another when we were getting started as young working musicians. Jeff was a role model – high school class president, touring with performing youth groups, and more. A warm and good heart was always reflected by his warm smile.

It was perhaps twenty years since I had last seen him. When I heard the news of what had happened, and what he had done in the course of temporary insanity, I felt compelled to find him and to visit. County jail, prisons, and state hospitals for the criminally insane were something that I had only heard about in movies. The experience of entering them to see an old friend was bone chilling at the least. At one point, he had even tried to take his own life.

Sometimes during our visits he would verbalize a kind of distant realization about what had happened. Even though seemingly to him only a bad dream, he would discuss it, though quietly. Apparently he felt a kind of trust that I would not be repelled, and that I would remember who he was before his demons took him over.

One day while visiting in Northern California, I watched him rolling a cigarette; I said: "Hey Jeff, I didn't think I'd ever see you rolling a smoke."

He smiled mischievously and expressed something to the effect of: *I never thought that I'd be sitting here rolling one myself.*
It did lighten the moment somewhat, and even in the tragedy of it all, there was some humor. On one visit, he expressed that doctors say the *spirits* that he hears, those that tell him what to do, are only imaginary; he then followed his thought with how real they were to him.

It was nearing my mother's birthday in March of 1987, and I was visiting her during a short hospital stay. She was no older than I am now [2012], and I was unaware that she was very near her last days.

I said to her, for whatever reason: "Mom, I'm going up to see Jeff again tomorrow; does my going there ever bother you, or how do you feel about that?"

"What do you mean?" she asked.

"Well, you are a mom, and you know what happened; but yet you never seem to be uncomfortable with my visits to him."

She seemed to believe in such things as demons, and felt empathy for him; she then said something to the effect of *One day you will understand.*

Some of my own friends disapproved of those visits. And so goes a saying: *Those who feel they deserve love the least need it the most.*

My mother passed in the spring soon after those visits, and shortly thereafter Jeff wrote to me saying that he felt he had taken advantage of my friendship, and that he wanted to terminate all contact with outside people. I wrote back to him and said that I would honor his request. He will most likely spend the rest of his earthly life in that institution, which somehow seems to have become his place of comfort and refuge. Yes, there are demons that can destroy good people, make no mistake of that. And through all of her own tortured state of mind, my mother knew that very well; she understood my friend even better than I realized at the time. Perhaps I have my answer as to why she always seemed happy about my visits with him.

The 1980's kaleidoscope begins to close - a reflection

I began learning to fly in about 1987, the same year that my mom passed. I also started going on backpacking trips near that same time. Yes, I mentioned poverty, so how could one afford a luxury such as soaring lessons, considering $100 to $200 per week was not unusual? Well, I rationalized that there is a reason why God invented plastic cards that go into slots on little machines.

When my mother passed, the emptiness was so pronounced that had it not been for Victoria, and other friends such as Robb, I would have been devastated. As told earlier, the flying was not simply something fun and exciting to do. My nights were constantly plagued with dreams of airplanes falling out of the sky. That began in 1953 and continued until 1987, then later and beyond. So with Victoria's encouragement, it was time for some real aeronautical head shrinking; and so it came to pass, plastic cards notwithstanding. The one benefit I never expected from such an experience was that I learned more about being a music teacher by becoming a student, than from all of my education and teaching work put together. Some music instructors prefer to not accept adult students for various reasons; having become an adult learner myself, empathy for helping them with their musical aspirations and dreams became a priceless asset for me, and a benefit that I have tried to pass along to them.

Things to come - a preview

I had nearly paid off the flying bills from the eighties when I founded the Braille Music Division at SCCM. But for the period between BMD founding in 1993 and its decline beginning in 2005, I had ran up well over a whopping new $45,000 in credit card debt. No, not with more flying lessons, caviar, ocean cruises, and trips to France; my partner and I had both put ourselves aside during this time, and while concentrating on what we had to do to bring students and visibility to our school, we had little time or energy left to be concerned about how to make our livings. When tax estimates were due, we charged them. When the penalties for not paying enough arrived, we charged those. When credit card statements came for the taxes that were charged, we bounced them to other cards, and on and on it went. On the surface, we appeared to have gained enough grants for every scholarship, thereby attracting blind students and their families to our program; some were able to pay tuition, and others were not. It was our make-believe scholarship foundation that funded many of them; all we had to do was appear successful.

Grants began to come in slowly, but would never alleviate the financial mess that both of us had gotten ourselves into. If it had not been for our director initially, the program would never have gotten off the ground in its early stages. She set aside $6,000 for us to use as scholarship money; this would be applied towards a limited number of blind students that we served in an outreach. But once the money was used up, the school at which our classes were conducted produced more and more deserving children, and we simply taught them for free. Most of that money had gone to purchase equipment for the program, and to finance attending annual conferences at which we would present our work each year.

A little help from a few friends

Although enduring personal losses during the period from 1978 to 1990 and beyond, those times also brought special friendships and acquaintances, not to mention some unique honors. These are not credits or honors that I earned, but rather that in the form of celebrated individuals who crossed my path resulting from my work as a music teacher. In some ways – although they may never be aware of it – their presence and energy helped to prepare me for the exciting and yet very difficult professional times just ahead.

I'll close the early summer period of my remembrance by sharing a few things about some very special celebrity people who wandered in and out of my life before 1990, and a few thereafter – those who will always remain warmly etched in my memories. I have decided to list them in a random order, as any kind of priority, impact, or chronology is really not relevant.

Special People; just to honor a few

Clair Huffaker: Clair came to me for music lessons in the mid seventies. He was a prominent author, and wrote numerous screenplays for folks like John Wayne and many others. His only non-fiction book was beautifully titled: *"One Time I Saw Morning Come Home,"** which he signed and gave to me as a gift. It is the true and passionate story of his family and parents growing up in a rough and early Utah. Clair passed away soon after reaching age sixty-five, April 6, 1990. (*Simon and Schuster - © 1974*)

Jonathan Waessil: Jonathan Waessil was also a fine author, and wrote for movies and many novels. He produced and directed the movie, *Wolfridge* (1994). Strangely enough, while searching for accuracy of facts on Clair, Jonathan's amazing likeness of him in one photo strikes me; his even more close likeness to John Wayne is uncanny. His daughter is Victoria Waessil who I've written about in this remembrance. Thank you, Jonathan, as she is a gift to us all indeed!

– *For all too soon,* Jonathan Waessil passed in 2010.

Lee Weaver: I met Lee while teaching jazz guitar classes at Los Angeles City College. Lee is a fine and very talented actor, and to his credit are parts in many movies such as *"The Onion Fields."* He has appeared in at least 120 film and television productions. Lee became perhaps one of my longest enduring adult students of the guitar.

Dorothy Lamour: I only met Dorothy once, but it was such a special meeting that I somehow felt I knew her. She co-starred in the wonderful *Road* pictures series long ago with Bob Hope and Bing Crosby, and other films as well.

I was playing with a band that was hired for her fiftieth year in show business celebration, and we chatted some. It was held at a pool party in one of her children's homes in the valley. Many celebrities were there, and I was dazzled to be among so many of them who had been enormous stars when I was only a young child.

Julie Parrish: Julie was one of my childhood make-believe fantasies. She was a stunning red-haired girl who appeared on wonderful shows such as *Dobie Gillis* (1959-1963), and later in movies with Elvis Presley, TV with James Garner in *Rockford Files*, and others.

My last public performance was at an event that friends put on for her; it was an effort to raise money to help her with expenses from a life-threatening cancer. Our last contact was when I had loaned her my signed copy of Clair's book, *"One Time I Saw Morning Come Home."* According to my Internet research (tonight, June 12, 2011), Julie left us in 2003.

Billy Regis: Your response: let me guess; "Who is that?" Billy was an excellent trumpet player for starters. He and I played a number of casual gigs together, and we never had anything less than bundles of laughs. Stories about Billy were abundant among musicians; on one trip to a gig at a military base, I thought I would run off of the road laughing at stories of his antics from a drummer who knew him.

This year, 2011, actress Jane Russell passed away at age 93. She was a very prominent movie glamour girl – the one with the bathing suits and long, long legs. There was a movie in the fifties that was called *"Underwater"* that Ms. Russell starred in. The theme song was recorded with the popular mambo king, Perez Prado. The title of the song was: *"Cherry Pink and Apple Blossom White."* There is a very famous trumpet solo on the melody, and I've yet to find anyone who's heard it that does not remember the long descending and rising slurred note on the introduction. That solo was performed and made famous by Billy Regis! I still have an old 45rpm recording of it with his name on the label under the title. I was only a hopeful teen growing up when Billy recorded that hit song.

Rachel Flowers: Rachel is blind, and was 4.5 years old when she came to SCCM in about 1997. Now she doesn't know that she's considered to be a celebrity by some of us, and that is just as well.

Rachel came to us on the first day of a concert season featuring blind performers when we first began using our new estate campus – the *Story Yet to be Told* campus that our Dr. Burgess made possible.

We were setting up for the program, and Rachel had never seen a concert grand piano. She sat down to it, feet dangling from the bench, and began to play the opening movement of Moonlight Sonata by Beethoven, and then the Toccata and Fugue in D minor by J.S. Bach. History is certainly interesting, but perhaps the following little article that we submitted to several venues will tell it best.

SPECIAL NEWS ABOUT SPECIAL PEOPLE - AND MUSIC
... And about October 27, 2007 [Source: Article, SCCM Braille Music Division]

Saturday evening, Grant and I were honored to be invited guests at the Thelonious Monk Institute of Jazz, International Jazz Trumpet Competition. This was an intimate dinner gathering, and part of an all-weekend event and special Tribute to Herbie Hancock.

Our reason for being there was their featured artist, our own Rachel Flowers. Her proud mother and father watched as Rachel shared her incredible gift, and very deep understanding of the meaning of jazz, with such icons as Quincy Jones (Host), Herbie Hancock, Thelonious Monk Junior, Herb Alpert, Terence Blanchard, Roy Hargrove, Hugh Masekela, Clark Terry, and so many others.

Many great personalities were present, not to mention our generous financial supporters, Lou and Kelly Gonda. Refreshingly, Rachel was clearly accepted as a fine young artist. Rachel is blind from birth – it is part of who she is. And who she is musically touched every person in the Paley Center for Media during those precious moments.

Share with us the moment watching this young child stand next to Clark Terry in his wheelchair. He held her hand to his face - looking straight ahead - for what seemed to be a lifetime. Quincy Jones stood behind Rachel with his hands on her shoulders, watching Clark Terry - a jazz icon - absorb her incredible energy – truly a moment never to be forgotten.

Herbie Hancock has been one of Rachel's musical idols since she first discovered jazz only four years ago. There he stood hugging her, and saying over and over that few ever play the right chords at the ending of his tune, "Dolphin Dance." She was apparently one of the first. All of this happened only because of the music. No other reason - not for philanthropy, nor charity: just the music, a little girl's love for it, a man who inspired her, and who continues giving to all of us.

DRIVER READS BRAILLE

MID SUMMER
XXV. The other miracle on 34th Street

The eighties: a decade in retrospect

After moving from the West Hills house in 1979, I spent about eleven years living in a Van Nuys neighborhood near where I grew up. There were no air raid sirens any longer, and I was indeed fortunate to find the little 1928 duplex house owned by the very wonderful old-country Italian landlady, Bruna. Having left the role of homeowner and most material belongings behind, to not be renting in a large complex was a fine blessing. It was also close to my mother and stepfather, so the nearness of family was very helpful; this was good later, as when they became ill, my proximity was essential to them and to me.

The house had a nice backyard, private garage, and Bruna was very tolerant when I wanted to construct some antennas for my radio hobby. Neighbors came and went during that time, but there was always a constant awareness that I was no longer living in the same times as when a child. The neighborhood was rich with transient tenants; break-ins and crime were always a threat. My unit had been broken into and robbed three times during that period. One burglar turned out to be my neighbor next door whom I had even helped after his wife left him.

On one occasion, I was summoned to court as a witness; two men that had broken into my apartment were caught in the process by the police – thanks to someone across the street (I was not at home at the time). The policemen chatted with me in the hallway of the trial court, and warned me not to feel sorry for them. Nonetheless, it was still a bit touching when I was told they insisted that someone tell me how sorry they were that they had caused such a problem for me. Again I thought: *those who seem to deserve love the least need it the most.*

The eleven years in the little duplex was never without interesting events. But all things change, and the neighborhood was slowly becoming worse than when I moved in. Writing was clearly on the wall (and on a few fences) when someone came beating on the back window right over my bed at 4am in the morning. Apparently he was convinced this was the place where he was attending a party the night before, and that he had lost his wallet here. I rolled up the shade and sleepily talked him into realizing that it couldn't have been, as I had been asleep here since 10pm the night before. I then decided that even though I believed I'd never be able to own my own home again, I needed to leave Van Nuys, and soon. However, it would not be before a few more rather entertaining events would take place, including the cockfight meets across the street at 3am.

Back home, we just blow 'em away ...

On one side of my duplex, a kind of backwoods family had moved in. They were rather pleasant people, but the two young boys of the house liked to shoot at birds and other animals from the kitchen window. Slowly my reasons for leaving became more intense. I would hear the sound of small gunfire from their yard very close by, which was disturbing to say the least. Watching pigeons tumble from the telephone poles just didn't cut it. I spoke to them in a friendly way, and indicated that they could get into trouble by shooting guns in a residential neighborhood.

Aw we ain't doing nothin' wrong, was their attitude.

Once again, I asked myself: "*Why is this?*"

One day a kindly lady came to me and expressed how sad she was to see what they were doing. She showed me a little shoebox that contained two injured white turtledoves. The neighbor boys had shot the doves for fun, causing the birds to fall into the lady's back yard behind theirs. She told me that she had gone to them showing the injured birds, and pleaded with the boys not to continue doing this. They had little feeling or remorse, only to say: "Well, from where we come from we do it all the time. What's wrong with it?"

My mom passed away a few months later, leaving $4,500 dollars to me from her small savings; I decided then that I would begin a search for a home of my own, no matter what it would take.

But why is that?

In his compelling novel, *"The Voice of the Coyote"*, J. Frank Dobie expresses an observation that emotional regard for wildlife has not been a very strong factor in our American heritage. (Mr. Dobie's book is published by University of Nebraska Press.)

He points to a novel from the mid 1800s where the author expressed the thought that there surely must be some good in seeing wild animals other than killing them. Mr. Dobie's writings are sure to produce much thought, especially after my story about the Van Nuys "hunting safaris." I most highly recommend the book to everyone!

Miracles do happen – sometimes

I searched for over a year and finally found a mobile home that I wanted, and in a unique woodsy area outside of city limits. The community is situated in a secluded canyon, and homes are separated on terraced slopes. During the escrow period, I would maintain contact about the progress with my realtor, Pat, who represented my interests. The home had been abandoned and was owned by a bank. It had been neglected some by the previous owner, and during the time that it had been on the market.

In the last few days of escrow, I was given a go-ahead to enter the home so as to do some cleaning before moving. I knew that I'd need soap and water, and would probably have to purchase some area rugs, as all of the existing carpet had been removed leaving bare floors. It would take time to make it livable, but as exciting as the prospect of my own home was, I remained undaunted.

Pat was holding an open house nearby, and I met her there in order to borrow the key to the new place. It felt good pulling into the driveway; after parking, I unloaded my buckets, brushes, and cleaning things then approached the rear door of the trailer house. Upon opening the door, I suddenly saw a glimpse of what appeared to be very attractive new carpet. Confused and bewildered, I thought: "Uh oh, now I've done it, I must be in the wrong place." Nope; this was definitely the right house. I opened the door completely and stood in absolute shock and amazement. Having had so many things go wrong while leaving the West Hills house behind in 1979, and losing many of my material assets to thieves, this could not possibly be happening. I then thought: *when something goes right, why does it always seem so confusing?*

Apparently, Pat had convinced the bank that the home should be completely refurbished before it would sell. I was quite happy to go in "as is," but never did I expect to walk in that day and see several hundred square feet of home completely dressed in brand new wall-to-wall carpeting, and every fixture, sinks, and floors sparkling clean. When I went back to the open house to return the key, Pat just smiled. It seemed that for so many years, all I knew was losing loved ones and being defeated by greed; ever since that day, my time in this home has been blessed with good energy and in a place of peace. I have hiked the mountain trails that are a short distance from my driveway, and quietly been left to author my textbooks in blessed solitude. But what does *34th Street* have to do with it?

Long ago there was a movie called *The Miracle on 34th Street* – 1947, Maureen O'Hara, John Payne, Edmund Gwenn. Essentially, Kris Kringle tries to convince folks that he is really Santa Claus; of course he's laughed at, but tolerated as an eccentric. Somehow he is hired for a gig to play *himself* at Macy's department store in New York. A little girl makes a request to Santa to someday have a house of her very own. Christmas morning comes, and she drags her parents out in the winter snow to 34th Street; there the house stood, just as she had described it to the old man who supposedly was playing Santa Claus at Macy's (Kris Kringle, the old man that no one believed in).

Everyone knows that cows are not intelligent

As soon as I moved into the new home, I began exploring the hills and canyons nearby. Climbing up the ridges immediately adjacent to the mobile home park, I discovered rich fossil fields of ancient sea life. Apparently, the area had been a part of the ocean or at least an inland portion of it perhaps millions of years ago.

Across the old Highway 99, now known as "The Old Road," is a continuation of the same mountainous region, then soon to become a state park. Many of the locals would hike in quietly, as until it could be publicly designated, hikers were not yet officially welcome there. Range cattle belonging to ranchers from high in the hills above the San Fernando Valley still roamed the canyons to graze; they would then make their way back to the upper elevations at dusk.

I had been covertly hiking all day, and it was now nearing dark as I made my stealthy way back toward the entrance of the wilderness area. As I approached a turn in the trail, several cows, a calf, and a steer were coming towards me on their way back into the canyon for the night. They stopped; the steer snorted and patted his hoof in the dirt, while the cows stood and waited for me to give them the right of way. I was not aware of the entire situation yet, and stood for a moment just looking at them while they watched me – a kind of standoff of sorts. Apparently the little calf was frightened, and ran up the slope to my right. He somehow became caught between a bush and a rock about halfway up, nearly what appeared to be about 35 feet high. The mother cow looked my way, then back up at the calf in watchful concern. The others just stood and waited for the saga to play out, but darkness was coming fast.

The little calf tried to work his way down when mom would moo up toward him. Each time, she would glance at me, then up to him and moo. Her baby was in serious trouble, and with one wrong slip he could tumble to his death. The situation now became dangerous, and as she continued to look back and forth at the calf, I sensed an attempt at communication of some kind. There was no room for me to pass on the trail, so I decided to leave the path and cross the stream, thereby removing my immediate presence that seemed to be holding up the rescue. Every time the calf tried to move, rocks and dirt would tumble from the precipice, causing him to become more stuck each time. I began to panic, as I felt that I had caused it.

A few minutes later, darkness approaching, the mother suddenly turned around and left; she walked back down the trail and disappeared around a bend. The calf was calm at this point, as I was no longer a threat; the others were just waiting, not unlike onlookers at a baseball game.

Nearly forty minutes passed, and suddenly I could see the mother cow appear above the calf on the ridge well over his head. She had strategically explored what may have been one of their earlier trails, making her way deep into a canyon. She apparently hiked up the back side of the ridge somehow knowing about where the calf would be – even though not in view, and at least a quarter of a mile away. She had worked her way above the little fellow, well knowing that if she mooed at him from above, he might be able to go up, whereas he could not descend the steep slope below him.

Slowly and carefully, hooves slipping precariously, he made his way safely to a heartwarming reunion with his apprehensive mother above. Soon the two disappeared again. The others stood quietly in the moonlit darkness while I sat in the sand waiting for something to happen. At least another hour went by, and still there was no sign of them. Suddenly far down the trail, the silhouette of two animals appeared making their way towards the others still patiently waiting, as though knowing what the outcome would be. Here comes mother cow, calf, and a huge sigh of relief from me, the one who caused it in the first place. But then remember that cows don't think. Not much, they don't!

To this very day, each time I pass that spot on my way out of East Canyon, I think: "Yes, miracles can happen – sometimes."

Photo taken of the steep hill that our little calf nearly tumbled down from

XXVI.
The early days of SCCM Braille Music Division

Prelude

While still settling into my new surroundings on *34th Street*, the SCCM *Braille Music Division* was continuously stirring in my mind, although not officially given birth until about 1993. Its original and legal name was "Braille Music Programs," as was the DBA given to the project by an attorney on the school board of directors. Later, I asked to alter the title to "Division"; I felt that it created a more personal entity specific to the school itself, as opposed to a commercial product that the word "Programs" seemed to infer.

From the beginning, I was firm on the idea that an academic braille division should never overshadow the conservatory so as to create a false image of a school for the blind. The entire uniqueness of the idea was that SCCM should remain a music school first and foremost – "*... in which resides a special division within the mainstream of its general academia.*"

Schools for the blind are well known, and many have wonderful music programs for recreation and beginning players. But generally they are not designed for serious music students to study either as a formal part of their education, or if pursuing careers. Conversely, primary, secondary, and postsecondary schools that require music reading skills for blind students usually cannot provide the teaching of it. Thus the idea of my program to establish a fundamental concept whereby a blind student could attend a school of music where their special needs could be met, and with respect to literacy, would simply speak and teach their language. The division would be capable of providing curricula, producing braille on site, and remain completely self-contained within the school. Preparatory training for blind students attending other schools would also be included.

SCCM was originally patterned after the great European conservatories, in which a child might enter at a very young age and remain in the same school throughout the college level. As such, our children could be given music disciplines whether sighted or blind, and those skills would become an active part of their whole educational picture – whether or not they would pursue music as a vocation. To the day of this writing in 2011, even though now substantially reduced due to economic priorities, SCCM – were it still fully intact – would remain the only school of music worldwide with such a program as an integrated part of curriculum [Closed 2013].

But I must add that there was always constant pressure upon me to segregate our blind students; many people still do not understand that in today's world, they simply do not want to be set aside and put out of the way. Follow now, as I invite you to walk with me through some of our lonely journeys – those that have been said by some, may have actually changed the course of history in our field.

The Literacy Movement –
What Does Braille Music have to do with it? [1]

"When this 1994 article appeared in 'The California Music Teacher' [journal of the Music Teachers' Association of California], *no one could foresee the impending dramatic and rather aggressive demand for academic independence, equality, and career/employment opportunities that would soon overwhelm those of us in the field of music education and visual impairment. This demand would come from those we serve – the blind young people who have refused to remain lost in the 75 (approx.) percent unemployment rates among the blind population. These are the musical few who have learned of published research in music education and brain development – those who now are not afraid to pursue a once often laughed at music diploma, and to brave with confidence, the corporate business world or education and teaching professions. These are the blind young people who KNOW who they are, and that they are unique and special – not in spite of the fact that they are blind – but* [often] *BECAUSE of it!"* [2]

Heroines and a Hero

"But Richard, you don't have any blind students yet"

When the program was just in the beginning stages of taking shape, I would sit in a small corner at the back of the original conservatory location. My friend and colleague (later to join me as co-director) would often come out of his small teaching module directly across the way, gazing perplexedly at the strange little dots on the computer screen before me. To him, it appeared like some kind of alien form of communication; one day he stopped to ask what I was doing. I explained that it was a special computer program that makes it possible for us to produce braille just as with a word processor for print. He was intrigued, and began to wonder how his own career might one day become involved.

I had no idea where all of this was going yet, but as I made contact with people I knew to be in the field of education and blindness, all were extremely fascinated with the idea of teaching music braille along with lessons in a dedicated music conservatory. I then began to obtain letters of endorsement and wonderful support from many distinguished professionals whom I respected and looked up to.

The program and its implications had been brewing in my mind for over twenty years, but until now I had not been able to produce materials that might one day be used for blind students. I hadn't yet finished my music certification, and stood fast on the principle that we could not announce a formal program until (1) I was credentialed in music braille, and (2) had a basic library from my own curriculum with which to work. I had no computer myself, and the director made certain that one was provided to me; a little corner next to the janitorial supplies was made available for me as the official headquarters of the new braille program.

Two of my heroines

Kitty Johnson was the wife of our composition department head, Hal Johnson. She was also the acting fund-raiser for SCCM. She would say to me that, "I could maybe make a grant proposal, but I can't seem to justify it until you have some blind students."

"Well, Kitty, it's the chicken and the egg here; I can't serve students until I have some equipment, but I can't get equipment until you get funds."

"What do you need the most?" she asked.

"I could use a Thermoform machine."

"Why?"

"Well, that way I could make copies of some things that I can't emboss from the computer yet, as an embosser costs about $5,000; a braille duplicator is only $2,500."

"Oh; let me see what I can do; but without blind students, I don't think that I can ..."

In the beginning, our director was very enthusiastic about the whole idea, and just what it could mean to her school. However, once the *braille tail* began wagging the proverbial dog some time later, caution clearly did set in. Meanwhile, Miss B was never less than completely supportive of my crazy idea.

One very early morning my phone rang, waking me from a deep sleep. "Richard, Richard! Kitty just got a grant from the Robinson Family Foundation for your Thermoform machine!" She was so excited, that even before my first cup of coffee I couldn't help expressing much of my own excitement. Thus the program was born, and now it was full speed ahead!

That first year, I designed special SCCM T-shirts that resembled the traditional ones with a circle of fifths on the chest; but above the circle were the large letters S-C-C-M in braille dots, and below the circle was the name: *Braille Music.* Imagine my pride, when the Godmother of Braille Music, Bettye Krolick herself, came strutting into a state conference for VI teachers wearing one of those T-shirts!

Loretta was also on our board. She was one of the director's church friends, and part of a somewhat prominent family. Some of her children had studied at the school throughout the years. Her job on the board was that of publicity, and no one has ever been able to equal the fine media coverage that she produced for my work. As soon as we officially opened the program as part of the school,

Loretta was able to bring attention and media coverage from some of the following venues, just to name a few:

Channel Five Television – KTLA: We were still at the humble storefront school in Sun Valley when Loretta contacted KTLA News. A very popular newscaster brought his technical crew to the school for interview and to televise one of my first classes in music braille. The live broadcast was aired on the ten o'clock news for Saturday night, a highly rated news program. The class was composed of mostly adult students, and showed four enthusiastic blind women sight singing using braille music. The youngest was about 16, the oldest, in her forties.

Channel 22 hosted a television show called "*Daytime Dialogue*." I was asked to appear on the show for an interview telling about the work and how it all began. Although it only aired twice, it was a fine opportunity to show the school and to promote our work in music literacy for blind students.

KUSC radio (University of Southern California, Los Angeles - USC) aired a somewhat energetic program with the successful hostess, Bonnie Grice; her program was generally comprised of commentary for classical music. I was invited to be a guest on that program in June of 1996. I had been training a young man from China in music braille and theory from books that I had transcribed; he later returned to his country as a musically literate flute teacher. As the interview progressed, Chi Wei's beautiful performance on baroque flute could be heard in the background.

The Daily News: A full-page article in a section for several Los Angeles area cities appeared describing our new program. My photo was included, and a wonderful story about the school and the new Braille Music Division attracted much attention for us.

Other publicity was brought through these efforts, and with conference lectures and other presentations for Lions, Kiwanis, and others, the program grew, and grew. Thank you, Loretta and Kitty,

223

for bringing attention to our work for those who would one day see their lives changed because of your contributions.

A very special friend and un-sung hero

My heart is heavy when I think of my friend, Cass, and the selfless hours and effort that he donated to SCCM and to my early work. I met him as a student at City College during my teaching there of commercial guitar classes.

Cass was a computer specialist, and came to study jazz guitar with me privately in the mid eighties. He took a strong interest in the school, and later offered to help our director set up improved computer systems for office records, and just about everything that would help the SCCM become more efficient. He would spend time after his evening lesson, sometimes into the early morning hours, working to update and implement computer systems. He would donate most of his work, and often absorb costs of new devices, not to mention his valuable time and expertise. One of the computers that I used was one he built for me in 1995; it had a very long life, well into the millennium.

Cass built machines, serviced them, and stood by vigilantly. Were it not for him, my work, my publications, and our worldwide coalition, *Music Education Network for The Visually Impaired –* MENVI (www.menvi.org) would not exist today. Yes, that means that our Natalie, the young blind violinist, would not have made history as told earlier, nor could Maria have pursued her dream of becoming a piano teacher.

Peeking ahead just a little

When SCCM began setting up its new campus on the large estate in about 1995, Cass offered to build eight computer stations in order to equip our new computer music class soon to begin for blind students. Late one evening, he met me and another faculty member at the developing campus. Through a misunderstanding, the teacher had already made previous arrangements with someone else to provide similar machines, but Cass and I were both unaware. The machines that he had built for us were waiting in his car.

He had invested enormous time, his money, and caring expertise in building and bringing these specially designed computers to us; time that he could have been home resting after his day's work, and spending with his family. I've never since heard from Cass.

---

[1] Article title appearing in *The California Music Teacher,* Volume 18, Number 1; Fall 1994; content was subject of numerous lectures and conference workshops – referenced here by permission of the author, Richard Taesch

[2] Excerpt taken from lecture and workshop presented by Richard Taesch at an annual conference for California Transcribers and Educators of the Visually Handicapped – circa 1999 – 2004

XXVII. The great Quake of 1994

As progress for the new braille division began to gain momentum in 1993, I began presenting workshops at state conferences through encouragement from new colleagues in the field. Much attention was being given to the work, but as a result my own personal finances were slipping and becoming quite precarious.

I sat down one day to add up my income from the school and other sources: gigs, and such; I compared them to what I needed to spend on site rent for my home, groceries, and mounting credit card debts. Suddenly I realized that the debts were increasing at the rate of about a $500 a month deficit.

The director was in need of help, but I was reluctant asking to be hired temporarily as a weekly helper to maintain the school. She also felt that it would compromise a professional image as faculty member and guitar department chair. However, once I indicated that I was becoming desperate and could not withstand the deficit much longer, we agreed that I would work one day a week for her at about $400 per month, or $10 per hour. Now bear in mind that all of this was just a precursor to the debts that Grant (my colleague) and I later piled up giving scholarships once the division moved into the new campus in 1995.

I crushed my pride, continuing to teach and develop curriculum. My duties ranged from fix-it man to plumber, to delivery boy, electrician, auto mechanic for Miss B, and much more. Sometimes I would spend hours on her computer while she taught her children's musical theater, creating and updating school catalogues and brochures. Having led two lives before in the real estate work, I was somewhat prepared for the split personality. That extra money is what kept my "lips above water," so to speak, and allowed me to continue building the braille program for the school. After all, I once dodged bullets at the rifle range and jumped off and on trucks delivering distributors' newspaper bundles, so who needs pride in a crisis?

Mom! My guitar teacher just crawled out from under Miss B's car!

227

Not more than one month after settling into the role of resident janitor, I was awakened at 4:30am in January of 1994 with my bed rolling and tossing about the room. A massive earthquake was occurring, and Californians are no strangers to them. Oddly, the first thing I thought of was the new paint job that I had just finished the night before for the school bathroom – "I wonder if the shelves I just put up came down; I wonder if the school is ok? ...". For one year following that morning, life as I had known it was changed dramatically, becoming very difficult at best.

The exciting new venture continued to grow, but will still be there to tell about in Chapter 28; my humble dual-life servitude also continued faithfully until about 2005. However, time out must now be taken, as life in my shaky new rural home – although perhaps not quite as interesting as the Circle Oh Ranch – is certainly worth a side trip as entertainment and storytelling goes; not to mention an inseparable part of my work and its progress thereafter.

Such an experience does remain a constant reminder for the tragic disasters that others have endured in recent times. By comparison to Hurricane Katrina, tsunamis, Haiti earthquake (home of one of my favorite contemporary guitar composers, Frantz Casseus), and other similar heart-wrenching events, this was really no more than a small inconvenience. When one works daily with blindness and disabilities, particularly in the arts, one becomes very sensitive to how others have dealt with extreme changes. A person's peripheral view of the world around him or her becomes somewhat expanded.

Shake and bake: some first impressions

At 4:29am – 1/14/94, Braille Music Division was accelerating, and my teaching schedule was full every weekday; but on that morning, many of us South Californians simply had to temporarily *drop all agendas,* and come to attention.

To set the scene, on the day of the great quake, the weather suddenly turned unseasonably hot especially for January. The media tagged the daily events with a flippant heading, "Shake and Bake."

A memorable event, and there were many, was one that surrounded our mobile home park manager, Angie Leano. Angie is another heroine that I will discuss more in a moment; but she was, and still is to those of us who have lived here near or over a quarter of a century, a most remarkable lady. In the midst of recurring chaos, Angie came towards me one shaky morning waving a Daily News article on my work; she seemed proud that I lived here, and wanted me to know it.

Bear with me as I may seem to stumble, but the story is bound to make you (us) cry some and laugh a bit too; heroes and heroines were many, including the American Red Cross, without which we would not have had hot meals in this community for nearly a year after the quake.

Consider that folks just over the hill in the San Fernando Valley town of Northridge just had the upper level of their apartment building fall upon them while in their beds; others were thrown from freeways to their death. Immediately in front of this mobile home park, the Gavin Canyon overpass of the Interstate 5 freeway fell before our eyes, while cars dropped from over fifty feet high becoming crushed on The Old Road near our front entrance – no need to describe the occupants. A motor home was stranded on what remained of the suspended portion of the freeway between two sections that had broken and separated. That became known in history as *The Island in the Sky.* Pictures of it later appeared in magazines and on the cover of a Los Angeles telephone book. Those of us living here were now caught in this canyon, which suddenly returned to the isolation from which it emerged before the noisy interstate freeway had cut through surrounding farms, ranches, and peaceful countryside many years before.

At that time, Angie was quite different as mobile home park-managers go, and a very special lady. Having worked in real estate and mobile home sales, I saw the good, the bad, and the ugly in management on power trips. And even though full of fond memories of my home in the seventies, I had decided that I would never live in a mobile home park again – that is until I met Angie and moved into my home in Crescent Valley, otherwise known to me as *34th Street.*

It was now nearly 5:30am on that historic morning as the sleepy homeowners began collecting their wits. Somehow, at least 15 or more people gathered in front of Angie's home waiting for some kind of leadership from her that many of us had come to respect. Others met in the streets to make hot coffee on camping stoves, while hoping power would be restored for news and updates.

Clocks ticked, and still no appearance of her. The home was at least as large as many three-bedroom tract houses; it was now tilted severely from the quake, and obviously quite damaged. Was she OK? Was she alive? No one knew. We waited and waited, until suddenly a small flashlight glow shone across the window of her bedroom. We stood in our nightgowns, shorts, and just about anything that covered us, while keeping watch near her front patio. The ground continued to shake, and the high ancient hills directly behind us were still thrusting and throwing rocks and dust downward; this would last well beyond several days.

Suddenly Angie's doorknob began to turn, and with flashlights and the rising sunlight, we could now see her working to open the door, pulling it, and holding on to whatever was available so as to overcome gravity in the tilted home. To those of us that morning, this was the only world we knew. Later we would find out how our neighbors and families in the valley below were, but for now, this canyon became our primary point of reference.

Angie, now fully dressed, appeared in her distinguished age of about seventy-five; a resounding cheer went up unexpectedly from all of the people anxiously waiting to see if we still had our leader. Sleepy residents included doctors, day workers, and teachers who all looked towards a lady who they had come to depend upon for community direction. Of all the many things that had just happened, and of the troubled year of problems that lie ahead of us, this was indeed a moment to remember! Families were separated, loved ones' whereabouts were uncertain; our immediate future was clearly not known, and yet that cheer for the grand dame of Crescent Valley rose loudly and upward toward the dust cloud from the thrusting hills, and was definitely the greatest comfort of that moment.

Vignettes

I'll describe some of the highlights of life in Crescent Valley that occurred during the remainder of 1994 in the form of little vignettes. The chronology of recollections is not exact, but serves to create a kind of progressive accounting of a community so affected by this event, that it was publicized nationally in newspapers and on CNN newscasts as well.

Day 1 and beyond

My neighbor, Chip, had become a good friend and faithful helper. The first thing I remember as the shaking subsided somewhat, was Chip pounding on my door: "Richard, are you alright? The mountain behind your house is slipping, wake up, please!" Well, the mountain was moving, but seemed to still be where it has been for centuries, so I assured him that I was OK, and quite wide awake. He had awoken literally in midair with blankets still draped over him, and two heavy stereo speakers flying past his head from the shelf behind his bed. For the rest of that year, Chip and I remained in the community with Angie and a few other neighbors, long after most of the residents had left.

After regaining our wits, we realized that we were stranded in the canyon and would soon need food and water. The downed freeway bridge partially blocked old Highway 99, and no emergency help was around. The wilderness to our north had a dirt trail through it that was used for inspection of power lines. We tore down the gate that closed it off, and took Chip's small pickup truck making our way to whatever outlet we might hope to find. Apparently, an alert highway emergency worker had taken down a fence that would lead to an escape onto the freeway off-ramp at Calgrove Blvd. We made our way into town finding most of it shut down. We found some food supplies, but could not locate much water or soft drinks. Well, the next best thing (relative to one's point of view) was to purchase as many cases of beer that we could convince the store to sell to us; at least it was liquid, and those at home might just have to "tolerate" it (what a shame).

231

We had no natural gas, no water supply, and no sewer, as the septic system was ruined. Electricity was restored the next day, but the former three would remain absent for much of that entire year.

In the days that immediately followed, we settled into daily barbecues in Chip's driveway and drank much beer, as there still was no water. Angie suddenly remembered the most wonderful stories of early park days; others that would join us shared our substitute water as therapy

Ruth was a neighbor that I rarely saw before the quake; she was an elderly lady, and yet seemed quite active and trim. It turned out that she and her late husband had been aerial trapeze artists in their native country of Holland long ago. Yes, quiet folks who normally do not drink can suddenly become quite talkative and sociable.

In the months following the proverbial *Day 1*, most residents vacated the park, leaving their homes to the possibility of looting and whatnot. Chip and a few others of us were fortunate enough to acquire Andy Gump portable waste tanks and weekly service; Red Cross and the city would soon begin bringing water in for us, but only for drinking, as no running water for toilets or washing would return for several months. If one had a small electric hot plate, some cooking could be done in one's kitchen. And so, life continued as such for many, many months. Chip and I would make several trips a day to our swimming pool in order to lug buckets of water up the hills to our homes and to Angie as well. For a time thereafter, that was the only way that toilets could be flushed. Dramatized? Not a bit!

Day 2, Month 2, et al

A portable toilet was needed on each street that still had brave residents; my home was chosen to be the block host. I was still too traumatized to sleep in the bedroom where I had been violently shaken out of deep sleep, so I decided to bunk on my living room couch. All night the door to the portable water closet outside would bang shut with customers making use of it. It had actually become somewhat of a landmark, as on two of the CNN telecasts there were photos of my home and the resident crapper as a decorative icon.

Later, the city of Santa Clarita was able to arrange portable shower units to be brought in; they are often seen as trailers, and used on location of movie sets or forest fires for convenience of fire fighters. Those showers were being provided for months on end at a cost of over $1,000 per day, but were a Godsend for those of us who chose to remain in Crescent Valley.

We became good friends with the young men who had been taken from their families in northern California to tend the showers for the duration of our declared disaster area. Yes, they were a daily part of the barbecues and gold-colored water that we drank – even though we now had bottled water brought in.

Day 3, Month 3

Work slowly began on restoration of the park, but the scene was grim at best. Trees had fallen; streets were torn up; pipes were exposed everywhere and large doublewide mobile homes sat in ruins for months. My teaching work at the school continued, as most folks in the San Fernando Valley below had gotten somewhat back to normal.

Here, however, one could not just leave or come home without a Highway Patrol escort. The roads and freeways leading through the Newhall Pass were so damaged that there was no practical way in or out for anyone to safely use. One would simply make his or her way to the entrance of the park then wait for the hourly CHP escort to pass by. Late in the evening about the time I would generally come home, I would drive into old Newhall and wait at the freeway off-ramp until a few other drivers might gather for an escort to bring us safely through the dirt ruins of the canyon.

Late one night, I was following my CHP escort through a dark canyon when he suddenly pulled over and came back to talk to me; apparently he had received an emergency call and, apologizing, asked for me to wait until he returned; I had little choice as I had no idea where I was. An hour passed while I sat in the darkness, not more than a mile from home. He returned then led me back as usual.

My teaching studio in the valley was approximately 13 miles away. One evening during construction, the trip took over seven

233

hours to make. Folks became quite accustomed to the routine: cars slow to an idle and sit on the freeway; one does not continue to creep as in normal commuter traffic. You simply stop, shut off engine and lights then wait – sometimes for hours. If one needs to relieve oneself, it's really not a problem. Nobody shuddered at folks getting out of their cars and watering the center divider. Chatting and visiting with strangers simply became a common activity on the freeway parking lot in early 1994.

Meanwhile, work continued on the roads and on the Gavin Canyon overpass with the sound of construction around the clock. The Old Road, normally a deserted old highway in front of our park by day, became the alternate route for the Interstate freeway. We would wait for several minutes to enter the road upon leaving our little community once the escorts were no longer needed, and even longer to return. The speed limit on the old divided highway was now 35 mph; however, 70 mph was common; heaven help you when needing to make that turn into the park. Those who were left here still remain largely bitter towards the drivers who were so intolerant. Sadly, amongst offenders and speeders were even school bus drivers and family vans bringing children home.

I was told that the contractor for the overpass project was given a monetary incentive to complete the bridge within one year. He did, and with some time to spare at that.

The "cherry patch" and another kind of hero

Human nature is truly interesting, and in times of severe stress, it becomes even more difficult to understand. There were perhaps no more than fifteen residents left in Crescent Valley during this time. Let us look back momentarily to before the highway work had begun, and while The Old Road was still deserted.

All traffic had been temporarily re-routed to the other roads and freeways nearby. It became apparent that strangers had been seen frequenting some of the abandoned homes, and absentee owners' items and cars began to disappear on a regular basis. A sheriff called such a place a "cherry patch," as the deserted homes became easy targets for people who would make them temporary headquarters for larcenous activities. Once we realized this, several of us formed a kind of self-appointed posse, one that would make a patrol round each night.

We became aware of one particular person who was seen roaming about the park, and later observed taking belongings and a car that had been left in a deserted home's driveway. Once a day and time that we were sure he was present could be determined, we began a vigil to put an end to the plundering that was going on here. Suddenly he was noticed trying to leave, and became aware that someone was following him. Several of us gathered to quickly set a plan: Chip was stationed at the entrance of the park, others at different homes. I was assigned to hike through the wilderness area, as I was most familiar with the trails that someone might use to escape.

As I made my way along the trail, I noticed that a helicopter was circling overhead. I stopped and watched it, well knowing that they probably thought I was the bad guy trying to get away. They landed on a small knoll nearby, and sure enough it was the sheriff deputies. I confronted them, explaining what I was doing. One of the officers radioed back to call Angie to verify my story: "Yes, for heaven's sake, that's one of my tenants. Please look for the bad guy, and leave him alone!" Off they flew, and my patrol continued.

Meanwhile, Chip spotted the man trying to leave the park on foot beyond the entrance where he was posted. He drove off to catch up with him, pursuing slowly in the truck while the man ran desperately away in front of the vehicle. Chip stopped, jumped out of his truck and shouted: "Stop now, as I have a gun!" The man complied, and Chip ordered him to drop to the ground. There was Chip, one foot on the fellow's back, his gun – hand shaking – directly pointed at him.

At that point another of our posse had called the sheriff, and soon they came through the deserted and blocked off roadway. Instinctively, they seemed to know what, who, and why an armed citizen had this man apprehended. They promptly cuffed and removed him.

Chip then said to them: "Well now, I guess I'm in trouble for brandishing a gun, right?"

The officer looked at him, over toward the culprit then remarked: "What do you mean? I don't see any gun."

As it turned out, this fellow had been behind the looting operations here, and with other badly damaged homes in the area since the quake happened. Again, miracles do happen – sometimes more than once on 34th Street.

The Gavin Canyon Bridge of Interstate 5, January 14, 1994

A typical street scene in our mobile home park on the morning of the quake

A rare photo of the "Island in the Sky"; note two automobiles that fell from the bridge; the park entrance is immediately to the right of the photo, in the foreground.

237

Richard E. Taesch

*Angie Leano passed away in Crescent Valley
on August 6, 2013
(She was born March 3, 1924)*

Outtake

In her last few years, Angie became unable to walk due to a broken hip bone. She spent much time in her home, and became dependant on family and healthcare professionals. Dementia began setting in, and her memory became somewhat selective. I had so hoped to complete *"The Great Quake"* for her to one day read before it was too late.*

Not completely edited at that point, I managed to print out a draft and give it to her daughter on my behalf. I am told that Angie read it at least twice, then quietly set it aside, making no comment.

Other family members also read the chapter, and one afternoon someone said to her: "Grandma" did all of this really happen?" She thoughtfully looked up; her answer – with little hesitation – was:

"Oh yes!"

"The Great Quake ...,"with excerpts about Angie, appears here with approval by her daughter, Adeline.

238

XXVIII.
The birth and death of a 35 year-old dream

Prelude

As my kaleidoscopes open and close, little microcosms within them seem to take on journalistic accessibility for me mostly at times of either walking in nature, or during morning practice sessions. Pages and pages of outlines and scrambled notes adorn many notebooks, but just how they will go down here often doesn't happen until those moments.

The growth of our programs and the struggles for the school pursuing the new campus in the mid 90's, seems to be dominantly intertwined with my own personal life, as little else existed for me then. Hiking trips, nevertheless, remained the place of spirituality, meditation, and creative energy. It was at those times that many of my textbooks, curriculum ideas, and journal articles were conceived.

Yesterday (July 11, 2011) before beginning this chapter, I lay napping on a shady ridge in the mountains near my home. The spring grasses have dried, and hiking off trail causes one's socks to collect those little pointed stickers we call *foxtails*. I carried a notebook in my daypack in order to jot down some ideas, as I had somehow run into a block on how to write about the notes that I had made for Chapter 28.

Suddenly my foot began to itch wildly, and there was no choice but to remove my boot and extricate several foxtails that had lodged themselves within it. Unexpectedly inspired, I jumped up with a "Yes!" that could have awoken a hibernating bear. The direction for Chapter 28 was magically born – due only to the annoying little foxtails. I scrambled for my notebook, wrote the idea down then proceeded to crawl into a shady thicket to resume the nap before planning the five-mile hike home.

I fell deep asleep for near an hour, as restful sleep continues to elude my nights. I opened my eyes slowly regaining the where, how, when, and why I was here, then suddenly turned to see a young rattlesnake peacefully curled up within eight to twelve inches from my head. They are plentiful here in the summertime, and knowing the nature of this type, I was only mildly alarmed. One must never be complacent about such things, but having had many close encounters with them, I felt that I was not in any danger. I simply began to move and raise my head; his one little eye opened and watched me. Both of my big eyes watched him! I saw that he was not threatened or agitated, so I sat up slowly and spoke in a quiet voice as he continued his nap. I picked up my notebook while carefully moving a foot or so away then let him lay peacefully. I was still unaware that he would later contribute to my newly inspired notes. *The troubled years* includes an episode that gives special meaning to that unexpected and natural moment.

The troubled years

Preamble: The times from 1995 until about 2003 were mixed with wonderful events at the new campus, but were sadly sprinkled with stress, internal conflict within our board, and agonizing legal problems. The good years were blessed with love and loyalty, and are too special to tell about along with the troubled ones, yet both share the same microcosmic time frame. I have chosen to get the troubled times out of the way so as to cleanse the pages for the good ones. Soon enough, late summer in 2005 will bring more challenges and the untimely death of much of the little school as we once knew it. None is depressing, however; as with all challenges, some humor and new lessons is the windfall.

I haven't had foxtails in my socks since I was a kid!

It was approaching lunchtime during an emergency board meeting being held in our new conference room. The area was once the grand dining room of the old Tudor estate home, now slowly being converted to what one day might become a primary campus for the SCCM. Large windows looked out upon acres of green and the beautiful rock-lined swimming pool somewhat resembling a small lake. Across from the pool was the little two-story "Sleeping Beauty" cottage that looked like a miniature castle. The building was the home and headquarters for the burgeoning Braille Music Division. It housed thousands of braille books, our braille production center, and was my personal office and teaching studio.

My partner and I had made each other a promise that, once the struggles during purchasing the property were over, we would lower a case of beer on a special rope down into the creek behind the cottage. The cold water was to chill the beer, and we would sit on the bank to celebrate the arrival of a dream. That time never came; *for all too soon,* the dream became a nightmare, as the new campus – now in the throes of uncertainty – was nearing the end of its short life.

This meeting was to be only one of many critical board discussions that were becoming commonplace. Finances were nearly depleted due to failed attempts to obtain city permits, and the passing of Dr. Burgess, the facility's main supporter. It was inevitable that if funds were not obtained soon, the school would be forced to sell or abandon the unfinished campus.

It mattered not to the man who sat at the head of the meeting table, that blind children and college prep students had found the right home for their musical needs – perhaps the only one of its kind anywhere in the world. He was called during one of many desperate searches to find interim funds to save our dream. This was a ruthless businessman who would make short-term loans, then repossess a property for a late payment, or if the money could not be completely repaid within a few months.

The board decided to recess, then take the gentleman out to the far reaches of our property to tour its possibilities. We walked past green grass, the many fruit trees, and our tennis court in order to view a backfield; the field was in a natural state with brown weeds and vegetation. Suddenly the man reached down to his feet to see why he was being rendered uncomfortable. He seemed to stop in an unexpected kind of childish moment, looking into the distance as though reliving a past experience. He then exclaimed: "… I haven't had foxtails in my socks since I was a kid!" For a moment he was a child again, long removed from the mission for which he was invited to lunch with us on that day. Soon after that, the meeting resumed while our director proceeded to have meals delivered.

241

"Now, sir," a board member asked, "what are your terms, and how much can you invest here?" He would advance the school just enough money to uphold perhaps 2 to 3 months of mortgage payments then the loan would immediately come due.

"Will there be some grace period if we should be delayed in repaying the entire amount?"

"No, there will be no extension; I will definitely take the property, as this is why I'm in business you see."

There was no further comment as he continued to munch his complimentary tuna fish sandwich while smiling kindly. His casual friendliness and wonderful return to childhood seemed somehow lost on most of us at that point. He had done his homework, and knowing how desperate we were, was confident that he would soon own the multi-million dollar property. Sadly for him, another bandage loan was acquired. Although I was tempted to now ask him to pay for the lunch (with compound interest), he was called and greeted with a "thanks, but no thanks." All efforts were eventually unsuccessful; SCCM and its blind children still lost their campus.

My own opinion of human nature clearly took another setback that day. It always seemed to me as a child we learned that *business* was defined as a kind of "fair exchange." One would provide a service for which he or she would be paid in return. Profit was fair, as it would enable the businessman to propagate his craft and to create more products to be sold again. "An eye for an eye, and a tooth for a tooth" were values that we learned as children.

Our modern world has taught me a new meaning of what I once respected as "business ethics." I have become increasingly more aware of an observation that the honest ethic of business may have been re-defined by some, in that one must only maximize profits no matter the cost to the consumer. Could it now mean that to be successful, one must strive to take as much as possible, and to give back as little as is absolutely necessary - or, nothing at all? Make it cheaper and charge more; put less coffee in the can and raise the price, and so on.

Observations: A homeless person who is hungry can be arrested for stealing a loaf of bread; but creative labeling can be deceptively misleading, and quite justified as marketing strategy, not to mention discarding that loaf of bread to waste if not sold by a certain date. A maligned creature such as my earlier nap-partner can be so feared by humans, that it is often destroyed on sight even without cause; but the *ethic* of a ruthless lender is considered to be merely *business as usual*.

What does a summons have to do with anything here?

Many concurrent problems were now confronting our school, including a lawsuit brought by a student whose SCCM degree became invalid due to changes in state education requirements. A longtime loyal and faithful helper also felt that he was treated unfairly when he was asked by our director to move from the property in order to satisfy permit requirements during applications for re-zoning. He brought a lawsuit against her, and later was successfully awarded damages.

Trying to remain separate from these administrative woes so that we could concentrate on our teaching, Grant and I worked tirelessly to maintain the braille program there on Saturdays. Meanwhile, the school had spent nearly a quarter of a million dollars during the application process – all efforts to be turned down.

Not yet discouraged, SCCM maintained communication with city planners, feeling comfortable to continue as a satellite facility until it could satisfy their requirements. Meanwhile, the degree and helper's lawsuits continued to loom, and with all other problems ongoing, were approaching determination. [See "*The Sacramento Files*" on Page 248.]

I was teaching a young learning-disabled blind girl one afternoon in the little cottage, when what appeared to be a stranger suddenly came jogging across our yard. At that moment, I needed to return to the main building to acquire some fresh braille paper.

"Excuse me for a moment, Joanne, I'll be right back; just keep trying to read through your music."

As I opened the cottage door, the man ran toward me. While running in place, he said something like: *Oh, are you Richard?*

Someone gave me this note; I think it's for you. I took the note as he mysteriously jogged off, never to be seen again.

It was not a note; it was a summons to appear in court as a witness for the school helper's lawsuit. My partner was teaching in the main house and also received one. Until this point, the friction between the director and the helper was uncomfortable, but did not directly impact us.

Even to this day, I am shocked at how I reacted to that moment, and how the following several weeks were affected. I stared down at the summons thinking to myself: "My god, just what does this have to do with that poor child in there; what does it have to do with any of this – I just don't understand it; what have we done wrong, and why is everything so difficult?" I was not concerned about appearing in court, as after visiting prisons, that was not even a remote thought.

Hundreds of images raced through my mind as I stood there, door open, and little Joanne working away inside. She had been on a full scholarship since a small child; she was part of Grant's and my make-believe scholarship efforts. We had given up everything for this program; my debts were mounting into the tens of thousands of dollars, and suddenly a jogging trespasser brings this news.

I continued to stare at the paper, and at that point nothing made sense, and nothing could fix it. I returned to the cottage and quietly sat down next to the girl. I looked at her and thought once again of words in the song, *Bless the Beasts and the Children.* I then said to her: "Joanne, I have to end our lesson but I can't explain why." She began to cry; she was frightened, sensing that something terrible had just happened. We walked slowly toward the kitchen of the mansion where her caretaker was waiting.

Joanne was living in a foster home, as her mother was unable to care for her; moreover, her father was now lying terminally ill. She was perhaps about 14 at that time. I brought her into the kitchen to the waiting caregiver that she called grandma. "Arlene, something has just happened, and I can't explain; but I have to leave. I'm so sorry, but I'll explain later." I turned and left, got into my car, and was not heard from for nearly three weeks.

I went home and turned off all phones; I sent one email to my friend, Valerie, who was working at the school so as to let her know

I was safe. It was during that time I completed most of the Part II edition for "*An Introduction to Music for the Blind Student*" course series. All I could do was to write, and write, and write; it was the only way that I could try to justify any valid reason to go on, as the reality of how such an event could be so removed from the blind children and those that we wanted to help simply could not be reconciled. For the first time, I lost faith and belief in Ernie's words to me: "*Just do the work Richard, and the rest will take care of itself.*" We did the work, and now I was asking why.

I returned to SCCM after about a month. I then wrote a formal letter to all the parents of the children explaining not the reason, but only that I had returned, and would give it my all. No one asked where, why, or what; somehow they all knew, and respected my reasons.

Perhaps you may want to once again read "*A Story yet to be Told*" from Mid Spring on page 92. That story was written for public consumption, and designed for promotional interest to grant writers; now that you have been invited inside to peer behind the scenes, you will no doubt observe the underpinnings in a much different way. Only later did I learn that I had undergone a complete psychological breakdown.

The stories surrounding these troubled times are so complex and so many, that it might be well to tell just a few of them in a section of short vignettes. As promised in the Introduction, you may laugh, you may cry; but be assured that the author will be laughing and crying along with you as he writes about, and re-reads, these very real and special moments. Beyond that, the good years were so abundant and full of heart-warming success stories, that I believe they need special attention; and so will they have in Chapter 29. Now should the chronological kaleidoscope of chapter 28 seem a bit unstable, that is only because it is, and exactly how it appeared to those of us who survived it.

Following is one of the many exercises that I composed for some of my students during the weeks following the summons:

WALTZ FOR MALISSA

A braille music reading session with Sebastian
Photo courtesy of Luradine Rogers &
Dancing Dots (Used by permission)

Vignettes

Noah's ark

Valerie is a very special friend who I met quite by accident. She was conducting a survey of postsecondary schools and blindness on the Internet, while completing her master thesis at New England Conservatory of Music. I responded to her through our Music Education Network for The Visually Impaired, and we immediately became lifelong friends. [Story and name used with Valerie's consent.]

She later moved to California from Boston, leaving an administrative job at Berklee College of Music. She was to take a very low paying job with us as Director of Development, and would live at the new campus in a combination residence/office suite. We shared laughs, delightful company, wine, and commiserated when necessary about the many problems we confronted day to day.

247

Valerie was in the process of losing her sight due to a congenital cause. She could see in some capacity, but nevertheless required a guide dog and a cane.

Not being completely aware of the many hidden faults that had not yet been corrected in the large house, she was often unable to anticipate inevitable problems. Once everyone had left for the day, she had little support should *it* suddenly hit the proverbial fan. This home once had thirteen bathrooms; hers was the size of some bedrooms, and housed within her 900 square-foot quarters. The tub was not unlike a Roman spa, and marble was quite prevalent. But one of many flaws was that the contractor had never installed an overflow for the tub – you know, that which prevents a major flood should one become ill and fall asleep while filling it with bubble bath and hot water.

The recital hall was directly below her suite, and contained a very expensive concert grand piano. Well, as the water flowed through all of the upstairs rooms and through the floor, it did miss the piano, but not before causing $40,000 in damage to the hardwood floors throughout the main level. Poor Valerie woke up from a deep sleep that was caused by a massive migraine headache. Realizing that she had left the water filling the tub, she jumped up and found her feet over the ankles in water. For weeks fans ran, workmen toiled, and Valerie was thereafter fondly dubbed with the nickname, *Noah*! However, only Noah and her guide dog were passengers on the ark that night.

The Sacramento files

SCCM did not grant many degrees during its state-authorized lifetime, but those awarded were very well earned, and led to fine jobs. Miss B was quite steadfast, and a driven director; she believed in the quality of education that the school provided, and remained vigilant to its reputation.

When degree authorization was removed due to changes in the state education policies, she was in the midst of completing a diploma for a man that had come to SCCM on my own reputation. She began a new application process, but overlooked the fact that a degree could no longer be granted without re-certification being intact – a very pricey project. She continued to complete a graduation for the gentleman, including his senior recital. In all fairness to her, however, an official from Sacramento had supposedly assured her that if the school went through with the new application, his degree *should* be valid. Well, either he wasn't clear, or perhaps she was unable to comprehend the new requirements.

Upon applying for the teaching job that the new graduate was promised, the degree was rejected; he sued the school, Miss B, and was quite unhappy with just about everything that had anything to do with it. Hoping to pull things out of the fire, the guitar teacher – me – with Valerie's help, volunteered to put together a new application which might have redeemed things. It was months upon months of demanding work, dotting every "*i*" and crossing every "*t*." There was constant consultation with the representative from the education department – a new bureau still not completely familiar with all of the revisions itself.

The lawsuit was looming at the same time, SCCM was out of money as usual, and the application was abandoned upon advice of the attorney. The musician who earned the degree was awarded a substantial sum, which came from a small inheritance Miss B's brother had left to her, money she was only saving for the good of her school. Miss B never took a salary, and lived like a homeless person most of her life; she literally gave that life for SCCM. Somehow the irony of that has always remained far over my head.

Fiddlers on the roof

Among several temporary occupants of the quaint roof-top apartment over our campus garage, was the family of a long-time violin student. They lived close to the would-be school in a nearby neighborhood, and had made arrangements with the board to reside in the apartment until their new home was complete.

On one particular day, some plumbing work was being done and all water in the building had been turned off. The workers proceeded to leave the premises for their lunch, but carelessly neglected to inform anyone that there was a reason the water was off, and NOT to attempt turning it back on yet. Upon arriving home from a long day, someone decided to take a shower. *Strange, the water is off again;* was apparently the thought. *Well, no matter. I know where the valve is I'll just turn it back on; the gardener must have forgotten again.*

Turn it on he or she did, then proceeded to enjoy a shower in the upstairs apartment while - unknown to anyone - an open pipe elsewhere gushed water violently throughout the main house causing another flood that, although not quite as interesting as the *Ark*, did another $25K in damages to the building. The pageant was playfully referred to thereafter as *fiddlers on the roof.*

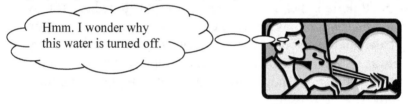

A soccer field, you say …

During the time that Valerie lived and worked in the building (pre-fiddler days), she had the opportunity to visit with folks who would come in to view the place out of curiosity. A lady came in one day who seemed somewhat familiar with zoning issues and development. Valerie mentioned our challenges during the process of obtaining permits to quietly exist as a school. The lady said that the only reasons she could think of might be the zoning change, and that she once heard that someone had long considered the property to be appropriate for recreational purposes.

SCCM was now in the throes of financial ruin, and an offer to buy our property was brought to Miss B one afternoon. Several *"suits"* (the kind that contain businessmen) gathered at a table that included our realtors. They said that they were from a foundation that was authorized to purchase private land for recreational use.

They apparently knew that we were desperate, and offered very little for the property. As it turned out, they represented interests in the search to acquire public parkland. It did appear that they had been considering this parcel long before our time. Meanwhile, a backup offer had been accepted from a private party just in case, and the property was sold to them.

Our property was sold for about 1.7 million, but within six months, was perhaps worth about 5 million dollars – enough to have endowed the school for the rest of its existence. SCCM recovered only that which it had saved for over thirty years, and that was spent in wasted leases within two years.

Postlude: the troubled years

Miss B's first and last real home

Miss B had lived in a rented room within the large home of one of her past voice students for many years. She was suddenly forced to move out, as their property had been sold. For a short interim time, she was able to room in a home with an old friend that she knew from her church. Soon after, Valerie left the SCCM as director of development and returned to her home in Boston.

After some convincing, Miss B agreed to move into the upstairs suite in the satellite *un-campus*. It was one of the few times in her life that she had private quarters of her very own, and best of all, it was on the owned property of the school she herself founded long ago. She slowly became attached to the suite, and even began to put some of her personal belongings there, including artifacts and musical things around her.

As described above, within less than a few months *"it"* hits the fan, and the property was sold. Miss B was again homeless, but now there was nowhere to go – no one to offer a room – and no money to rent, as her savings had been spent on problems resulting from the helper's, and the rubber degree settlements.

Lurrine literally stayed the rest of her days inside the original storefront building of SCCM where she founded the school in 1971. She was able to contain the secret for quite some time before her death. But it was soon to be known that, when everyone would finally leave in the evening, she would quietly unpack a hidden cot; her school office became her last bedroom. She was found collapsed in the bathroom shortly after and – *for all too soon* - passed away slightly *thereafter*. She was 79 years old.

I would like to share a little reading that I recited to the attendees at her funeral; it is called *The Donkey*.

THE DONKEY*

One day a farmer's donkey fell down into a well. The animal cried piteously for hours as the farmer tried to figure out what to do. Finally he decided that the animal was old, and that the well needed to be covered up anyway – it just wasn't worth it to retrieve the donkey.

He invited all of his neighbors to come over and help him. They all grabbed a shovel and began to shovel dirt into the well.

At first, the donkey realized what was happening and cried horribly. Then, to everyone's amazement, he quieted down. A few shovel loads later, the farmer finally looked down into the well and was astonished at what he saw. With every shovel of dirt that hit his back, the donkey was doing something amazing. He would shake it off and take a step up.

As the farmer's neighbors continued to shovel dirt on top of the animal, he would shake it off and take a step up. Pretty soon everyone was amazed as the donkey stepped up over the edge of the well and trotted off!

Yes, life is going to shovel dirt on you, all kinds of dirt. The trick to getting out of the well is to shake it off, and take a step up. Each of our troubles is a stepping-stone. We can get out of the deepest wells just by not stopping, never giving up!

Remember the five simple rules! To be happy:
1. *Free your heart from hatred.*
2. *Free your mind from worries.*
3. *Live simply.*
4. *Give more.*
5. *Expect less.*

The source of this reading is unknown to me. Thanks to the author for sharing it wherever he or she may be. Your inspiring work has brought smiles and tears to all of us upon whose ears it has fallen. [RT]

According to Internet searches on 2-14-13 and 3-13-20, the author of "The Donkey" is unknown. The above version is only one of many that I have seen.

Child reaching out to comfort an abused donkey

(I asked one of my young students to describe her image of the donkey portrayed in the story; the rough sketch above was how she explained it to me.)

Richard E. Taesch

The little cottage that housed the Braille Music Division for seven years; thousands of braille books lived in the upstairs portion

An occasional visitor (photo taken left of the cottage above)
[Photos courtesy of Gayle Pinto]

XXIX. The Good Years
- 1995-2003 -

*"The trick to getting out of the well is to shake it off,
and take a step up."*

Prelude

Events and struggles marking the years beginning with the purchase
of our new campus unveil two faces of one microcosmic framework;
we've already read about one that ends with the turbulent loss of
that dream; however, along the journey through those years, the
love, good will, and many historic achievements of the time clearly
shaped many lives. Positive changes in music education for the blind
have occurred in recent times, and many of those can be attributed
directly to SCCM having left its academic footprint.

I had been putting off beginning this chapter for quite a while, as
I seemed to come upon yet another wall of some kind. I would carry
my little book of notes into the woods as I so often do, and yet still
come up puzzled and confused. My notes contained many subjects,
and worked with my overall outline to include in *The Good Years,*
but no cohesive theme or story was coming to be. "Richard," I
would say to myself, "you lived those times; why are you having
such struggles writing about them? After all, you conquered the
problems writing about the troubled times in Chapter 28, didn't
you?" So I waited, somehow knowing once again that the answer
would come in some unexpected moment.

As the past kept racing through my mind for whatever reason,
the cause for the writing block became somewhat more apparent.
Instead of focusing on the "good" of the good years, I was dwelling
upon the many things that had been slowly eating away at my spirit
– things that I cannot (nor feel that I am willing to) dismiss quite yet,
but tend to become distractions and form a cloud. I had truly
forgotten that *"my initial objective was to drain the swamp."*
Apparently, the alligators and anger demons were still quite busy
nibbling around the edges of my mind.

When I finally stopped feeling sorry for myself, I realized why I
could not begin to write this chapter. Even though relatively short-

lived, energy and love coming from everyone working together became the life-blood of *The Good Years;* perhaps I had been looking toward inspiration for Chapter 29 in the wrong direction. So stand up, Richard; brush the dirt off, and just like the little donkey, get your own self out of that well!

Dawn of "The Good Years"

The Setting: At that time, the new campus was still under development. Although we had not yet acquired final blessings from the city to conduct a private school there, we seemed to be tolerated, as attempts to gain permits were in process. The idea of a cultural contribution to the community, and in an aesthetic surrounding of the old Tudor mansion appeared to be welcomed by most people other than some neighbors whose fears were unfounded.

A Concert Season of Blind Artists: Young virtuoso pianist, Stephanie Pieck, was the first in our concert season of blind musicians to perform at SCCM, and came all the way from New York to stay at the mansion for several days.

During the day before the concert, little Rebecca Dawning then 4.5 years of age, came up the stairs from the parking lot below the swimming pool area stretched out over her father's shoulders. He was holding her by one foot. Her little cane swung behind his back, and she resembled a child's mannequin being carried by a movie set worker. Grant and I met with the family, and Rebecca's musical gift seemed nothing less than startling! She is now 17 years of age, and has just left to attend a summer jazz camp at Stanford University. [She turned 23, 12/2016; story is with her family's permission]

Some Impressions: A few days later, Rebecca's mom, Jenny, wrote the most wonderful email to a special Internet list for parents of blind children. She described the feeling of coming up the tree-shaded street and into the quarter mile long driveway of our facility. She described the peaceful atmosphere and the wonderful new "home" that was there for Rebecca's music. Each Saturday the family would bring the little girl, and my colleague, Grant, would work with her. Little by little he was bringing Rebecca out of her cloistered self. About a month later, Jenny wrote a very personal email to me; apparently she was troubled and felt a need to share something, as a trust had grown between the family and us.

Some well-meaning folks of her church – good God-fearing folk – had written to her. The gist of the message was that of: *have faith; we must all pray for Rebecca, as God will make her well and bring her eyes back if we have faith and pray;* it went on to express compassion for her "defects," and that *we must not question God's reasons.* Having now observed the unique and special gift that Rebecca was given, I wrote a response back to Jenny; following is a summary as best as I can recall:

Jenny, don't be troubled by this; above all, you must not believe that there is anything wrong with Rebecca; she has come to us as a gift from God, and there is nothing that anyone or anything can do to change that. Rebecca doesn't need "fixing." She is so far beyond anything that any of us will ever understand, and we should thank God every day for sending her to us. As you believe in your church, like his own son, he has given Rebecca to the world.

This was in about 1998. After we had lost our campus, and in the subsequent leased facility, she again wrote to me about another troubling situation. I was able to find the 1998 email message, and sent her a copy reminding her of why she is here, and why Rebecca was born to her and to her father.

Uh Oh! Paint is about to be thrown on Rebecca's wagon ...

Intimidation has been said to be a very powerful tool, and I have been told, is often used in war strategy. I am reminded once again of my friend who would return to his parked car at night after a long hike. He would come down the trail holding one flashlight in his mouth, and two more – one in each hand. His philosophy was that of appearing as three people should any wrongdoers be in the process of breaking into his car. Paranoid? Perhaps just a little; but the technique of the clipboard can truly go a long way to create an official appearance, and perhaps be applied to many situations.

Rebecca's flute teacher was preparing her to take the first *Music Certificate* examination. These are very prestigious certifications that can show very well in a child's transcripts for college later on. Rebecca had never taken an examination in braille before, and apparently her school had yet to prepare her to understand textbook format, or take a written exam of any kind. This is not untypical, as I have observed schools preferring blind children to have math problems read to them, as opposed to taking the time sooner to teach them the braille code that would enable them to do what sighted children do in print.

I carefully prepared several early-level theory exams from the flute program for Rebecca; we would spend time on Saturdays reading through the materials together, becoming familiar with concepts of intervals, figured bass, multiple choice, matching columns, and dissecting the oddities of braille format. I wrote special transcriber notes tailoring them especially for her, knowing her level of understanding, disabilities, and that which she had not yet been prepared for in her school district. Her first exam was Level Three of the program; the exam took all day for her to complete, and many tears were shed. The answers were sent overnight to New York, and Stephanie Pieck, my blind musician friend, corrected them. Rebecca passed with honors, even though much was still to be done.

We worked together for the following years towards her eventual Level Ten pre-college exam, and each year was a little better than the one before.

There is no doubt that the child would have remained musically illiterate had that process not been undertaken – a process that the chairperson was, at first, adamant should not be used. They did not want to take the time to use resources they were not familiar with, and preferred to have the exam "read" to her. (Wonder why there has been a 75% unemployment rate among the blind?) This happened at least twice during the examination years, and each time I would pick up my proverbial clipboard and advocate for Rebecca's right to literacy.

The final experience was during her second of two tries for the Level Ten examination. She had made it to the highest level of the pre-college process, but unfortunately a new chairperson was in charge. In an exchange of emails, the program chair recommended that neither money nor time be spent on braille transcription, then rendered a decision that the exam would in fact be read to her. The bloody fight in the streets of North Hollywood once again reared its ugly, but powerful head. "No, not this time you don't," I said to myself. "This is her shining hour, and not you or anyone else will take it from her!"

I put on the gloves one more time – tired as I was from the battles within, and becoming powerless to make changes that might turn the tide in the inevitable demise of my program. The letter that I wrote to the official certificate chairperson in 2010 went essentially thus:

Dear Ms. ...

Thank you so much for chairing the Certificate program this year, and for your response on behalf of Rebecca Dawning. I would like to respectfully ask that you do NOT "waive" the written examination requirement for Rebecca. This child is musically literate and quite capable of taking a written exam just as is any sighted child, and she has successfully done so for all prior exam years. If you should choose to have the exam read to her, it could result in much vocal protest from the blind musical community. Please be aware that United States ADA laws protect the rights of blind individuals as well. If this is a matter of transcription cost, I am more than happy to volunteer my time as her transcriber, as I have done before.

Sincerely,
Richard Taesch
SCCM Braille Music Division
Headquarters: "Music Education Network for The Visually Impaired"

Perhaps a little dramatization was used to intimidate this willful chairperson, but is there someone who would find me wrong?

* * *

The Good Years have so much to tell, and as said before, were short lived; but true magic was always in the air for all of us; curriculum was developed, classrooms were full of happy students, and blind children were succeeding in ways never before thought possible.

Nevertheless, my time then was always under much stress: how to pay bills, how to deal with our board, and on, and on, and on. My best therapy for rejuvenation was, as always, in my escapes to the

259

mountains and hiking long and hard trails. My next chapter will share some success stories of the good years, and here and there throughout the remainder of the book, I will take a little more time to tell about some of my animal friends: the wild ones that gave me so much company and comfort in the many solitary hikes and night adventures. My Sunday cathedral was their home in the forest.

I clearly remember walking just before darkness and stopping to talk with the man upstairs; I would ask for blessings on the school, and a long healthy life to do the work that I was here to do – the work that Ernie told me I must do. I would pray that our director would live to see the day that our school would realize her dream to build a campus of its own where it could do what *it* was "supposed to do."

The following little vignette is somewhat inspired by Rebecca's plight with the certificate chairperson. Had I been less than lucky and a little more knowledgeable, perhaps my unintentional intimidation with a forest bear may have not worked out quite as well as did her certificate exam.

Vignette

Maggie and *Scarface* are two rather elderly bears that dwell within our Angeles National Forest backcountry. Many California black bears roam the Angeles wilderness, frequenting the more remote trails that most casual visitors never see. I have seen the couple a number of times, and we simply go our own ways. I've lost fear of them, and they *seem* to say, "Oh there's that silly night hiker again."

This particular day I had been hiking very high in an area beyond what is called *Little Jimmy Trail Camp*. It's an area where backpackers on Pacific Crest Trail can stop and sleep for the night. It is also familiar to long-distance folks that make the trek on PCT yearly from Mexico to Canada, a walk of about 1,500 miles. A fresh water spring and pleasant camp facilities welcome the weary trekkers every season.

I've come to enjoy day hiking by going in somewhere near midday and returning well after dark. I had been hiking along PCT to a peak called *Hawkins Summit,* and was on the return trip just slightly before nightfall. I was approaching Little Jimmy as I passed a high ridge-crossing called *"Windy Gap."* It is a ridge saddle that has another trail crossing it, which then descends several hundred feet south into an area called *Crystal Lake.*

It was a chilly evening at over eight thousand feet elevation, and I had just donned most of my layers of warm clothes – hooded jackets, wool shirts, a ski vest, and heavy gloves. I was approaching the cutoff to Little Jimmy when I spotted movement in the shadows near a camp stove. No humans were there at this time, and it was obvious that this was not a marauding raccoon.

My trail was quite narrow there, and the slope to my right, although not a great drop, it was somewhat steep; the slope to my left was very steep upward and could be navigated, but not easily. I then realized that the shadow that I saw was, indeed, a full-grown California black bear. He stood within thirty feet, seemingly wanting to come toward me. My old pilot instinct took hold: I calmly stopped in my tracks, held my flashlight down to the ground, and looked straight at him. He looked straight at me – and I looked back at him. He seemed to start coming forward toward me then would stop. Not knowing his intentions, I just stood firm and continued to look at him.

Strangely, fear was not there; I just held the position and waited – kind of like the towrope disconnection with the emergency landing. He seemed to rock back and forth on his feet, and just let out a few non-threatening snorts; he then continued to watch me. I must have looked quite menacing to the poor bear, as I would simply not budge, nor would I allow any intimidation on my part to show. After perhaps five minutes of this little dance between us, he let out another "grumph," did a 180 then walked back into the darkness toward another trail. Once he was out of sight I was on my way, never looking back until safely at the trailhead where my car and a thermos of hot coffee were waiting. Whew!

Sometime later I spoke to a friend who was quite well versed in such things; he said: "Richard, couldn't you see that he just wanted you to stand aside so that he could pass and continue on the narrow trail that you had just came from?" Duh! Now I understand that the poor fellow was just trying to return to Crystal Lake before dark where he probably came from; he had been on a day hike too, and most likely had hopes of raiding the trail camp for some food scraps left from the seasonal PCT backpackers – an event that he apparently mounted each evening before returning to his den in the canyons far below.

Had I been a little more aware, I could have simply climbed up the slope and watched him pass. Well, neither of us was carrying clipboards, but either one of us could have done a fine job of convincing Rebecca's chairperson that we were indeed in command of that situation. Long live Acme Carpet Cleaning! (By the way, I do hope that they don't clean bear rugs.)

* * *

Do you have any kids?

Oh yes, this question has been asked by just about everyone, and I always give the standard answer: "I sure do! My students are my kids, and I've been a part of raising them all."

My teaching career has been quite well blessed with wonderful students, some stellar, some not; but even though my work now spans well over half a century, *the good years* began the winding down process of a very satisfying professional life for me. I'll write more about "what's ahead" in late summer, but for now the wheels are pleasantly slowing, and will hopefully provide a *poco ritardando,* with an eventual segue into the *fall* movement of my sonata.

As to "my kids," there were more than I could ever describe: the little girl who started classic guitar at 5 years old and remained a student with me until age 18; I later attended her wedding. In one memorable incident, I was preparing her for a recital; my colleague Robb opened the door to my teaching module and said to her: "Hey Michelle; where are your pedals – you know, the fuzz maker, and the wah-wah?" She was about 8 years old at that time.

She looked up at him with big eyes and replied: "*I don't need all that funky stuff.*"

Incidentally, in over 10 years of diligent study, Michelle NEVER missed one quarterly recital, and performed with my classic guitar ensembles continuously from about 12 years of age until becoming an adult.

Then there was little Tyler who was also 5 when he began. As a gift for his middle school graduation, his dad borrowed all of the VHS tapes of every recital that he had participated in (from about 1983); he then surprised Tyler with a compiled and complete digital video history of his son's musical performances. The young man went on to apply at Pepperdine University, and to study under the renowned guitarist, Christopher Parkening.

The last significant guitar student of my career was a little girl who was the daughter of a long-time associate. I taught the child since she was perhaps ten years old, while remaining with me well into her teens.

During the years at the big campus when her lessons were finished, she would beg for me to give her "jet rides," as she called them; we would ride through the many acres of the school grounds on a cargo cart with large wheels. I would push her up and down hills until delightfully exhausted, and she was in wonderful laughter and joy. She was like my own child, and never having my own by birth, all my students were "my kids."

She was not a diligent student, but while growing more mature she was beginning to develop a strong technique, and would soon be able to perform the *Asturias* (Leyenda) by Albeniz. This is a work often reserved for concert guitarists and senior recitals. It was a fine showpiece, indeed, and I had great hopes of reviving my ailing guitar department by having her perform it under my tutelage.

Although the performance I anticipated did not take place, the girl went on to study a wonderful Chinese instrument called *Pipa* (pronounced: *pea-pah*). She has become a brilliant player of that instrument, and would often perform on it as a prelude to her classic guitar selections on our student recitals. So yes, I do have kids – lots of 'em.

Just a few of my special "kids"

(This photo courtesy of Gayle Pinto)
Used by permission of the students and the instructor
(The guy in the middle)

XXX. The magic was everywhere

"Magic" was a word that our dear *Noah* (the name affectionately given to my very special friend and distinguished colleague, Valerie) would use to describe the energy that was in the air on Saturdays at SCCM Braille Music Division. Saturday mornings at the original storefront school several miles away, were alive with dedicated children rehearsing for end-of-quarter musical theatre runs. But at the (underground) satellite campus – far removed from Miss B's administrative oversight – we were on our own much like the early American colonists, and growing faster than the little school headquarters in Sun Valley was able to keep up with.

Blind children were busily going up and down the two majestic staircases in the main facility, heading to and from their classes during the morning hours. *Computer Music Arts*, where they would study simple orchestration and write music by using screen readers; *Listening Lab*, where they learned to sit quietly and absorb a symphony, then discuss the music with their teacher or student aid; *Music Reading*, at which several blind students would often gather to sing canons and trios using their sight reading skills in braille; private piano and braille music reading lessons, along with other instruments, were all activities that were going on everywhere at the same time. Sighted students also volunteered as aids in classes.

At its peak, BMD had eight paid staff and teachers working on any given Saturday, and at least thirty or more children in attendance; some families would bring them from as far as 100 miles away. Magic was the right word, and it could be felt at every turn. Resident students in preparation for college were regular guests at the mansion, and the many bedrooms and suites made for comfortable quarters during their stays.

Intensive resident programs consisted of as many as eight to ten blind educators and students who would attend one- or two-week study sessions in computer music under a celebrated and pioneering specialist in orchestration and composition for blind musicians. These programs were particularly exciting, as parents of the young adult college students attending would form cooking teams, working together with Valerie to make wonderful meals for the troops.

Often the evenings would be graced with music playing and jam sessions; at other times, the outdoor garden spa was a favorite.

During the concert season, attending resident students would be among those invited to enjoy the concerts as a part of their program. Here they would see accomplished blind musicians, and enjoy opportunities of visiting with them and learning about things that they themselves were looking forward to one day doing.

On a normal Saturday, the large kitchen in the house served as a waiting area and gossip center for the families of our children. Anxious parents who wanted to chat and ask many questions were constantly corralling teachers who would visit the kitchen for coffee or a short snack. It became quite a valuable skill for staff to learn the many hidden doors and exits so as to avoid being detained when we were on tight time schedules, and with only a moment to grab a short break. At one time the home had over thirteen bathrooms, and though only about nine remained at this time, there were always many ways to avoid detection by the chatty folks when the need arose. Guide dogs were always part of the scenery, and would sometimes visit with children when they were not working. And yes, *the magic was everywhere*.

When I think of the environment and academic accomplishment of this experience, it becomes a sheer tragedy to know that none of it mattered to those who eventually turned us away when vigilant and tireless efforts to pursue compliance and necessary permits to continue, failed. Some of our own advisors even discouraged the resident program, and yet many students went away with skills to land fine jobs in education, corporations, or music-related professions – jobs that became possible through the special dedicated resources that no other music school in the world could provide in quite the same way. Perhaps such a concept simply exceeds the point to which today's business environment seeks to find merit. And again I ask: "Why is that?"

Curriculum was being developed even during the time that classes were in session. There was truly no precedent for integrating music braille literacy into mainstream music education, and methods with special approaches had to be applied on much of an experimental basis. As time progressed, new ways to prepare blind students for their educations were perfected, and perhaps the first curriculum of its kind was born out of these renegade years at the controversial facility; *renegade*, because we were constantly in fear that someone might consider some kind of zoning violation against us while permits were being sought; as a result, "under the radar" became the mode of operation. Imagine: even some blind professors of music were educated there, and only because of persistent, yet cautious and respectful use of our own property – a facility that a world-renowned surgeon was working to make possible. As a result of this perseverance by dedicated faculty and staff, "*An Introduction to Music for the Blind Student*" (a full course for the teaching of general music using braille code) was born at the Southern California Conservatory of Music in the year 2000. (See: www.dancingdots.com for publisher's information.)

But most of all, recognition coming from myself – the author of the courses – must go to the blind students: the children and adults who taught me and my colleagues how to teach them. It is through their trust in us, and their loyalty and dedication to the school that these efforts continue to help teachers and students throughout the world. Thanks to David Pinto, a brilliant pianist and innovator who chose to channel his talents and resources into research and experimentation that would one day provide accessible computer music technology for blind musicians; and, for teaching our students the computer tools that they need to help themselves. As put forth in the acknowledgements of my course books, a personal tribute will continue to reach out to our students, my colleagues, and the many teachers who participated in the development of this work.

A one of a kind library is born

Over time our reputation grew, and respected colleagues were expressing much support for the mission of the school and its special program. Several music braille libraries were donated to us, and to date [2013], there may have been as many as five thousand titles in our database. Blind teachers retiring from their work would send us hundreds of print and braille books that they had used during their careers.

The Janet Cross Library is only one of the many resources that we received from blind educators. The University of Illinois at

Urbana contacted me to donate a special library that had been given to them by the respected blind musician, Donald Heitler. Pianists Stephanie Pieck, Robert Smith, and Karen Gearreald gifted hundreds of braille collections and albums to us, as did so many other donors. Over 200 boxes of new materials came from one school that had received them from American Printing House for the Blind. APH was in the process of scanning their braille music into electronic files, and was ready to donate the hard copies of them. SCCM became the beneficiary of many similar efforts. Later, once one copy of each book from the APH collection was placed into our library, SCCM - with Stephanie Pieck's oversight - shipped the remaining boxes of books to a special school for the blind in Krakow, Poland. Board director, Jeffrey Skinner, generously provided the labor to complete the shipping project.

Perhaps one of the most unique collections was that of two very distinguished blind educators: Mr. John de Francesco, and the late Professor Carlton Eldridge. Mr. de Francesco was a lifelong educator, an opera singer, and conductor; he was also a music proofreader for The Library of Congress before he died. After he lost his hearing, he decided to give thousands of choral works in braille to SCCM based upon the recommendation of my friend, Bettye Krolick. Bettye initiated the donation from the widow of Dr. Eldridge as well.

Long ago, a disagreement over how braille vocal music was to become formatted and formally put into code, raged on between John and Carlton. John insisted that the words should be set at the margin, with music to follow on subsequent lines. Dr. Eldridge, also a professional vocalist as well as church theologian and university professor, felt that the music should be presented first, and the words should follow it. As I understand it, the debate went on for some time, each man hoping to see his recommendation accepted by The Library of Congress officially. History proved to show that Mr. de Francesco won, and today the official format is as he wished, that of words first and music following. The significance of this story is that, SCCM is [was] still in possession of both libraries that belonged to each of these distinguished blind educators!

268

Measure numbers in vocal music? Preposterous!

Richard can only imagine the significant changes that folks like John and Carlton accomplished; but in one very small way, I can understand a little of the gloating that one might enjoy when feeling victorious upon such an outcome as was theirs.

It was one of the glorious times during the good years that a similar controversy was going on – one that recommended vocal music in braille should rarely show measure numbers at the margin, as it was considered unnecessary clutter to the reader. At that time, our official codebook didn't discount them, but did not encourage the practice of transcribing measure numbers into vocal works unless shown in the print. Journal articles rarely addressed the subject, and some specialists seemed to avoid it altogether.

As I was learning and teaching, I worked daily with blind students, and could see inside of certain teaching situations that many braille specialists and transcribers are not often in proximity to. Transcribers seldom meet the readers that they braille for, and rule makers often work only on the periphery of music braille pedagogy.

Being the natural rebel that I have always been, I began to resent the fact that it was becoming increasingly more difficult to work with my blind students using old vocal transcriptions due to the practice of avoiding measure numbers on every parallel. I gave this much thought before inciting a civil war, but since our MENVI discussion list for the network was becoming quite busy, I decided to launch a *capsule* into orbit. "Let's see what happens when I *innocently* put this one out."

I then sent a message to the MENVI discussion list particularly aimed at several blind professional singers that I knew – ones that I believed to prefer measure numbers. I wrote something to the effect of: *A question has arisen regarding the recommendation to minimize measure numbers in vocal braille music.* [The question was, of course, hypothetical.] *How do singers feel about that practice, and what is your thought?*

I knew what the result would be, but as soon as I threw my firecracker into the fray, I disappeared from the list for about a week. Email went back and forth, and the general consensus from those who sung professionally was something like: *How can I work with my accompanist if I or he doesn't know immediately where either of us is during a rehearsal?*

A short time later, a statement appeared written by a specialist regarding the no-measure-number preference; the gist of his comment was essentially: *Has anyone seen the recent discussion on the MENVI list regarding measure numbers in vocal music? As a result of this discussion, the committee has decided to consider the use of them to be included in the new training manual.*

To bring The Good Years to a warm conclusion – and regrettably they did conclude – I would like to present some short readings in the form of little vignettes that you have become accustomed to. Perhaps you may think of changes that you would like to see; but mostly, just enjoy this short journey along with me.

Vignettes

So how does one individual bring about change? I suppose that one must first feel a need to make something better than that which it is to begin with. Now at times, some self-proclaimed intelligent folks might hold their IQ's over the rest of us. High IQ's, however, don't necessarily guarantee high common sense – a rather useful ingredient for most positive change. I once expressed the thought to our Miss B that smart people seemed to like gloating over that which they are smart about, and that others may consider such a practice to be condescending.

She said to me, "Well, yes, smart people like to do that."

I thought about it for a while then responded with great caution: "No, those are not really smart people as I see it; they're just smart-asses." (Now, no offense is meant to our little donkey that pulled his own out of that horrible well.)

Truly smart people do, however, have unique ways of getting even with the fakers. In one example, a musician was said to have used his smarts to get even with a very antagonistic bass player while on the road with a well-known band.

Now Mario did not appear to be a scholar, and would not necessarily be attracted to the *Mensa* society, but he was quite smart in his own way.

The bass player loved to make condescending comments to him, whether it was about his wrinkled suit, or whatever. This went on and on, and at one gig, Mario showed up with a pair of glasses to read his music charts with. The bass player looked on curiously then finally asked him why he was suddenly wearing glasses. [Dialogue is playfully reconstructed as described to me long ago.]

Mario said to him: "Man, haven't you seen these yet? These are my *transposing glasses*."

"What do you mean, Mario?"

Knowing that the man had a musical weakness transposing written parts from one key to another, Mario had gone to a drug store and purchased a pair of phony glasses. He somehow carefully etched what appeared to be five music staff lines across each lens. As he sat reading his charts on the gig, he would move his head slightly up or down as though experimenting with them during a performance.

The bass player finally asked: "Mario! Man, where can I get some of those? How do they work?"

"Well, you just move your head up or down so that you can see the notes on different lines of the staff, and you can transpose anything into any key."

"Oh man, I gotta have some of those! Where can I get 'em?"

"Just go to any music store and ask for transposing glasses; they'll know what you mean."

The next day before the evening show, the antagonistic bass player searched the town over, going into every music store and asking the very puzzled clerks if they would sell him a pair of transposing glasses.

A little angel named Angela

During the good years, my partner, Grant, and I would travel to a special education school for blind children to provide outreach teaching. SCCM had received a special "partner" award from the Los Angeles Unified School District for the work that we were conducting there. I represented SCCM when receiving the award on public television. This was also the school from which the music teacher would later retire, and come to work at our Braille Music Division as a piano teacher.

Among the children that she would bring to us each week for the outreach sessions, was a little Asian child named Angela. She stood no higher than perhaps my elbow, and never said a word. She was brought into my music braille class several weeks late, and although I didn't express my discomfort, I was somewhat annoyed that I would need to backtrack in order to bring Angela up to some level that we had reached with the other children.

I passed the music sheets in braille to her, and gave a very short explanation for the first five scale steps in music notation. As the rest of the class began to slowly do their best to read and sing the notes in *do, re, mi* solfege, little Angela began to sing. She had immediately gotten the code, and sang each and every note perfectly, and on pitch! When I said to her: "Angela, that is wonderful! Did you read music before?" she just stared ahead through her blind eyes and smiled sweetly.

"No, but you explained it very well."

There was nothing I could say; I was lost for words. The following weeks resulted in Angela literally leading the class in sight singing on a level that could have put an adult community college music 101 class to shame.

I was then able to convince the music teacher to let us make contact with Angela's family; we would offer to give her a full scholarship at the school and teach her music and music reading. I can remember her coming to the original storefront school in Sun

Valley, as this was just before our new campus was ready to accept students. For several weeks Angela would come in with her parents, dressed in a precious little pink dress, and sit with me; fully prepared, she would sing her exercises perfectly: a rare joy to behold for a weary music teacher, is an understatement.

The following week Angela did not show up; this was strange, as her family was so very happy to bring her to me. I called them and they said that she was ill, and they were sorry for not letting me know, but that she would be there next week. Next week came, and no Angela. I made a call to the family, and a relative of the child answered.

"Richard, I'm sorry to tell you that little Angela passed away yesterday."

I have attended funerals for children before, but never have I wept as I did that day. And so it came to pass that – *for all too soon* – our little angel was gone.

Happy birthday, dear Omar ...

Yes, how does one bring about change? The good years always found me hiking alone in the mountains to recharge my proverbial batteries. Much like the *"return of the iris meadow,"* I did what I could to make a difference where possible; picking up litter to repairing trail switchback cuts made by irresponsible hikers was routine.

Among my pet complaints is the finding of airborne birthday balloons that have been released by whoever, high in the mountains. Such a practice is supposed to be illegal, but year after year hikers find them lodged in trees at high altitudes in the wilderness. Most of us will interrupt our hikes to scramble and struggle up hills, climb trees, and do what we can to retrieve these invaders into our forest.

I was hiking along the Waterman trail a few miles east of Pacific Crest Trail, when I spotted one of the shiny aliens up slope in a young pine far above me. I looked for a while, trying to decide whether I had the strength to tackle the mission. Once making the decision, I removed my daypack and began the climb upward toward the glistening object in the peaceful surroundings; this was

273

just as well, as anyone observing this caper would have surely called the sheriff to report someone trying to steal pinecones.

Upon reaching the balloon, I cut it down from the little tree; suddenly the alien came alive: "*Happy birthday to you; happy birthday to you; happy birthday dear Omar, happy birthday to you*" came belching out from some kind of mysterious audio device contained within the trapped packet. I yanked it down and began beating on it to silence the obnoxious noise, but it would not stop. I then took out my little pocketknife and began sticking it to see if somehow I could return the forest to its peaceful state; it still did not stop.

Finally I was able to silence the horrible invader; I then yelled joyously as though victorious in a battle. Now if the sheriff didn't arrest me for stealing a pinecone, he surely would have thought me to be an escapee from the closest honor camp. Quietly and proudly, I hiked back to my pack and continued with the day.

Upon returning to my car at the trailhead very late that night, I began to empty my pack of the litter and balloon that I had felt so proud to save the wilderness from. It went promptly into the bear-box (bear-proof trash container), and as I began to retreat to my car for my thermos of hot coffee, I suddenly turned around in complete amazement! From the bowels of that bear box in the dark and quiet night, came a return from the dead: "*Happy birthday to you, happy birthday to you; happy birthday dear Omar, happy birthday to you.*"

"Aw, Shit!"

Mass at Saint Gabriel's church

My dear Aunt Frances was such a devout Catholic, and as my legal godmother, she made quite sure to quiz me often as to whether I was attending church regularly.

"Oh yes, Aunt Frances, I do that every week!" [Uh, well, sort of.]

"Do you go every Sunday?"

"Oh yes, surely."

"What church do you go to?"

My aunt knew all of the churches that I was near to as a child, and she could not be fooled in any way. As said earlier, my cathedral is within my mountains – sometimes the Angeles National Forest in the San Gabriel Mountains.

"Richard, what is the name of your church?"

"Uh, uh, Aunt Frances, it's called, uh, Saint Gabriel's; you know ..., the one that's up in the forest."

"Oh yes, I think I've heard of that. That's just wonderful, as I just wanted to make sure that you are keeping your faith. After all, I am still your godmother."

Whew! Got through that one; she passed a few years after my mother who was her only sister.

Postlude: *The good years*

The good years were rich with rewards, but never without struggles. I often bucked our board, Miss B on some issues, and was always disappointed when some teachers were not willing to support me, such as perhaps using my books in their classes.

An important meeting was taking place this day in my co-director's office at the new campus. The meeting was concerning typical school business, and a discussion about the direction that the "tail-wagging" BMD was taking appeared on the agenda. The president of a foundation was there; he was a fine gentleman who had served on our board for many years.

The discussion was positive, and at one point when the accomplishments of the braille program were under scrutiny, someone made a statement directed at me to the effect of: *This is very good; now this young man can go out and promote his program in order to bring more funding to the school.*

We had worked tirelessly, created published curricula, appeared on public radio, television, and in newspapers, all on behalf of SCCM. I had attributed my books to the school, amassed enormous debts, and bypassed a possible family life for myself. Along with my colleague, Grant in his department, we all worked and sacrificed together for this special cause. My response to the board following that statement at this moment went something like:

Uh, oh no! We've created, devised, developed, and otherwise breathed our life into to this program for the school. I have now brought it to you, and have laid it here at your feet. My question to you, gentlemen, is: Now what are YOU going to do with it?

I will always wonder what my attitude that day may have had to do with why the foundation later forsook us following Miss B's death. But perhaps in my own way, I must have been doing some things right, as in the year 2003 my biography was selected to appear in the 57th edition of *"Who's Who in America."*

I had tried so very hard to make our school advisors aware that the possibility of someone wanting our new property for other purposes was indeed a real one; but that would only seem to incur annoyance and impatience from them.

One day after all had come to pass, Lurrine (Miss B) and I were driving together to do an errand for the school. In a rather unexpected moment she turned to me and said: "Richard, I want to thank you."

"Thank me, for what?"

"Just thanks for not saying I told you so."

I smiled back and just replied: "Well, Lurrine, how could you have known?"

No one needs to be right, ego notwithstanding, especially when what you were right about ends up contributing to your own demise. The tragic irony of knowing that our ship would hit that iceberg, and not being able to turn it, was a reality that SCCM and its faithful crew lived with daily during the *troubled years* and the *good years* alike

* * *

Speaking of Godmothers:

Today – August 6, 2011 – I learned that Bettye Krolick – the godmother of braille music – passed away last evening. Flashback/Replay: On one of the first conferences at which I presented a workshop on behalf of SCCM and its new Braille Music

276

Division, I met Bettye in the hallway of the Marriott Hotel. She was proudly wearing one of our SCCM T-shirts that I had sent to her: The letters SCCM (in large braille dots); the proud circle of keys logo that Lurrine designed, and the words, *"Braille Music,"* were etched on the bottom.

Photo & permission, courtesy of Bettye Krolick's daughter, Kathy

So in conclusion, just what did we accomplish through "The Good Years"?

Circa 1994: Richard was appointed as State Music Specialist for California Transcribers and Educators of the Visually Handicapped – CTEVH, following the passing of Ethel Schumann, former music consultant for CTEVH.

1997: Music Education Network for *The Visually Impaired* – MENVI – was founded, becoming the #1 meeting place, watering hole, and registry for blind and visually impaired music students, teachers, parents, and administrators; by the year 2011, overall membership had grown to near 1,000.

2000: The first published course of its kind, concentrating on music braille pedagogy and music education using braille as its medium was launched: *"An Introduction to Music for the Blind Student,"* (Part I) was the first of an ongoing series that has enjoyed worldwide acceptance; the course was inspired by curriculum development at SCCM during the good years, and dedicated to its director Lurrine Burgess, Bettye Krolick, our staff, my colleague and co-director, Grant Horrocks, and to our blind students who were the real authors.

2003: Richard's biography is selected for inclusion in *"Who's Who in America,"* 57th edition.

Circa 2005: SCCM formed a special partnership with California State University, Northridge – CSUN – specifically serving the needs of the college's blind music majors; the first to graduate was trained and prepared by SCCM.

2006: The book, *"Louis Braille, A Touch of Genius"* by Michael Mellor, celebrating the bicentennial of Louis Braille's birth was published (National Braille Press). Richard with his friend and mentor, Bettye Krolick, contributed substantial input for the portions of the book dealing with music braille.

2008: Richard presents his last workshop and lecture for CTEVH – a re-visiting of his second workshop in 1994 called: *The Literacy Movement – What does Braille Music have to do with it?* A special series of journal articles completing this effort on the state of music education for the blind child was concluded in early 2011 (see "Music in Education," a periodical column published in the CTEBVI Journal at: www.ctebvi.org

Co-director of Braille Music Division, Grant Horrocks, begins serving a four-year term as President of California Transcribers and educators of the Visually Handicapped – CTEVH, later to be renamed: California Transcribers and Educators for the Blind and Visually Impaired – CTEBVI.

For all too soon

Summer

I am quiet – noisy – hot – cool – a time for different things – a time to remember the coolness of winter, and to anticipate the new beginning ...

SUMMER

See if you can picture blind children happily going up and down these stairs to and from their computer classes such as:

This one

"... even the nighttime darkness of a remote forest trail can become a very magical, friendly, and warm place."

LATE SUMMER
XXXI. Transitions

The transition following my last view of the just-vacated five-acre campus as seen in the rear-view mirror of my old 4X4, to the subsequent loss of our leased facility where we continued to share what we had learned through our blind students, was nothing less than totally consumptive. Only one young man is [was] still with us from even before that era. He is Jamie Smith, born blind with cerebral palsy, and now over age thirty. [Story is by permission.]

When beginning the braille program, my original interest and mission was that of providing the means to music braille literacy for academically capable children and college-bound students. Jamie will never read braille, and yet he is [was] the only remaining student from when BMD began in about 1993. He is a very gifted pianist in his own right, and blessed with a wonderful family – one that continued to donate regularly to support our program or what exists [existed] of it.

During the time that students were coming and going, history being made with blind children graduating college through our work, technology being developed, and music braille literacy at SCCM gaining national attention, young Jamie Smith continued to come to classes week after week, growing on the peripheral effects from the energy that was infectious to everyone who walked through our doors. It was once thought that Jamie would never overcome the cerebral challenges to right and left hand neurological brain coordination, and yet he plays the piano beautifully with both hands. As usual, somewhere along the way, the experts always seem to miss something significant with respect to musically bent children diagnosed with various forms of brain damage.

Jamie would attentively absorb an entire symphony in his Saturday listening class; he could learn proper scale fingering on an instrument that he already seemed able to play naturally from birth. Jamie has perfect pitch, and through the efforts of his dedicated piano teacher, Grant, he has learned to use both right and left hands in ways thought very unlikely by some neurologists.

And though he does not read braille, I have been [was] able to teach him to write words and thoughts in a basic format on a mechanical braille writer – a right- and left-brain skill that one with cerebral palsy is not usually able to perform; but then so the bumble bee – like SCCM – should also not be able to fly according to the laws of physics. Since normal typewriter keyboarding is still very challenging to Jamie, the skill of using simple six-key braille writing in basic letter combinations may one day – through modern technology – become his only way to share thoughts using the written word. Impossible? Have you ever listened to the beautifully musical sounds that come from the delicate wings of a little bumblebee in flight?

Ya' mean you'd even talk to wild animals?

My little animals have taught much to me about my work with children like Jamie, and so many others. They have kept me company throughout the turbulent and dark times of late summer, and have taken me into many places of peace and inspiration. Jamie and all of our blind children and adults walk daily in darkness; yet they see so much more than any of us can imagine, and more than many of us see with our eyes. In the Introduction of my book I have said that, "... *even the nighttime darkness of a remote forest trail can become a very magical, friendly, and warm place.*" This *place* has given me unique insight into what their world must be like. I have come to understand in some small way why they seem quite happy and able to see things that I can see, and at most times, even more clearly.

Packing into the woods in the day and returning after dark often allows evening encounters with wildlife that few are privileged to see. My blind students have taught me that darkness is not to be feared; it is something that I have learned from them. It is only through this kind of therapy that I have found any form of serenity in these troubled times; in the light of day, it often seems as though much of what I have worked for in music braille has come crashing down around me. One stop at the MENVI discussion list, however, is always another step up from that dark well.

As night began to fall, again I would stop on a high mountain perhaps ten or more miles from my trailhead to pray as one might do on a visit to his or her church: "Bless the school, and please let us continue to help the children that we have been gifted with enlightenment to reach." As darkness came, I would imagine them navigating the way from one place to another, and be thankful that I could at least see shadows, and for the lights that I carry to see the trail when in a dark forest canyon. The silence would sometimes seem almost deafening, and yet became warm and comforting. A frightening wilderness to some would become for me like the world of a blind person in the presence of friends – the trees, the sounds of nocturnal animals, and the blessed peace.

Just before dark one evening following my visit with the man upstairs, I spotted a young bobcat cavorting like a small kitten. I was on a ridge above him, and he could not see me. He jumped and played just like any young cat, and I was truly fascinated by him. He was alone, and now in the early spring, was most likely in his first year of being a typical youngster.

I returned to that place a week later, and while walking along the same route I noticed what seemed to be movement on a little rise just overhead to my right. It was no less than the same little fellow peering down at me. I stopped and thought that I might try to get a better look at him before dark.

Quietly, I walked up to a rise on the opposite side of the trail. As I carefully peeked over to where he was, I could see his ears ducking down so as not to be seen – not unlike a playful domestic kitten. This went on for several minutes, and soon he became quite comfortable to not hide. We just looked at each other for a while, and from what I thought was a safe distance, I spoke a few words to him. He looked curiously back, but just blinked like any young cat in a somewhat relaxed or sleepy state. Soon I decided to hike on as I had many miles yet to reach the trailhead, and was becoming weary as well.

The following week I decided to hike back to that area to see if he was still there. I saw him again briefly, and our meetings became quite regular throughout the following season.

By this time, he appeared to be near the size of a guide dog, and very likely approaching that teenage time. I was making my way along the trail when suddenly I spotted him walking ahead of me at about 100 feet. He was yowling as male cats often do when looking for a mate. I stopped and said somewhat aloud: "What's the matter, kitty?" Alarmed, he turned quickly not expecting company, but seeing and hearing what seemed to be a familiar sound, stopped; he sat on hind legs and just looked at me.

A few similar encounters occurred thereafter, and for a time when I would spot him, I'd stop carefully and speak aloud. As soon as he would hear my voice, and as long as I was hiking alone, he would stop and clearly recognize the sound and my presence. I related this story to a naturalist friend and his reaction was not surprising. No, he did not say – as did some of my more conventional friends: "Oh, Richard, you must be careful; that is very dangerous." He said something to the effect of: Oh of course; he recognizes your voice. He knows you mean no harm and has no fear of you; moreover, he's probably come to expect your visits.

Perhaps it's not unlike our Jamie; he stumbles into the library annex and waits to hear my familiar voice. "Hi Richard," he says to me even before he knows where I am. Incidentally, his Uncle Marty drives him for a round trip of over 100 miles to see me, Grant for piano, and his voice teacher every Saturday. My hike of 10 miles to visit my bobcat friend somehow seemed much the same.

* * *

The troubled years return

After the closing of the never-developed campus, there was a hiatus for the BMD of about two years while renovation of a dilapidated leased building was taking place. Even though the original 1971 headquarters remained, any opportunity of keeping our blind students in any kind of learning program tutored by SCCM had been lost. This was largely due to delays resulting from failure to acquire teaching space in temporary locations. Many of my own sighted guitar students were also lost, as I did not have a home studio like some of my colleagues.

I was not in a pleasant state of mind, and became unwilling to return to the original cramped quarters in Sun Valley; as a result, there was no choice but to accept some retainer funds offered to me (and my colleague) from the school during the interim. Had Lurrine and the board not supported this, Grant and I would surely have gone into bankruptcy, as all of our resources had been applied towards expanding invisible scholarships while building the enrollment of blind students. For retrofitting the leased building, the school was only able to recover about $250,000 from the sale of our estate, which is about the same that had been saved in the original building fund over a thirty-year period.

As with most projects that confronted SCCM throughout its history, the reconstruction of the leased building was constantly plagued with problems, and conflicts from within the administrative board itself were commonplace. There was serious mold found in the framework calling for attorney services; there were building code issues, unexpected costs, and on and on.

On the positive side, I was able to spend much more time at my home office during which my book, *"Jazz and Chord Symbol Reading for the Blind Pianist,"* was written and subsequently published (see: www.dancingdots.com). Much planning and outlining for Part III of the *"Introduction to Music ..."* series of my courses was also taking place at that time. Part III is a detailed teacher-training program designed for educators of music braille; hopefully publication will occur sometime in 2012. [Publ. 2014]

Little in the way of good energy emitted from the relocation project. But once the building was complete, for at least two years thereafter, some of the magic and spirit did temporarily return; however, that can only be attributed to the children who came through our doors – sighted and blind, as the morale and heart of me and my co-director was terribly depleted.

Battles raged on over whether or not the BMD was overpowering the general school. As a result, music braille materials were boxed up and removed from the library annex; I felt that this would help to demonstrate that the braille collection was not intended to crowd out the print materials that were part of the music school. By that time, we had packed and unpacked hundreds of boxes many times, and all was now tucked away in our dusty warehouse. Each of those moves required rented trucks, backbreaking labor, and often the hiring of itinerant help. I injured

---

myself, although not seriously, twice in the process of climbing high up to try and retrieve a work needed by a blind student. On one occasion, the boxes came crashing down as I fell nearly ten feet to the floor, buried under piles of books and containers. On and on the frustration continued, until the materials were once again moved back to the annex for the last time.

Lab funding: *Now you see it; now you don't!*

Just before closing the unfinished estate campus, a foundation provided a grant to our program for the second time (about enough to fund most of a three-month quarter). Along with donating our time for scholarship support toward needy families of blind children, other foundations were beginning to grant money through the efforts of our fundraiser. Although much too late for my own financial situation, the project was beginning to see more ongoing funds for offering programs that would not require tuition from blind students. Once the building was complete with special classes, instruments, trained faculty, materials, and labs organized, we were able to apply the waiting grant money, thereby attracting some of the lost student body back into the Saturday program.

We then set out on a mission to convince our administration that not charging tuition for the Saturday labs would attract not only students, but also more funding from grantors. Not everyone on the board agreed, as it was foreign to them to "teach for free"; they felt that tuition should be charged no matter what the situation.

As board support grew stronger, my colleague and I managed to have this one our own way. Had we not conducted the labs and classes for blind students on fully funded scholarships, there is no doubt in my mind that the program would have failed within the first month of re-opening. The eventual failure of our program and closing of the teaching facilities came quite later, and due primarily to the well-known downturn in economics affecting our funding sources in about 2008. We were not alone, as the collapse contributed to the demise of numerous similar non-profits throughout the country.

The program and its mission were strong; funders were attracted to the fact that we had channeled many of our resources and unique skills into this special division with academia specifically geared towards blind music students. Whether or not the students' families drove expensive cars, the children were blind and in need of that which we had invested vast resources and skills to provide for them.

The passing of an era

The following editorial appeared in our MENVI Journal following the closing of the Saturday program. However, that issue was never published due to resistance of some advisors; they determined that it portrayed a negative image. Of course I disagreed, as I often did, and inserted it into another journal. As a result of my protestant behavior, a concert was given in our name, raising $500 towards support of the worldwide MENVI network.

THE PASSING OF AN ERA - an Editorial

It is with great sadness that we announce the closing of the primary teaching facility of Southern California Conservatory of Music. The well-known Braille Music Division continues in name, and will be represented only in limited off-site outreach programs at this time. However, plans for re-development are encouraging. SCCM was founded 37 years ago, and has lived a colorful and creative existence, but never less than a relentless uphill struggle for survival.

The SCCM-sponsored coalition & network, "*Music Education Network for The Visually Impaired*," MENVI, continues its free services for the time being; however, funding shortages threaten its existence as well. Print and braille news journals could be discontinued, relegating the network to only an on-line service for those with computers. Sadly, this would leave out nearly half of the membership in many parts of the world.

The SCCM music braille library contains nearly 5000 titles in its database. The school donated over 200 boxes of music braille scores to a deserving school in Krakow, Poland, last year. Some limited teaching continues amongst the crowded walls of print and braille books in a combination small library annex and recital room, but no special program of braille music instruction is offered at present.

SCCM was believed to be the only school of music offering braille music education, production, and transcription within the mainstream of general academia. Not dubbed as a school for the blind, it attracted highly motivated blind music students, many in preparation for college entrance and graduate school studies. Some have gone on to professional careers and employment in the teaching profession. Blind children, whose families believed in the significance of music education in their lives, once filled the classrooms on Saturdays with laughter and learning. The times have taken their toll, and once again the arts have become reduced to a peripheral frill in the hierarchy of educational economic priorities. The classrooms are now silent, and the children's laughter and sweet sound of "do re mi" is now only a distant memory. [R.T]

* * *

Many a night since these things have come to pass, I find myself waking up in a cold sweat from a dream: I see my father on that dusty trailer park street lying in the dirt with blood on his face – but the person is not him; it is myself – down just one too many times to get back up and fight again. But when morning comes and I am enjoying my first cup while playing the scales, I can't help but to smile; I then remember my father sitting with my mother gently cleansing his face; instead of pitying himself, he turned and asked me: "Son, are you ok?" I smile just slightly, and once again try to remember:

Stand up; brush the dirt off, and just like the little donkey, get your sorry self out of that well!

The legacy lives on

In 2018, the SCCM does continue to exist as a non-profit entity. Through the generosity of its donors, it supports some special outreach programs throughout each year.

For all too soon

A WALTZ FOR JAMIE

Richard Taesch

© 2000 by Richard E. Taesch – *Introduction to Piano for the Blind Student, Graded Studies Book 1; used here by permission of the publisher, Dancing Dots Technology – www.dancingdots.com*

Even the night time darkness...

XXXII. Is there life beyond a conservatory?

Prelude

Surely there must be. But why has such a question suddenly begun to monopolize my thoughts? As I study my notes for the remainder of summer and the happy closing of a good remembrance, I feel at a loss to separate far too many school dilemmas from the other adventures of my life. And yet, instead of feeling uneasy as one growing older sometimes does when professional usefulness lessens, I look ahead quite eagerly to my fall season. However, each pathway to another episode in summer seems more and more difficult to write about without first passing through a kind of fog. At those moments, the school and my long obsession with the work there becomes analogous to what it must be like living in a city like London – one where deep fog and dampness is present much of the time; not necessarily a negative energy, but a cloud to one's vision, nonetheless.

In the beginning there was delightful growing up. And although mixed with air raid sirens and youthful fears, there was also love, radio communications, new technology to learn, kit building, and telegraphy skills not typical of pre-adolescents in the fifties. There was young romance, music, youthful hormones, and the healthful pursuit of what finally came to rest as my lifelong career in music – work that still continues to be a driving, although fading passion.

And yet I still rise every morning to at least three hours of intense music practice. I have absolutely no intention of ever stepping up to a performance stage again. Even the thought of performing with my own few students in recital is now uncomfortable, as a motor disability has taken a toll. But as I play the scales each day there is a kind of "grounding" that occurs. It simply helps a man return to his roots – those roots that are the base of all life expectations and inspirations.

So again the teacher inside of me reaches out to my students whoever and wherever they may be; that teacher hopes that we can all learn to release the negative effects of adversarial struggle – those that even I became far too willing to submit to. Yes, life does exist beyond anyone's mission and all of its challenges; but my lesson learned is that I began allowing them to become my only point of reference – one that traveled dangerously beyond my career, and well beyond the ever-fundamental need to simply make a living.

Each of us requires points of reference – (translated) a reason to get out of bed each morning. But do be kind to yourself. Recognize your constraints and your own *troubled years*. Accept your eccentricities, but do remain cautiously aware and critical of them. They are yours alone; either you will choose to rise above them, or allow them to bury you deep in that well. And I might again add that, you will have no commiseration company from the donkey. He found his own way out.

* * *

A living analogy: Rising above that London fog

Winters in South California are generally mild compared to other places, but for those who love the out-of-doors, even the short rainy season can put a damper on some things. When a bit more adventuresome, I would often drive to the National Forest on cloudy and even rainy days. Knowing that the clouds would top off at a specific altitude, I would pack my hiking gear and begin the drive to high country places through our mountain roads. The first time I was apprehensive, as it had been damp and raining for several days. But I had also become accustomed to some rather unusual adventures, and was quite familiar with the late night returns to the trailheads even when rain would begin high up in the mountains.

Up and up I traveled: 3,000 ft; 6,000 ft; now past the timberline and ski lifts at 7,000 ft. And sure enough as I had hoped, the car suddenly emerges from the top of the cloud cover. Bright sun was everywhere, framed with a sky more blue than I could ever imagine. I pulled into a turnout just to look below me and see the tops of mountains sticking out of the clouds; the scene was no less than surreal, with the high peaks at 7,500 feet and above appearing like small islands in a sea of white water. Folks who are frequent air travelers probably see such sights often but rarely spend any time there. Later I arrived at my trailhead, a crossing of the famed Pacific Crest Trail. The hike lasted an entire day, and as usual, I returned to my car quite late into the night. However, I had forgotten that while returning from the heavenly place, I would need to descend through the clouds as I navigated the dropping altitudes.

I did finally make it home safely in the wee hours, but not without much adventure. As I descended into the cloud, it became a very thick fog. Visibility became more and more difficult, until the yellow line on the winding mountain road became impossible to see in my headlights. Steep drops were on either side of the road, one that is notorious for cars going over the side even in good weather. Indiana Jones says his usual "S" word, but as the script goes, manages to come through in true movie style.

I could see that no one was ahead or behind; and if another fool such as me should appear, I would likely see him in time. I grabbed my flashlight and opened the car door slightly while driving at a snail's pace. I would shine the light down at the ground to the yellow line in order to see when and where the road was curving to, thereby steering accordingly. This was strictly IFR (Instrument Flying Rules) for nearly five miles until the fog broke, which was the cloud ceiling at the lower altitude. Whew! Of course the rain was heavy, as the weather below was unlike the other world that I had just come from. Perhaps I must re-think this journalistic analogy; could it be that we might not take advantage of these liberating adventures quite often enough during our late summers?

The little gray fox

As the years pass growing ever closer to fall, life does indeed seem to continue beyond the conservatory and the music teacher person that I became. Each night following my teaching day, I would look forward to traveling home to 34th Street, anticipating the peace and warm summer evenings cloaked with the lovely sound of crickets and the coyotes' songs in the hills nearby. Often a family of wild raccoons would greet me while searching for water.

My nest in Crescent Valley is somewhat removed from the more conventional communities that many folks come home to each day. The grandiose Stevenson Ranch and other areas that are now near

Santa Clarita seem very remote to us here even though within short distances.

One evening I was traveling home while passing the Van Norman Reservoir north of San Fernando Valley; it was a typical commute following a day of teaching music. Suddenly my headlights picked up what appeared to be a small animal in the road ahead of me. *Road-kill*, as many have heartlessly taken to call crushed wildlife in the roadway, is common here and one generally makes an effort to avoid adding to the carnage. Birds of prey, coyotes, owls, and other of nature's friends usually take care of man's careless leftovers.

I could somehow see what appeared to be the glow of eyes peering toward my approaching vehicle; I slowed down to take a closer look. Fortunately there was no one currently traveling on the deserted road near the turnoff to my destination at that moment. A great weight suddenly came upon me, and I knew that this was not the time to steer around the common crushed sight; I pulled my car carefully to the side, thinking: "Now what am I getting into?" I cautiously stepped out and approached the little creature in the middle of the roadway. To my enormous surprise, it was a very young gray fox no larger than a full-grown domestic cat, lying somewhat in rest; he appeared to be injured, but somehow I could only see what looked like blood on the tips of his little paws.

The animal looked up at me as I tried to observe him in the darkness. He did not appear crushed, and it was likely that he had tried to cross the road in an attempt at refuge beyond the fence that protected open space for the reservoir.

My thought was: now what do I do? If I leave him here, surely the next car or truck that comes along will either avoid him, or kill him. That was not an option. Do I pick him up and carry him to the side of the road? Do I wrap him in a blanket and find a sympathetic veterinarian? If I pick him up, in his fear he may surely snap at me, and just what I need is a rabies treatment. "Great! The next trash truck on the way to a late night delivery to the nearby landfill will ruin both our day." Something needed to be done and soon, as sure enough headlights were clearly bearing down in the distance. I had no gloves to pick him up with and no blanket to wrap him in.

Well, perhaps St. Francis was checking us both out, and I simply decided that this was one of those times when one just does what one must and hope for the best. I reached down to him and very slowly placed my bare hands about his body, clearly noticing the bristly fur common to a fox. He again looked up at me and strangely seemed to have no fear, only concern. He was apparently somewhat in a state of shock, but it seemed that the injury was merely that of an attempt to cross the road with a very close call, resulting in his front paws only being bruised. I started to lift him, but miraculously he began to rise up on his feet. He then began to move even though still quite stunned by the event. He just stood and looked at me as though to say: "What to do?" The only thing I could think of was to try intimidating him to cross the road, and flee to safety beyond the reservoir fence.

I stomped my feet and uttered words like: "Go; move; please!" He looked up to me like a child who has been sent off to school for the first time: "why are you sending me away?" After a moment or two he began heading toward an opening in the fence, turning and looking back at me with each step or two; my car continued to idle, and headlights lit the area. A great sigh of relief was now in order; somehow it now seemed to me that he would survive. Off he limped under the fence while pausing to lick wounds, and continuously looking back at this weirdo who tried to intimidate him to: get up on your feet and just move – PLEASE! He did; and off I drove to savor a relaxing evening following a very unusual day's work. [Revised 8/16]

The original meaning of the word "rest" room

After my mother's passing in 1987, I began to backpack with the family of a special musician friend and fellow educator. As summer has worn on, hiking is still a weekly adventure for me, although backpacking is not as likely now. A back injury several years ago has rendered the body a bit more breakable (of course, nothing to do with becoming a geezer now is it?). One- and two-week treks into the high Sierras were quite special during that time. Richard never did much camping as a youngster, and since his scouting time was

297

cut short by that infamous knock on the door at ten years old, there was really no one to camp and scout with until much later.

Observing new hikers adjust to the strangeness of outdoor plumbing in the wilderness is always quite entertaining to those of us who have already gone through it. On his first trip, it was clearly Eric's turn; and even though day hiking for some time, he'd never dealt with this side of a trek where there were other people nearby.

We arrived at camp about 3pm after packing from the trailhead since 7am. Needless to say, Mother Nature was having a discussion with him, and this was not one that could be engaged in while ducking behind the nearest pine tree. Off came the pack while other comrades began to settle into the business at hand. He grabbed the token trowel, a hank of *film* (tissue) then dashed into the woods searching for the obvious.

When new at this skill, one continues towards a destination while looking back so as not to become lost; but mostly to make sure that he or she is out of sight of everyone else. Eric must have hiked about a quarter of a mile in search of the perfect place (ever watch a dog go around in circles, making sure he's found his?). Settling down to business in what seemed complete isolation and privacy, it seemed like a good idea to take one more peek around the big pine against which his back was resting. No more than ten feet to another tree, a familiar face came peering back from around her selected spot; it was one of the ladies on our team! There they sat staring at each other, both thinking that a moment before there was no way he or she could be within any proximity of another human.

On a different occasion, feeling quite immune to such embarrassing situations, I had wandered quite far away as there seemed to be one of us in the group at just about every tree within a quarter mile. Suddenly I began to hear voices. I parted the thick high bushes next to me only to see a band of backpackers merrily trekking on the main trail no more than a foot away. Oh well!

Left to right: Greg, Fred, Karen, RT
(Photo by: camera with timer)

A view from above that fog
(Twin Peaks Saddle - Angeles National Forest)

XXXIII. Was there life before a conservatory?

Most definitely there was, and as I slowly reach backwards to bring those times into present focus – some of which I waited to tell in late summer – I see two different lifetimes: one was that of a simple music teacher, later pioneering a new department of guitar in a developing and promising academic institution; the other is that of an entirely restructured career – one that required new education and braille certifications; one for which there was no precedence or demography; nothing to compare to, and no model to pattern an idea after. Venturing into the unknown, there was no way to know if there would be an audience for such an idea. Nor did I know how many years ahead might require more study and preparation.

The pursuit of a *Braille Music Division* completely consumed my energies, and the possibility and hopes for a new family life following divorce gradually became a very doubtful likelihood. Relationship after relationship failed, as it was obvious Richard was being slowly drawn to another mistress – that of his newly born work; work which – still unknown to him – left too little room in his life for the wonderful people he was so fortunate to know.

The music store days

Music store teaching before (and during) the conservatory, and my college gig was always a bit hectic, but full of good memories and great stories of simpler times.

Center of Music closed just after the Great Quake of 1994, and was the last descendant of the 1940's *Adler Music Academy*. As described in an earlier chapter, the new owners that opened the store following Adler's closing in 1970 inherited the teaching faculty and the students who followed them. *LeDonne's Center of Music* was to me like another port in a storm before and after my divorce. Vince and Grace, the husband and wife team who owned the store, seemed to consider all of us as though part of the family. Their son, Tony, was a musician like his dad, and we often played gigs together. After many years they retired and sold the business.

Other stores and owners spanning about 1985 to 1995 were generally from musical families as well. One was a well-known instrumentalist who played with many fine bands during his career. Jim was a typical commercial musician, and the atmosphere at *that* store was always fun with plenty of music tales to swap.

Gene, the store manager, kept a small refrigerator well stocked with cold beer in the repair shop near his office; visitors would stop by each week for cheer and joke telling. Needless to say, laughter would come pouring out of that room on a regular basis, and with business beginning to wane toward the end of the store's life, more social time than sales was common. Many small family-owned music stores went bad during those years, as large conglomerates ruthlessly smothered most of them.

At times, neurotic customers could truly become trying to a salesman, especially with day-to-day boredom of selling guitars, picks, and the like. Folks would often come in with a chip on the shoulder, demanding answers to questions that would really frustrate the salesmen. On one occasion, a somewhat brash fellow came in insisting that he had been sold a defective electric bass. His contention was that the strings kept going out of tune, and since the bass was new this should not happen. Gene asked the gentleman if he had ever had the first string "aligned." (By the way, there is no such thing.) Knowing that the fellow didn't have a clue as to what he was doing or even how to tune a bass, Gene said to him: "Let's take the string off, and we'll align it now."

He then asked the man to hold the string firmly on one end while he slowly held more and more tension on the other. There they both stood: Gene with an unbelievably straight face, holding and seeming to stretch the string until he now says "There; I think that will do it; now just be sure to buy this new tuner to maintain the alignment." Meanwhile in the back room, staff is doing all possible to keep the laughter down. The man thanked him profusely and went on his way. The next time he came into the store the salesman asked him how the bass was doing.

"Great," he said, "I really appreciate you aligning that string for me."

On another occasion, a gentleman came in asking to return the saxophone that he had just bought from the store last week. Gene expressed regret that he wasn't happy with his new horn, and asked him what the problem was.

"Well, the damn thing goes faster when I play down the scales than when it goes up."

"Oh is that all. Sir, that's normal; didn't you know that?"

"Whaddaya mean?" says the irate customer.

"Well, you understand the principle of gravity I'm sure. On a fine horn like this, the notes are going downhill when you go down the scale, so they will seem to go faster; conversely, when you play up the scale, the gravity increases; which means that you just need to practice more in order to overcome the inertia."

"Oh; guess I never thought of that. Thanks, man; I really am sorry to have seemed so dumb."

Stories from music stores are endless, but the best is yet to come.

As the neighborhood in some parts of town became less and less desirable, transients were common. It was not unusual to see a drunk passed out on a corner next to the pawnshop or in a back alley.

It was a rainy day, and management was about at wit's end with such folks dropping in just to be annoying while passing time. In front of the store, the awning had been raised in order to create a shield for customers who might want to come in. Water began pouring down from the covering.

Gene suddenly looks out the front window of his store and sees what appears to be another bum standing out of the rain; the man has his back to the window, legs slightly apart, with both hands in front of him in a stance somewhat like one visiting a urinal; a stream of water seems to be coming directly from in front of the man.

At this point, Gene had run out of patience with such things; out the front door he charges, yelling at the terrified fellow something to the effect of: 'get yourself out of here and go pee on someone else's sidewalk!' Meanwhile several of us watched from inside the store, all along knowing the outcome of this. The man begins running away frantically with Gene, "ass n' elbows," in hot pursuit. Both disappear for at least ten minutes. Soon Gene comes back looking rather quiet and subdued, while preferring not to be questioned.

Staff: "Hey Gene, how'd it go?"

"Hey man, please don't ask."

"What do you mean? You did catch him didn't you? Did you call the cops?"

"Just never mind; it turned out that he was standing with his hands in his pockets and just waiting for the bus. Now look, I don't want to talk about this anymore. Let's just forget it and have a beer."

During the time that Jim and his wife Margaret owned the store they had generously decided to provide me with health insurance. This is something that I could never afford myself. As a result, I was able to have surgery to correct an abnormal sinus duct with which I was born. Since I was a small child, doctors were unable to do very much to alleviate concern, or to offer a solution to the problem. My mother agonized over my embarrassment as a child when peers would comment on my red "Adam's apple."

When I began dating again following divorce, the dormant lump on my neck grew, and again reared its ugly head sometimes spewing fluid externally. For most of my life, doctors would warn of tens of thousands of dollars in medical bills to correct the problem, and no assurance that surgery would be successful. But now that there was insurance, I decided to wander into the clinic where I was now covered. Following my mother's recent passing, I felt that enough was enough after forty-five years of living with this.

As I waited for the ENT (Ear-Nose-Throat specialist) to come in to examine the problem, I recalled the many doctors that my mom had taken me to as a child, and how she worried over the fact that perhaps it was a birth defect.

Quietly, in walks a young black man who was the throat specialist. I looked at him with confidence and thought: "OK, you are in his hands." He took one look, poked around on my sore neck a little, and said: "Oh yes, I've done quite a few of these."

I remember him saying that he would need a thyroid scan, and that he may have to remove a little portion of bone near the back of my tongue. I thought to myself: "Well doc, just don't shorten' it too much."

I can still remember the moment just before I went under for that very long surgery. I looked up to see to see the surgeon while lovely music was quietly playing in the operating room; he was saying "Oh yeah, this guy has lower cholesterol than I have." He winked, pinched me on the toe, and out I went. When I awoke resting peacefully in my hospital room, the first person that I saw was my friend, Victoria, quietly watching to make sure that I was OK. Dr. Lorenzo Brown had literally changed my life.

Jim and Margaret finally had to terminate the insurance, as the demise of the music store became imminent. I remember leaving the store late one night long after they had left; I placed a good bottle of wine at the door so they would find it in the morning, and a note thanking them for the many years that they had provided that insurance for me. They were confused that I would respond in such a manner, considering that they had just taken the benefit away.

(The chronology and sequence of events for "The Music Store Days" may be slightly altered, and some characters are fictionalized. Although the events were real, and some stories from other music stores, some playful ornamentation has been added)

Richard E. Taesch

Seems that love is all you need
(photo taken on a1995backpacking trip)

XXXIV. Was there ever life at all?

Closing thoughts for summer

Fall is still a ways off, but admittedly begins to stir thoughts in my mind for a September *someday* sequel to this first remembrance. And with summer still vibrant and hopeful, I have decided to begin a recording studio "fade," and quietly stray some from the chronology of my own life story that has unfolded before us. Perhaps both Richard and his readers (should there ever be any) can now retreat to a kind of random set of different places – those in the form of little stories consisting of observed points and views, some personal thoughts, favorite things, joys, some somber ponderings, and a few entertaining reflections that have come to mind; those without a need for fitting into any one particular recollection as before. Read them in any order that you choose – some, or none at all; but I am in hopes that anyone who may find them fun to read, might perhaps one day close the covers of this book with a little smile on his or her face.

So, which way from here?

Fall

I am mature, stately, and proud – my beauty can only be seen by those who walk with me in solitude – I am summer's memory ...

FALL

SHORT STORIES

Points & Views

The hunter

The telephone conversation began as usual. With an exchange of "what did you do today?" ... interesting trivia about the day's activities and accomplishments began to unfold between two old friends. After near an hour of conversation, I remembered a special event that occurred that afternoon on my weekly hike into the mountains nearby.

The joy of spotting wildlife in its protected habitat is quite exhilarating for me. Momentarily forgetting that my friend was sympathetic toward hunting for sport, I exclaimed: "Oh, I meant to tell you earlier; I saw another large deer, the second one this week; unusual in these lower altitudes especially in the dry weather." After the news was out, I then thought perhaps I shouldn't have brought that up.

My friend replied with what seemed to be a sharing of my excitement: "Ah, they are such beautiful and graceful animals to see in the wild." For an instant I felt a connection to share the moment, and perhaps some kind of alignment.

"Yes, this one was quite unusual for here as he was a large buck, antlers and all. I must have caught him off guard while grazing, as when I spotted him from the side of my vision, we were only about fifteen feet apart. He stood in a frozen position with antlers pitched high as if hoping that I wouldn't notice him."

"Hmm," replied my friend; "can you hunt in there? He would be a good catch."

My enjoyment of sharing soon turned cold and heavy; deeply disappointed, I longed for the opportunity to retract my revelation, but was only able to move to another subject.

She loved sirens

They would often visit friends when married, and conversations always made for fun afternoons on holidays or Sundays. This Sunday was no exception, and cold drinks with a barbecue enhanced the day. Suddenly a very loud siren roared close by the home where they were visiting. *I just love that sound* - Sarah expressed with emphasis, as she had sometimes done in the past.

Bill hated to hear anyone say that, but never had the courage to ask his wife why she felt that way. After all, to him a siren meant that someone was in distress, dying, or in a state of losing someone or something dear to them. Trouble in paradise was slowly creeping into their marriage, and definitive statements – though never deliberate – seemed to become more frequent.

Bill's own part in the demise of their closeness was something that he later realized much more clearly. He never blamed her, and often wished that he could have applied some of the same communication skills learned in the military while sitting at radio transmitters and conversing with strangers in faraway places. Perhaps they might have had a happier ending.

For the moment, the siren incident was put away only to revisit a very interesting return somewhat later. The time spent with friends continued that afternoon, and although Bill caught a slight wince from them when Sarah made that statement, they must have felt it best not to ask what such a bizarre thing could possibly mean.

Time passed, and during an intimate dinner, Sarah and Bill discussed things very close to their impending changes. Bill mentioned to her how one of his married musician friends that she knew was bringing a girlfriend to gigs with him; he was hoping that she would sense disapproval, and perhaps feel some renewed interest in their marriage.

"How can he do that to Kathy, Sarah?"

She seemed to respond as though not surprised, but that it might give them both a chance to explore other possibilities.

"After 20 years of marriage?" - Bill queried, puzzled and confused. He was stunned, remembering the earlier years that she would express concern as to whether he was happy in their marriage; over and over he would try to reassure her.

Things worsened over time, and she would come home less and less. One day feeling nothing to lose, he asked her: "Sarah, how can you find sirens so inspiring to hear? They are distressing to me." Bill knew that he would never rest well without finding out what this *dark* side of her was all about.

She looked up to him softly and replied: *to you that sound means hurt and suffering; to me, it means help and the end to a tragedy may be on its way.*

There is never a day Bill can recall that moment when a tear doesn't come to his eye. Show the way you feel – communicate, ask, and share – before it's too late.

One day while re-iterating this little siren story to a friend, he said: "Bill, for God's sake, put it away; that's just plain dumb. Besides, why are you thinking of that now?"

"Why didn't I think of it then?"

No reply ...

More loud noise (or a symbol of hope?)

"Hey Jim, pass me another beer!"

"Sure Richard; here you go."

Suddenly, a state-of-the-art war machine roars through the desert sky, seeming to tear a blazing path along the northern slopes of our San Gabriel Mountains – the only mountain range in North America that runs east and west. The sleek fortress of death is nearly invisible as it heads back toward Palmdale Regional Airport, probably on a test mission.

Jim and Bob look up to the plane with smiles and admiration; I cringe, clearly remembering the air raid sirens and horror stories of my French grandparents so long ago.

"Jeez; d'ya think that thing could get a little louder?" I exclaim.

"What's the matter Richard; don't you know what that means?"

"Sure; a lot of money and a lot of machismo."

"Now, now," Jim says while smiling patiently towards his momentarily opposed comrade. "Richard, that means *freedom* to some of us."

311

Slowly pulling another gulp from my cold beer, with wet eyes, I grin humbly then clearly remember my uncle Charles in WWII France and his work with rescuing downed American pilots. Perhaps the military dagger that he never talked about also meant *freedom* and hope that he heroically brought to those people too. There are always different ways to see everything, and fortunately, always very different *Points and Views.*

A reptilian point of view

She would often take short hikes in the William S. Hart Park near her home in Newhall. It's a lovely place with historic things and quiet open space. High up in the ridges above the little town below, Victoria and her Australian Sheep Dog, curiously named "Mountain," were both enjoying a walk there this day. Naturally, the spring season brings out the local rattlesnakes for recreation as well.

"Mountain! Stay close and please don't wander off where I can't see you" she called to the little Aussie. Suddenly, as the dog did just the opposite of her wishes, barking began in a very forceful way. Victoria turned to see Mountain facing what appeared to be no more than sagebrush; the sound of the rattlesnake made it clear what the dog was pursuing, and danger was at hand. "Mountain, come here, now!" she cried, well knowing that if the dog continued to antagonize the snake, it could strike at her. Cry after cry brought no response from the dog, as it was determined to flush the creature out. The rattling and hissing became more and more intense; the barking increased, and the girl was at a loss of what to do.

Suddenly a pitiful yelp came from Mountain, and with tail between legs she retreated from the snake. Blood was clearly on her nose, and it was obvious that she had been struck as the cornered reptile tried to defend itself. Still at least two miles from where her car was parked, Victoria reacted instinctively knowing that the dog could well be in danger of death. To make matters worse, even with carrying the heavy dog, there was the problem of finding a veterinarian on a Sunday; would she accomplish that in time? Making her way partially carrying Mountain and having her walk on

312

her own, Victoria finally made it to her car, and was able to find an emergency vet.

Immediately the dog was treated and placed on intravenous fluids. She would remain in the animal hospital for several days, and at a cost of many hundreds of dollars. Victoria asked the vet if this might somehow be a lesson to the dog, and perhaps a warning for the future. Paraphrased: *No, they don't learn that very well. But if that snake wanted to kill her, it very well could have. It only wanted to escape from the dog, and the very restrained slight prick to her nose was clearly evidence of the benign nature of the California Diamondback. They are not aggressive and evil as we humans make them. They will strike only when backed into an impossible situation and when in danger to their own lives.*

Mountain survived the adventure, and hopefully the rattler will make tracks in the other direction when domestic dogs approach; after all, snakes only know about coyotes, and *el coyote* is usually not a threat to them.

Some have only one view

The ranger was very glad that I had made the call to him. "Sir, it's good that you called to report this, as we have no other way to know; hikers are our eyes and ears out there, and we depend on you. You must never hesitate to contact us when there is trouble."

Partly in frustration, and partly in fear of the badge, many hikers will never make that call when disturbing problems occur in our protected wilderness. I myself had put the call off for months while feeling resentment towards folks that I've never met.

Some sections of Pacific Crest Trail near the western extreme of Angeles National Forest have become invaded with dirt bike riders. Even though scenic routes have been carefully set aside for off road enthusiasts, somehow the motorbike riders can't resist the intriguing crossings of our PCT – the 1,500 mile-long trail protected by law for backpackers, day hikers, and horse riders. The trail stretches from the Mexican border to the Canadian wilderness in the north. The United States designated PCT* long ago, and federal laws are clearly violated when any motor vehicle attempts to navigate it. (*National Trails System Act - October 2, 1968)

I was nearing a turn around the mountain when I heard the sound of motors; at times the trail comes into proximity with the off road reserves and the sound is not unusual. This day, however, it seemed terribly close. As I rounded the familiar turn of a blind switchback, I was confronted with two young men on their dirt bikes about twenty feet beyond, and heading straight towards me. The trail is no more than two or three feet wide with no quick way for opposing traffic to pass, as the drop-off is quite severe.

The bikes snorted, farted smoke, and growled their ugly aggressive way ever closer; suddenly the boys saw me and slowed as I frantically climbed the slope to my right like a frightened lizard.

"Oh man, we're sorry … are you ok?"

"Yeah, I guess so; just didn't expect you on this trail; kinda scared the hell outta me."

"Dude, is there anybody else up on the ridge ahead – uh, like a ranger or somethin'?"

"Oh no, don't worry; I only saw one patrol Jeep about an hour ago."

Of course I had quickly made up the story, hoping to coax the boys to abandon PCT and return to the motorway set aside for them. "Guys, don't you know that this is Pacific Crest Trail, and you could be arrested for violating federally designated lands?" I figured that the attempted lesson went in one head and out the other, as they continued on as though no one had said anything to them.

Hiking deep into another area near the same wilderness, some sections of PCT were becoming more and more degraded by unwelcome motorbikes. Returning late from a hike in darkness would often become perilous, as the foot trail had been so badly abused by them, that even with good flashlights one could not determine where the edge of the trail cliff was. More than one encounter with a horse rider would reveal the fact that some horses had sprained their legs in the wake of the bikes' deeply eroded tracks.

Week after week brought frustration, and one could easily see the attempts of some hikers to repair the damage, but to no avail as the persistent violators would return to destroy the work that had been done.

"Officer: I'm calling to report another problem." [I was never one to do this; I hated it, but fed up was now an understatement. Some folks I had met on the trail were even considering stringing wire across the path, a serious threat to the safety of us, and for the careless bikers.] "If the Forest Service doesn't do something about this soon there could be real trouble in that area, as some are becoming hostile towards these guys."

The ranger became quite helpful, and willing to chat in a way that could calm an agitated person. "As I said before, you should all make these calls more often so that we can do what we can to help."

"Officer, why do they do that?"

"Sir, you need first to understand this type of human behavior; no matter how you feel about it, there are those whose view is to do only that which pleases them, and with no awareness of how it might affect others. These guys have no feeling for our wilderness; they only want to ride and enjoy themselves in the moment. Accept that, and you'll be a lot less stressed. There are more good riders out there than bad, and the good guys so often take the rap because of the others."

About a month later I returned to the same area to find that volunteer trail workers and bikers had joined forces to restore the badly damaged slopes; my call might have made a difference, but then for how long? Yang; Yin: what one tries to polarize as positive, a different energy may reverse. The never-ending struggle of the ages continues, and each of us can only hope to "make it right" according to his or her own personal *point of view.*

A friendly message for "The GCP"

This view truly needs no explanation. Following is a hand written notice found in an envelope carefully attached to an oak tree; the location was slightly down a slope, and strategically just out of sight from the primary trail:

"A friendly message for the Green Canyon Pooper – AKA 'GCP':

The piles of poop are not a problem, no more those from the wildlife; however, the reams of tissue paper along the trail are un-acceptable. Rest assured that we know who you are, and if you insist on using our state park for your daily movement, at least kindly consider the act of burying the tissue paper. The toe plate of a good hiking boot near soft soil works very well for such things, just as we have been doing for at least two years in an effort to remove and bury hundreds of linear feet of such litter on your behalf.
    Sincerely,
    Your friendly State Park Volunteer Team Effort"

2084 by George Oh'Well

Dear Editor:

I'd like to thank you for your thoughtful editorial comment regarding those of us who... *clicking a mouse will never replace pushing buttons and turning dials.* In the eighties before my own work involved so many hours a day on a computer, I was thrilled at my first attempt at digital RTTY [radio teletype]; it was really fun.

A night or so ago, I dreamt that I was about to shower before settling down to a relaxing evening of ham radio. Knowing that Big Brother monitors our "Smart water meters," I first needed to step up to my 2084 computer keyboard (neatly installed in my water closet) in order to adjust the flow, set the time, and access the desired water using my conservation-defined software. After a 12-hour day on a similar keyboard, I had misplaced my special shower password. Drat!

I reached for my W/C Smart Phone (no digital pictures, please) to seek customer support in Calcutta. Sanjay was so helpful, and the shower took place about 3 hours later. Needless to say, 20-meter [licensed H.F. radio spectrum] propagation was down by the time I saddled my J-38 [vintage military telegraph key]. Sigh!

Sir, you are a criminal

Somehow an old public service television ad comes to mind: A policeman is seen stopping a car along the highway, suspected of drunk driving; he subsequently handcuffs the driver and leads him off to his patrol unit under arrest.

The man exclaims: "Officer, why are you treating me like a criminal?"

"Sir, you are a criminal."

In my puzzled mind concerning such things, I remember reading long ago in a school civics class, a statement that sounded like: One is "… innocent until proven guilty." Did I miss something in my youthful naiveté, or was the ad inferring that a trial was over before the booking? Perhaps today it might be simply called politically __in__correct.

Hiking the Garment District

A young man passed me on the trail as I began my journey today; he was dressed in a kind of uniform, perhaps a scout leader or youth director of some kind. He was carrying a rather large shovel, and I then thought perhaps he must be a volunteer trail worker as is sometimes seen in these parts. We traded greetings as we paused on the narrow path, and I couldn't help but to thank him, assuming that he was doing trail maintenance.

He responded ever so pleasantly: "No, I just carried this with me today, as there were still a lot of snakes last time I was here."

"Were you in danger of being bitten?"

"No, but it's just in case I see one."

"Well you needn't worry, just be watchful. They're not going to harm you; they are not at all aggressive as long as we don't threaten them. Rattlers are natural here, and protected as is all wildlife."

He smiled, and went on his way.

My day was nearly ruined, as my thoughts rambled while hiking on trying to cleanse my spirit from resentment.

Could this be a sample of those who teach our children about nature? Is it possible that someone would carry a shovel on a hike only to behead rattlesnakes whether or not they are any immediate threat? And just how does this fit into our violent world, one where video games with sport killing and destruction are popular as entertainment? Perhaps I have my answer.

I then thought that the young man might consider leading a children's nature hike into downtown Los Angeles; I hear that there aren't many rattlesnakes there.

Photo: *I think I spoiled this fellow's dinner, as he was stalking the tarantula that was near him. As you can see, he was quite willing to pose for me at less than four feet away.*

Family Ties

Hiking along a rather popular trailhead for families and children, a mom and her little boy were just slightly in front of my companion and me. The little fellow was no more than waist high – close enough to the ground for spotting litter along the way.

Unaware of anyone observing him, he would often bend down to pick up the careless leftovers, while seemingly quite proud of his contribution to our planet.

"Jimmy, stop that! You can't be picking up every piece of trash you see; please behave yourself, or we'll go back to the car!" exclaims mom in annoyance.

Obviously quite hurt and near tears, he turns to see if anyone might have witnessed his humiliating chastising. I smile ever so warmly directly at him, wink, and give a hearty *"thumbs up!"* Knowing quite well why, he peeks up at mom to make sure she's not watching, smiles wonderfully at me, and hides his own thumbs-up response to us behind her back.

Cute? Sure, perhaps; but ...

The Widow Maker

Point of view or just a curious observation for thought, the above title appeared as a caption on a billboard proudly displaying a photo of the state-of-the-art fighter jet. The billboard display was strangely removed soon thereafter.

Lockhart

In a sudden and surreal change, I slowly turn north away from the busy desert expressway. For a fleeting moment, I am able to imagine the experience of one passing into heaven after leaving a long and turbulent life. The little side road – lined with tall trees – shades the way, not unlike a planted arbor of protective vines and lush moist green; beyond the trees are endless expanses of irrigated land for the growing of man's sustenance. In the midst of *nirvana* is scattered a few old dwellings, and a general store to serve the last remaining families who have worked this land for generations. Here, time has virtually stood still for at least a century.

If you travel in spring, butterflies upon thousands surround your vehicle as though a halo, nearly clouding the view ahead, while painting the most colorful pastoral scene anyone could imagine; agriculture and moisture have created a natural refuge and breeding ground for them. I stop for a moment at the general store for a cool soda, and drink in the past and the peace. I often take drives into this area so as to view my vacant land beyond the little farm village; I believe that the drive through this lovely community to the desert beyond is indeed the best part of my trip.

Escape with me now, and imagine an old science-fiction movie – one about a remote country town where a strange craft from outer space has landed for a short visit. A lost traveler stumbles upon the village for gasoline and supplies, and discovers the residents to be in great fear of aliens who are slowly taking possession of their home. The driver speeds away, frantically trying to reach the next main city to tell his story; however, when he returns with journalists, the town is gone – nowhere in sight, and no one has ever heard of such a place.

Well, perhaps Richard's story is not quite as haunting, but after nearly twenty years of not visiting my nirvana, a friend and I decided to study maps, and to seek out my land for a campout.

I must have passed the location of my familiar turn at least six times; it was not there, and no sign was to be found. Taking a mere intuitive and desperate chance, I turned into a deserted road that vaguely resembled the general direction I sought. The pavement was full of potholes and appeared not traveled for decades, left in disrepair almost deliberately as though to discourage intruders. Nothing but barren desert and what appeared to be dried up fields could be seen.

Soon, empty shells of old dwellings and ruins of the familiar two-story general store came into view. A lone farmhouse was visible, fenced and still green, as though a neutral island amidst the sea of dried cornfields and wasteland. What happened? Where? When, seem to be in my mind as I tried to convince my friend that what I described did, in fact, exist at one time.

After a moment of quiet thought, he responded: "Richard, let's just drive a ways and see what's up ahead."

"Sure, if you want to, but ..."

Deeply disappointed, I was completely lost for any logical explanation. Suddenly there appeared to be the only possible answer to what happened here after the *aliens* came, raped the land, and destroyed nirvana.

Slowly we passed the remains of fences that still had the dried skeletons of once thriving vines; beyond them we could now see hundreds of acres of industrial solar panels, machinery, menacing barbed wire, and the stark reality of mass destruction of the secret garden – the once life-giving blood of families raised on the work that was no more. Crop growing and unimaginable beauty had been replaced with apparatus to power man's computers, video games, and insatiable thirst for energy. Was the land sold to the conglomerate, or were the inhabitants driven away from their home after generations of cultivating a perfect setting for the *new* corporate millennium?

As of this time, no evidence of Lockhart remains on some maps of the Golden State; but this lost traveler knows it did exist ... didn't it?

The bullet holes do make an interesting statement;
this beautiful trail sign was only one week old.

Pacific Crest Trail (Nocturne)

Richard Taesch

PCT at dusk, looking west towards Windy Gap

THE CODA
XXXV. Remembrances that dwell in the backcountry of my mind

The Circle Oh Ranch, July 4, 1998

It was in the year 1998, and I was spending some of my weekends camping at my pilot and ham radio buddy's dwelling far out in the remote Desert. One afternoon, I was standing on a high spot surveying the open space with a pair of his fine binoculars. Suddenly I spotted what appeared to be ruins of the old ranch property far off in the distance; only a vague memory of where it was located remained. I asked Bob if he knew what it was that I saw. "Yeah, that's the old place that your friend Ben used to own. It's been pretty much trashed by vandals now."

I asked what he thought about our taking a horseback ride over there early the next day, as I would like to see it once again. This particular visit happened to be, of all times, the day before Fourth of July 1998. It would be twenty years to the day that I had last been at Circle Oh, and since that memorable 4th of July party. *"How Deep Is Your Love"* somehow echoed in my brain, and though my heart was heavy as I recalled Ben's memory and how he died heart broken when his place became violated, I could not help but be drawn to see it once again as an adventure.

Bob's horse, Willy, would not cooperate that morning for some reason, so he suggested that I make a hike alone, but that we should stay in radio contact with our 2-meter handheld transceivers. I carefully plotted my return course with a compass; although only two or three miles away, when dropping in and out of the arroyos in that part of the country, one can easily lose direction in the vast expanses. While setting the course, I vividly remembered the imaginary spring caper that Ben and Woof escorted their guests to – the one that turned out to be just an old coil spring; Marcy's comment of *"Just wait. I'll fix his ass good for this one,"* brought a warm smile to my face. Awaking from the short reverie, I mounted the trail unaware of what lay ahead.

As I climbed out of the last arroyo, what looked like the little road leading to the Circle Oh on the higher ridge seemed suddenly familiar; again the reverie took over: *"Whips and Chains may be Required"* jumped out as though the signs were still there on that dusty road some twenty years before; but alas, nothing but a couple of old beer cans could be seen. Was this the right place, or did I somehow lose my way navigating the deep gullies? Nope! This was it all right.

While ascending the grade, the remains of the little cabin rose into view as I suddenly became overwhelmed with memories. The carcasses of Ben's old cars were still there, now riddled with bullet holes; what resembled a structure that would have held Grandma's legendary bell was there, and on and on.

I decided it best to stop for some lunch at this point and give Bob a radio call so as to let him know that I had arrived and was safe. I'd be perhaps a few hours before coming back, as I needed to absorb it all and would take some time returning.

"No problem, Richard; just do what you need to do, and I'll monitor the base station for your return plan." I sank to the ground in the shade of the cabin remains and reminisced as I enjoyed my packed lunch in the *somewhere-in-time* ruins and old memories that surrounded me.

Many things were still there to recognize, but could only be visible to someone who had known Ben: old pieces of newspaper were still lodged in some of the walls – those that my ex and I had saved in bundles and donated to him for insulation; some old red carpeting that we had given to him for the inside of the cabin, and much more scattered about here and there could be found under dirt and amongst the trash that had been dumped there by trespassers. As if the time warp was not rich enough, warm memories of weekends there with my wife also haunted me without mercy.

I spent perhaps an hour or so poking around with my camera, and trying to imagine how things looked before. Suddenly beneath the remains of the homemade bell structure, I spotted a shiny little object slightly protruding from under a bush. I carefully lifted the brush, and jumped back quickly when a large lizard greeted me and scampered away. Reaching in to retract the little item, I couldn't believe what I was seeing.

Twenty years later, winter storms with rain and snow, vandals and more, it was none other than the broken half of a little yellow ceramic bell that Ben said he bought as a joke with the word "*Liberty*" etched in black. He had hung it on the empty frame after Grandma's bell mysteriously seemed to vanish. I had only heard stories of a *new* bell, but I had never actually seen either one myself. Who would think that it would turn up twenty years later, on this of all days, buried under dirt and brush now to rest in the palm of my hand? I was so glad I had taken that sentimental journey; the little yellow bell now sits proudly on a bookshelf in my home in the year 2011.

With the help of my compass settings and making visual reference to Bob's high radio tower several miles away, I returned before dark with the little treasure in my pack, and to a very welcome stash of cold drinks. Now if you should think that little things don't matter, sure they do; they matter a lot to all of us, sooner or later. (Below: see a photo of the bell as I found it in 1998)

Outtakes from the back trail

After Alex's guitar lesson on Wednesday nights, we would sometimes trade a story or two. We are both about the same vintage, and having been raised in the same area, many fun and familiar places are remembered. Alex is also a hiker, and was a scout leader at one time.

"You did what? Wow, that's just crazy" was his comment that followed an accounting of my Condor Peak hikes at night.

I would begin the 7-mile ascent in the afternoon, and arrive at the Fox Peak saddle just before dark. After a short nap under the rising stars, I would grab my flashlight and continue west on the ridge, then towards the rocky Condor Peak high above the valley lights below. 45 minutes or so later, the peak itself rises perhaps 150 feet above the top of the ridge, and is mostly comprised of very large boulders. The ambient glow from towns far below would always provide enough light for the ascent whether a moon was up or not. Rock by rock, I would carefully climb to the top, raising my arms in victorious conquest.

"You are nuts, Richard!" exclaims Alex.

"Yeah, I know; but bet'ya a beer you'd do it too."

"Ha! Guess what? I did do it once."

"Aw, heck!"

* * *

One particular semester, I met the most wonderful student. Joe was a late middle age man who began attending my commercial guitar class at City College. He was more advanced than the others and obviously of professional experience in his younger days. At one time, Joe had studied with the iconic guitarist, Bucky Pizzarelli; we then immediately aligned musically.

He enjoyed my class, and decided to study privately with me at SCCM once the college classes had ended. He would come all the way from Los Angeles each week in his antique Ford Model A coupe, fully restored – a beauty it was! Great lessons, and his participating in my recitals rendered me quite proud, but I would always give honor and recognition to his prior background.

Joe soon began coming to lessons limping, then later on crutches. He shared with me that he had been diagnosed with cancer, but was hopeful, especially now with so much to live for. One day, he just could not navigate both the crutches and his guitar; he asked if I would mind carrying his guitar into our lesson for him.

Joe and his wife soon invited me to their home for dinner, as he expressed much gratitude and satisfaction in that which I had been teaching him. I was unable to make that invitation, and like little Angela, one day he did not show up. I waited, and was soon called to the phone; it was Joe's wife.

For all too soon, Joe was no longer with us.

* * *

78Y was a tie-down number inscribed on the wheel chocks found near the wrecked Beechcraft airplane.

I'd often hike high up to the 8,500-foot level of Sawmill Mountain west of Mount Pinos in the Las Padres National Forest wilderness. This particular day, I decided to approach the peak from a cross-country ridge north of the main trail. As I was navigating the area, I spotted what appeared to be the remains of aircraft wreckage scattered about. I began to explore the area, and it was apparent from finding some paperwork that the plane had gone down about seven years earlier, perhaps ca. 1992. I bypassed a sudden emotional reaction, and began to examine the slopes.

Many things still remained from the rescue: the transponder placard, parts of instruments, tools, personal items, and what appeared to be long human hair caught in some thorny bushes nearby. Portions of the plane were visibly crushed against a pine tree just below the ridge. It appeared to have crashed trying to gain altitude, perhaps in a storm while leaving the San Joaquin Valley far below to the north.

I left all that I found undisturbed; except, after recovering from a deepening sorrow, I placed the child's bracelet and one or two other artifacts carefully under a special place, thinking that one day I might return and perhaps make an attempt to find the family of the victims. From my own experience with such things, the family would only have had that site described to them; being quite inaccessible to most people, it would continue to haunt their imaginations forever. I could imagine a sensitive moment of having someone who had accidentally stumbled upon the wreckage in remote wilderness, suddenly present these things to them. After several sleepless nights, I returned and recovered the items.

So far, I have not been able to find the survivors of 78Y, but I still hold in safekeeping the bracelet, and two or three other keepsakes that probably belonged to at least one of the occupants of the ill-fated flight of Beechcraft Baron 55 in about 1992 or 1993.

* * *

Upon closing my eyes to remember, it's still quite easy to see the glowing eyes of the terrified deer lit by the headlights of my dad's car. As we slowly come into view of the injured animal blocking the way, I see her lying in a pool of blood on the dark mountain road directly in front of us as though resting, but clearly unable to rise up on her own – I was no more than four years old.

We were still living in San Diego, and returning from an outing that day in the mountains. Apparently the animal had been struck by a car sometime earlier, and it was clear that she was near death and unable to move. In those days, my dad would carry a handgun in his car while traveling alone with his family. We stopped in the road; he just looked ahead quietly at the animal as though thinking – what to do? What to do? There were no cell phones to summon help then.

Yes, I did relive that moment briefly when approaching the little gray fox told earlier. But this story in my early winter was not the happy ending as is in summer.

I remember a long silence; my mother said nothing. I may have been standing on the car seat between them, as I can see my dad seeming to have tears in his eyes. He looked at my mom and said: "Ann, there's only one thing we can do; I cannot let her suffer like that." No more words were spoken as he slowly removed his gun from the glove box and left the car. My mother gently placed me on the seat with my head in her lap; what seemed like hours went by; I heard a gunshot, and it was over – even at four years old I knew what that meant.

Soon a pickup truck came along and stopped to see if he could help. The man was a hunter and lived seasonally with his family close by in the mountains. He and my dad talked while he comforted us with what seemed to be great compassion. He said that he would take care of the dead animal, and that it would not go to waste. He invited us to follow him to the cabin where he would bring the deer, and then prepare it for his family for winter. He would later bring us a supply of fresh venison.

I remember a warm cabin, a fire, and a pleasant meal with kind people. My mother told me of the many times that I would ask whenever we were having meat for dinner, or at a restaurant: "Mommy, is it deer meat?" as she knew that neither of us could bring ourselves to eat venison for many years after that.

* * *

It had been at least seven years since my last gig with Lynn, perhaps one of the finest singers that I had ever worked with. We lost track of each other over time, and eventually I left the performance arena for good.

I would often drive high into the mountains nearby to hike, but would sometimes be sidetracked with an obsession to clean areas of trash that had been left by campers. This particular day, I hauled numerous thirty-gallon bags of trash up from the leftovers of the winter snowboard folks then searched for campground dumpsters. It's truly amazing to think that they believe if they bury their stuff under the winter snow, it just disappears in spring. Trashcan lids to beer 30-pack cardboards suddenly emerge when the snow melts.

It was a peaceful quiet day, and I had not seen a car or human anywhere in this very remote area for many hours. I spotted some throwaways down a steep slope near where I had pulled off the road. Down the slope I descended, rope and all; after retrieving the stuff, I climbed and struggled my way slowly back up towards the parking area.

As my head rose gradually into view, I spotted an old Lincoln parked across the road with a very familiar *canary* (vocalist) gazing at my car, as she apparently recognized it. There we were all but strangers of seven years earlier, and not another human anywhere in sight. And there I was, the guitar player without his tux on, pulling himself up a slope hauling a 30-gallon trash bag: first with gripping fingers slowly into view, then head, then the rest of me, little by little, climbing from the edge of the precipice back into the parking lot. There was no way she could explain how that looked from her perspective, and I didn't even try to describe mine.

* * *

Early one morning during our pre-class chapel music meeting, Father Phil began to gaze silently toward the large window overlooking upscale homes down slope from the school. Watching him curiously, I waited. Seemingly now removed from the purpose of our conference, he spoke quietly, starring ahead as if in a kind of daydream: "Richard, do you see those large homes in the distance?"

"Yes, Father, I see them."

"This is perhaps one of the most prestigious boys school in the country; here we accept only the highest achievers. They come from wealthy families; they work hard to make the *best* grades, graduate with *highest* honors, in order to capture the highest paid careers."

"What's your point, Father?" His gaze remained fixed as he continued:

"They strive to be the very best to gain the most in life; all so that one day they might afford one of ... [hesitatingly] those." He slowly points towards the impressive mansions below, then turns towards me: "What possibly can it all mean?"

330

Some of my favorite things

Hikes in the snow and long nighttime treks were a big favorite for me in the 90's. I kept a careful journal of all of them until about 2009. Here is a transcription of one that turned up in pencil writing from January 3, 1993:

Pacific Crest Trail @ Mill Creek Summit, west to Mt. Gleason; Time of departure: 2pm; return to car: 11pm

... Trails were like an enchanted wonderland; snow covered trail, but it was visible all the way. Most of hike was in new virgin snow with my footprints, the first there except for the tracks of small animals. All the trees & bushes were flocked with snow. Moonlight glowed on the snow & lit the darker parts of the forest and canyons at night. Easy to follow your own footprints back with only moonlight. A magical hike!!

* * *

I've spent most Christmas seasons alone the past fifteen years, and by my own choice for whatever reason that may be. It was Christmas Eve perhaps in about 2000, and I had chosen to do a short hike in the backwoods very near my home.

Nearing dark, I was relaxing in a quiet canyon looking up at the rugged low mountains ahead of me; thoughts of childhood, the smell of a Christmas tree, my mother and Doc, and other warm thoughts filled my reverie. As I turned on my hand held radio transceiver, I could hear local repeater groups playfully announcing the sighting of Santa Claus and his reindeer. "Ah," I mused; "it was so special then; maybe I should have accepted that nice invitation for tonight with Tom and Lisa – oh well, it sure is peaceful here."

Suddenly as I looked up to the steep ridge ahead that ascended the little peaks – those that I'd climbed many times before – I saw the most incredible sight: six deer in a single row were ascending the ridge as though in command of pulling an invisible sleigh.

"Sure glad I decided to spend Christmas Eve here this year."

* * *

Some Favorite Restaurants:
Taylor's in La Canada; *Backwoods Inn* - Santa Clarita
The Red Barn; now long gone, but a favorite of mine since about 12 years old
Georgio's in Palm Springs; also long gone
Lido Pizza in Van Nuys; quite alive and well; founded by a friend's family
The White Horse Inn; San Fernando Valley; long gone now
Ewing's on the Kern in Kernville California; fate unknown
Johnny's Pastrami on old Route 99 in Culver City California

Movies that have had an effect on my life:
The Fountainhead, 1949: Gary Cooper, Patricia Neal, Raymond Massey
The Young Lions, 1958: Marlon Brando, Montgomery Clift, Dean Martin
Bless the Beasts and the Children, 1971: Dir.: Stanley Kramer; Song: Carpenters
The King of Hearts, 1966: Alan Bates

Actors (many, but here are some from the past):
Gary Cooper; Marlon Brando; Noriko "Pat" Morita; James Garner (all movies and T.V.); Michael Douglas (*Shining Through*); Stuart Margolin; Joe Santos; Lee Weaver; Roger Moore; Lee J. Cobb; Dean Martin (a sadly underestimated talent for drama); Sylvester Stallone (*Rocky V*); Cary Grant (*Gunga Din,* 1939); David Jansen (*The fugitive* T.V. series); Ray Milland (*The Uninvited,* 1944 – Song: *Stella by Starlight*); Clint Eastwood (*The Pink Cadillac, Play Misty for Me*)

Actresses:
Meryl Streep (*The River Wild, Silkwood, Kramer vs. Kramer*); Lindsay Wagner; Hilary Swank (*The Other Karate Kid*); Bette Davis; Julie Parish; Cher (*The Elephant Man*); Lauren Bacall; Daryl Hannah (*Splash, Clan of the Cave Bear*); Elizabeth Taylor; Julie Harris; Haley Mills (*In Search of the Castaways,* ca. 1962); Kathleen Quinlan (*The Twilight Zone movie*); Amy Speedy (*Short Circuit*)

Old T.V. shows:
The Rockford Files; The Fugitive; Run for your Life; Peyton Place; The Saint; Knight Rider; Your Show of Shows; Steve Allen Show; The Hollywood Palace; The Deputy; The Twilight Zone; Hallmark Hall of Fame; many, many more ...

Less favorite things

- ❖ Wildfires and evacuations that happen where I live each year
- ❖ Big Brother hiding in your iPhone (and elsewhere)
- ❖ The slogan: "Save energy – Go online," while energy consumption from the digital age seems to be increasing more than any time in history
- ❖ When my back went out (Scary!)
- ❖ Giant gray spiders stretched across the Waterman Trail at night in spring
- ❖ Internet hype and dependency; computer games (big Yuk!)
- ❖ Ugly blinding blue headlights on cars
- ❖ Cars that go "beep, beep" every time drivers walk away from them
- ❖ "Clams" when I practice scales (clams = clinkers)
- ❖ Cars that emit pounding low frequency booming sounds
- ❖ Students that are always late
- ❖ Students that are always early

Two special memories

- ❖ The time I looked up to see people actually dancing to music that we were playing in one of my first dance bands
- ❖ Watching blind children frantically running their eager fingers across a page of music braille that I had prepared for them at my first outreach class in music reading

Internet service provider, circa 1942

A website for dreamers

XXXVI.
Observations, revelations, a few opinions

Looking ahead

I believe it best to not spend time regretting things that one has not finished. Although life is said to be short, it's also quite long enough to revisit those places and projects that were once left behind. To me, life is simply a little journey, a gift to use in the best way that we can.

"Time is running out; the clock is ticking" are words often heard coming from those who feel the pressure of their mortality; self-induced pressure that prevents them from appreciating that which they have accomplished, and moreover, any realization of that which they may still have time to do.

I sometimes imagine a day when all of my nagging projects are caught up; all of my creative appetites and longings being satisfied, and enjoying the luxury and relaxation of having no worrisome tasks lying ahead – time just to hike, do more ham radio, sleep, and … my God, how boring!

Come with me now, and place yourself in an imaginary computer game: you are submerged in *virtual reality*. In this game, all dreams, challenges, and life projects are finished and realized; you have no new skills to master, and only that which tickles the fancy from moment to moment. You may not take long to realize that such a game would be lost before it is played, and probably never sell very well. Consider the following two items: (1) a thought-provoking definition of boredom (source unknown); (2) a little quote for thought

Boredom: (bor'dum) n. a sensory deficit to stimulus [Whoops! – It looks like that one comes back on us, the bored ones, as opposed to blaming that which seems to bore us.]

"The only problem with having nothing to do is that you never know when you are through."

- R. Taesch

One morning while planning a restful Sunday of writing, I suddenly felt hopelessly confused as to where to start. I'd been looking forward to time for my writing once braille class materials and deadlines were up to date. Now this dilemma!

I sighed, opened the file for Chapter 36, stared at it as I'd been doing for several days, and quietly thought: "Where do I go now? Outlines are there, subjects are not a problem; Richard, you've got pages of notes that fit perfectly into this final episode of the book – shake yourself out of this; maybe I'll just go and make a cup of coffee instead!" Inertia, lethargy, a desire to take a nap – oh what a temptation!

Observation: An exciting idea for my next journal article for CTEBVI was brewing, but then so were other thoughts crowding in around it. I sat down and decided that I would just pick one of the scattered remembrances from the *backcountry* chapter and scribble out a few sentences. After all I could at least start, then spend the day writing my journal article if still at a loss. No such luck!

Revelation: Once the typing started the ideas began to flow, it became clear that I would be at my computer well into the night; inspiration was no longer a problem. Decision had apparently been the challenge, a periodic dilemma that confronts most of us during our lives.

Lesson: Pick your road for the day and don't look back, just give it your all – peace of mind guaranteed! However, do leave some room to change your mind; if you do, stick with it.

So what projects are ahead for me?

Among many to consider, are projects that were never finished, or those set aside that were not a priority due to life during, or soon after the conservatory. Which among them are still useful? Which ones are worthy of telling about, even though no longer apply directly to my work for Braille Music Division and the SCCM? Clearly, there are more questions than answers, but one project does seem to stand out.

Having written curriculum for our early degree program specifically for jazz, commercial, and studio guitar, I completed a counterpart book on the subject of college programs and the guitar. As written about earlier, it was to be published by a well-known publishing company but, due to my neglect, was never produced. For two years thereafter, I served as a contributing author for the journal of the Guitar Foundation of America called *Soundboard.* My column was called *The Commercial Guitarist,* and based upon the unpublished book; articles focused primarily on the chapters covering chord skills required of working commercial guitarists. One article following that series dealt with music braille and guitar in the classroom for the visually impaired. The commercial guitar column in Soundboard ran from spring 1992 to spring 1994, while the VI article appeared later in 1996.

The manuscript for that work is called, "*The Contemporary Guitar Gets Ready for College,*" with a copyright date of 1989. It is fully indexed with 189 pages and 16 chapters. It was an exciting project, and at the time it was written, I only had access to an old portable mechanical typewriter, and used hand-drawn artwork; just imagine, no batteries, no crashes, and only an ink ribbon for maintenance.

One evening while working quite late, our electric power went out during a period of intense creativity. I simply jumped up from my desk, lit a candle, and continued to work for several hours. Oh yes, an old toothbrush was necessary to occasionally scrub the typing letterheads clean. Following is the dedication:

Dedicated to ... professional teachers of the guitar who have given their careers to the highest standards of teaching and to the elevation of their profession and their instrument to a place of dignity within the academic world

At the time of conceptualizing this work, not even the classic guitar was yet accepted as a *legitimate* instrument for study in some schools; there were only a small handful of colleges and private schools brave enough to think that they could create recognition for commercial guitar in academic arenas. Since that time, however, many have succeeded. My book was an attempt to bridge that gap, and received much approval from some of those who had reviewed the outline and concept of presentation.

I completed extensive research on every college, conservatory, and music trade school that I could find in an attempt to learn all that I could about how such programs worked. As a result, Chapter 16 was to become a treatise on the subject, and was titled: *"The School of Guitar: What it expects; what you can expect."* Its purpose was to help prepare aspirants for entrance, and what might be expected of them as students.

At the time of completion, and once I knew that the publisher was no longer interested in the manuscript, I put it away for *someday,* and turned my attention to preparing myself for building my *Braille Music Division* for blind students at SCCM. Will I go back to the project? Most likely I will, as my journey is not yet complete. When, I cannot tell; but even if never, it remains a very active part of that journey.

In other plans, a new book in the *"Introduction to piano ..."* series called *"Introduction to Guitar for the Blind Student"* has been started, and became the inspiration for current articles in the journal for California Transcribers and Educators for the Blind and Visually Impaired – CTEBVI (formerly CTEVH). The book parallels my published (now out of print – *Jelloian Publications*) guitar method titled: *The Guitarist,* but is dedicated to the application of music braille reading with respect to the classic guitar.

As mentioned earlier, Part III of the *"An Introduction to Music for the Blind Student"* series is now in review and consideration as of this writing; it is a comprehensive teacher training course of near 500 print pages, with evaluations and planned certificates of completion [published 2014]; it is dedicated to teachers of music braille. Part I and II of the series will also be revised in the near future. [Part I - *Second Edition* - was revised and published in 2017.]

As to non-academic plans, Richard is planning to sell his home on 34th Street within a year or two. He is in process of preparing a home site near the shore in a somewhat funky area, but very proud little community called Salton Sea Beach. Once settled there, he will be fully retired as a music teacher (he thinks), and will focus on writing full time.

Salton Sea Beach at sunset
[photo taken in early 2012]

But I thought they said that the Salton Sea is polluted ...
[I guess the pelicans didn't think so in 2012]

Richard E. Taesch

Projects never completed

Among some unrealized hopes was my plan to develop a unique reading system for special blind children: those who have certain types of hand to brain coordination issues, specifically that of using one touch hand to read braille while trying to play an instrument with the other. Also, it can be difficult for some of them to sight sing, as they have been taught in school to use both hands to read their braille with. This leaves them without control of the reading when one hand must leave the page to check pitch location on a nearby keyboard.

A fine blind organist and retired college professor donated a full console two-manual organ to the school when at the large estate campus. The organ sat idle for most of the time then, but I was in process of formulating notes on how a lab project could be developed using the pedals for playing music lines where students needed to use two hands to read with. This would serve as an interim step until more digital independence could be achieved for them. The sheer size of the instrument might also serve to fascinate the less dedicated scholars, as the pedals can be set to produce upper-range pitches, thereby leaving both hands free to read on a specially devised surface just above the lap. The keyboards of a large console organ are generally high enough that a small reading surface can usually fit between one's lap and the instrument.

I kept the plan to myself, but became more and more enthused as I studied the problem that I had hoped that this could alleviate. I very much wanted to beta test the idea before proceeding, or before revealing the concept to anyone yet. I developed extensive notes on curriculum for the future, but never in my worst dreads did I think that relocation plans would exclude the organ as a part of the new building when the estate was sold.

A special computer tech station with adaptive technology was to occupy our facility; it would be a scaled-down version of the fine computer lab that we had at the large campus, but for training one-on-one. One of our board members donated a then state-of-the-art computer system for the project, but it was later discarded in a room only to catch dust. I asked for help to set the station up, and hoped

340

that someone would become interested in learning how to use and to teach curricula. But alas, that project was never realized

A one of a kind library lives on

Once it became imminent that our new West Hills facility would be closed, it also became a possibility that lack of funding could cause the closing of the school altogether. Prior to that, plans were begun with a braille production agency to include our library of music braille and music textbooks in both electronic format and hard copy in their database as a joint reference material project. This could serve to preserve the library in the event that the school did close. If not, the hard copy would eventually be scanned and turned into digital files – a lasting tribute to the distinguished contributors of their personal libraries, and a gift to blind students for generations to come. There were over 5,000 music titles in the SCCM braille database; perhaps more than anywhere else at that time.

Upon the final closing of the SCCM library facility in April 2013, all library materials were relocated and distributed amongst various non-profit venues.

A few things that I'm proud of

In 1970, my wife and I bought five-acres of desert land in hopes for a one-day investment return. The land became part of our divorce settlement, so I have now held it myself for over thirty years. The predictions for growth in that area never came to be, which is just as well for me. As time progressed, my attitudes about business investing and careless development changed. I made a pact with myself that I would donate the land to a nature conservancy before I would ever sell it – even for a profit – to a developer. Offers come to me several times a year, but I consistently refused to respond to them. An official county dirt road crosses the property, and it is indeed a strategic location for certain purposes.

Very unexpectedly, a non-profit organization called the *Transition Habitat Conservancy* contacted me in hopes that I would sell the land to them. The organization strives to purchase and preserve sensitive ecosystems for the protection of wildlife migration routes and transition. Although very pleased that my land would now lie in a conservation area, I was quite emotionally attached to it, and had hoped to one day perhaps visit there for campouts and such. THC offered more for the land than anyone else had, even though it was a fraction of what Sara and I had paid for it – the offer was about $2,500. I agreed to sell the land to them, and few decisions have ever brought such a smile to my face each and every time I think of it.

* * *

It was indeed a timely opportunity for SCCM and its *Braille Music Division* to have existed in the year of Louis Braille's bicentennial celebration – Louis was born on January 4, 1809.

In 2009, National Federation of the Blind (NFB) sponsored a wonderful video on music braille, and featured several blind musicians and celebrities. The presentation included the publisher of my own courses that were developed for our colleagues and students at SCCM. I was pleased to announce to our board and advisors that this had happened in our lifetime, and to be reminded of the 200 years of music braille education and its advances – much of which, in recent times, we ourselves had initiated and pioneered.

Our MENVI network and its purpose was a part of the organization's website, which recognized our school as a major player in the field; and how pleased I was to learn that a primary facilitator of the video project had been one of our two-week intensive braille music students. She has since earned her Doctorate in music, and performed at Carnegie Hall.

* * *

Amongst the many accomplishments resulting from colleagues working together at the SCCM during the early Braille Music Division, was that of a project to train blind orphaned boys at a special school in South Vietnam.

The director wrote to me, having heard of our work with blind students through our MENVI network. He asked if there would be a way that their guitar instructor could be trained to teach the boys to play using simple music in braille. They would then become able to perform on the streets of the city in order to help support themselves. Being a school, the boys would be encouraged to read basic braille chord charts, developing themselves academically so as to build independence.

Clearly, I would not be able to travel to the school and personally provide the skills and ear training that would be needed. However, knowing that the young men were being taught literary braille skills, I designed a short teacher-training manual using folk and pop music that I had compiled for my sighted guitar students. I then wrote for copyright permission from the publisher of a book source that I used, and was granted provisional rights.

Since we had just acquired our first embosser, we made about 10 bound braille copies of the music selections for the students. I then adapted a print equivalent for the teacher with braille facsimiles and print explanatory labels for the special symbols and signs. The teaching manual was created for the instructor, and a package shipped off to the school in South Vietnam.

Needless to say, my dear friend and supporter, Dr. Ernest Burgess, was excited about the project; his own work as a surgeon involved rehabilitation for Vietnam War amputees and veterans. Promptly, a response came from the school director. The package included photos of the boys poring over, and using the special braille books with which they were learning their new trade. Joyful smiles were quite apparent in the pictures, and Dr. Burgess was provided a report with copies of them. Ernie then took it upon himself to contact the school. He revealed his involvement, expressing praise for their efforts to educate and train the young men in such a way.

* * *

The early days of Braille Music Division at SCCM brought many rewarding new experiences. None was more fulfilling than that of one little orphan boy. [Some facts in portions of the following accounting are paraphrased as brought to my attention by others.]

While touring in the country of Guatemala, a young couple couldn't help but to notice the homeless children in rundown parts of the city. They would stop to speak with them, offering warm smiles and friendship. One particular child seemed to somehow captivate their attention; he was perhaps about nine years old, malnourished, orphaned, and blind. Putting all other plans aside, they began to inquire about the boy and what it would take to adopt and bring him home to America. Setting out undaunted by the fact that they had no experience with a blind child, much less that of raising any children of their own, the proud new parents returned home, now a family of three.

By time young Martin entered middle school, he had taken to study the trumpet. He learned to read music in braille fluently, and soon became first chair in the school orchestra! Richard had the unique privilege of transcribing all of his music throughout middle school, and parts of high school as well. What a joy he must have been to his new parents who gave of themselves in such a way.

"... to know even one life has breathed easier because you have lived. This is to have succeeded."*

- Ralph Waldo Emerson

*See Page 197 for this writing in full

* * *

Finale - Opus One

So many musically significant events occurred for SCCM when it was only as large as the original 1,700-square-foot building. Although the grandiose campus brought much expansion and notoriety to our new Braille Music Division, magical and musical things were still commonplace in the old location. Miss B's *Children's Musical Theatre* was a priceless example.

I would conduct jazz guitar improvisation workshops each Friday night: one week for intermediate students, and the other for advanced. All were adults, and many had followed me from my classes at City College in the eighties. Faithful students would attend recitals as spectators, and often pitch in to help make the quarterly performances successful. Sometimes fifty or more people would attend, and my helpers and volunteers would assist in bringing catered food and drink for our guests after the program. Needless to say, teacher and students would all glow with pride.

One of our favorite projects would be that of seven to nine jazz players from the workshops performing a solo transcription from one of our heroes, the late Wes Montgomery. Wes improvised many of his solos on his recordings in block octave movements, and my group would gather each session to study them. We would then perform not only the "head" (melody) of the tune, but then play the transcribed solo all in block octaves, and in complete unison with multi-guitars. I am not aware of many recordings that attempted this kind of thing. It was, perhaps, an anomaly.

Other students were composers, and our groups would often perform their compositions. Many of the young men were professional players in their own right, and truly made Richard look good; but the real credit must go to them, the hard working musicians who really made the events a success.

The guitar department had grown much in reputation. As a result, a quarterly newsletter called *"Guitar Times"* soon became an expected icon mailed to a fairly large audience, and an integral part of the SCCM.

Our classic guitar ensembles were also a source of great pride for the department. These would perform on Sundays following the Friday night jazz programs each quarter. Youngsters and adults of varied ages would convene for warm-ups, then step up to the performance stage to play everything from sixteenth century compositions, to the Baroque, and on to the more modern idioms of the day.

Following each recital, I waited until all attendees and students had left. After putting things back in order, I would sit quietly and re-play the videotape that we had just made of the program. Late into the night – sometimes two, three, or more hours – I would study the performances that had just taken place in order to evaluate my work, the students, and to contemplate what direction we were taking.

Generally well after midnight I would leave for home, but so proud of my dedicatees, and feeling partners with them and the school in so much good energy; all for the sake of the art, the students and my colleagues, ...*ever reminding me that their investment in themselves is only as rich and complete as we have all made it – together.* (Introduction, page ix)

For all too soon, **Fine**

April 2015
(Photo courtesy of Robb Navrides)

For all too soon

Testimonials for an author*

Re. "An Introduction to Music for the Blind Student"

"The intricacies of teaching music braille reading require materials that are consistent for quick and easy learning but varied for high interest and contain enough repetition for real learning. Richard Taesch has done all of that and more in his well graded lessons and study supplement for beginning braille music reading. Those of us who teach it are indebted to him.
Carol Tavis, Music Educator, Los Angeles, California

"Richard, you have hit the jackpot! ... This looks like a real winner. The copy is clear and clean and very accessible. I'm really excited and grateful that kids will get this kind of help with their music.
Bettye Krolick, Music Braille Consultant, Colorado

"I have used Richard Taesch's braille music course with several students with great success. Sighted teachers, who are not braille literate, can now guide blind students in their musical education. In the process, both the student and the teacher learn the braille music code. I highly recommend this extremely valuable tool
Music Educator, Los Angeles, California

"By setting high yet realistic expectations, Taesch has demonstrated that with proper instruction, blind musicians can and do perform at levels equal to, if not sometimes exceeding, those of their sighted counterparts."
Stephanie Pieck, Braille Music Instructor, New York

Contributed testimonials are taken from back cover material of the series, "An Introduction to Music for the Blind Student." Used here by permission of the publisher, Dancing Dots, and the author, Richard Taesch - © 2015

"I have used Taesch's Part I course to teach one of my students braille music. As a teacher of the visually impaired my training did not include braille music and I found this course extremely helpful in covering the code. I can read music but I don't consider myself a musician and I am unable to play the piano. The book is set up in a logical manner so that I didn't have difficulty teaching my student the basics."

Certified Teacher of the Visually Impaired,
Plano ISD, Texas

Special thanks from me to my family, friends, colleagues, mentors, and to my students for their contributions in making this remembrance possible - R.T.

The author looks ahead from 1985
(Photo courtesy of Victoria Seaborn)

PHOTO GALLERY

Family roots before Richard's birth – 1922-1942

Dad (violin) and Army Trio

Dad, warming up a trainer

*Uncle Charles (center)
graduation 1922 (France)*

Dad, Military Police

Some pictures need no explaining

Mom in convent school, ca. 1925

Left to right: Dad, Mom, Uncle Tom (the boxer & my Godfather); Tom's first wife, Pat

My grandmother (right) and her daughter

1942-1952

Dad and the author, about 1943

Young Richard and friends –
San Diego CA (lower left)

Grandmother & grandfather with
family at my uncle Lucien Paul's
wedding (Alsace, France)

Dad with his family; his last trip
home, 1951; Left to right: My dad;
his father; mother; brother, Carl;
younger brother, Lucian & wife

Family & friends at a
typical French village
picnic

First Communion, 9 years old

This is perhaps the last family photo
together just before my father's accident;
St. Elizabeth's church, Van Nuys
California

Father O'Dwyer (the tall guy)

Circa 1951

Top center: My friend Charlotte

ACKNOWLEDGMENTS & COMMENTS

Everyone's life story must surely contain a multitude of contributors, and to list them individually would be near impossible. Moreover, such would most likely become a mass *dedication* rather than that of an acknowledgment. Perhaps this is why autobiographies seem to rarely include them. However, those portions of my journey that have been career- (and/or) related adventures on a chosen path, clearly occupy their own unique microcosms within the story itself. It is with this in mind, that I have chosen to include this tribute to just a few of so many. And for those deserving people who may not find their names here, any preference or priority does not exist. I have included just a few that have – in more recent times – contributed in one way or another directly to this remembrance, and to those interests that continually motivate and remain a part of me. No order of any kind was considered, nor is categorically intended.

Much credit must go to my dear friend, Robert Walker, whose long life as a corporate pilot, electronics engineer, fellow Amateur Radio operator, musician, and very patient grammatical critic, has been an inseparable part of this story. My special companion and colleague, Robb Navrides, helped to lift a new Richard out of his turbulent times following divorce. Thanks to Robb, music took on a new meaning, and has remained a lifelong bond between us. He has climbed a ladder of success to the top in the entertainment industry, and yet continues to put our friendship on the highest level. Fred & Karen Carrington introduced me to the world of nature and hiking, without which, many portions of this story would not have been written. Fred, a lifelong and distinguished educator, musician, fellow bandstand companion, and his wife, Karen – a fine musician as well, included me as one of their family; they patiently taught me the rigors of backpacking, and so much more about real life than they will ever know. My dear friend and student, Bagher Habibi, served on our conservatory board during a very critical time in SCCM (*Southern California Conservatory of Music*) history; his financial support and very generous contributions to the school are significant, and his technological expertise and encouragement to me has made the production of this book a reality. Dr. Louis C. Vaccaro, Ph.D., Senior Advisor, University Committee for International Education USTC Hefei China, provided untold encouragement and priceless suggestions from his experiences writing his own autobiography. Thanks to my long time school friend and now colleague, David Vaccaro, who re-introduced me to his brother, Louis. My appreciation also extends to Lou's friend, Susan Bouton (educator and attorney), who helped considerably by providing an enlightened view from a reader's perspective. Recognition must go to my colleague and friend, Grant Horrocks; Grant worked closely with me in the victories and struggles of our work in music and literacy for blind students and musicians, without which, there would be no Braille Music Division to have written about. My dear friend and concert pianist, Stephanie Pieck, provided much encouragement on this journey; Steph was perhaps the first to know that I had strayed from only a method book author. Her editing of my music braille courses, and patient warnings about *"followed by"* and *"preceded with,"* continue to peer vigilantly from upon my shoulder as I type. A special appreciation goes to Victoria Seaborn, who's continuing contributions lovingly reach out throughout my story. A very special thanks to Diane Croft of National Braille Press for permission to allow the cover of the book, *A Touch of Genius,* by Michael Mellor, to appear in the background of my practice area photo; the book celebrates the 200th birthday of Louis Braille. My deepest respect and humble gratitude extends to Dr. Merlin D. Tuttle, author of *"America's Neighborhood Bats,"* who went beyond granting quote permission, and patiently walked me through accurate and updated information for my chapter IX, *"Why is that?"* in early spring. My special thanks to Bob Locke of *"Bat Conservation International,"* for my initial contact with Dr. Tuttle. Words alone cannot begin to express my gratitude to Casey Ogino. Casey established and maintained the first computer center and its applications for SCCM; without his contributions, continued growth and our braille Music Division would not have been possible. Many thanks must go to Ernest Koeppen, SCCM's computer technician in its latter years. Ernest gave his all to maintain our machines, working as though one of us in our unique cause. Even after his work for the school was terminated, Ernest stood an ongoing vigil to respond to my frantic calls concerning computer issues for my work. A dear person that I've saved till near last is my colleague, friend, and most patient listener, Janice Learned. Ms. Learned was a student when I joined SCCM in 1976, became a graduate of the composition department, and later served as executive office manager. Thank you, Janice, for your many years of loyalty, humor, and encouraging warm smiles, as you gave (and continue to give) so much to serving my projects during your years as SCCM Registrar; and by always *going that extra distance* to understand and care about the quality and meaning of our work and those it served. Much appreciation goes to my special friend and school companion, Greg Febbo, whom I've written about herein. After much rewriting and editing, Greg was able to become an active part of our story, adding important personal facts and accuracy to my accounting. Special recognition must also go to Adele Lun, who served on the SCCM board as treasurer, as well as an advisor on important committees for financial matters and fund raising. During the time that she studied classic guitar with me, she generously donated her time to create a Chinese edition for Part I - Lessons volume - of *"An Introduction to Music for the Blind Student."*

And lastly, deepest appreciation extends to my esteemed colleague, mentor, advisor, and constant source of inspiration, the late Bettye Krolick – known to many as *The Godmother of Braille Music*.

Cover photo: Twin Peaks Saddle looking west, above cloud cover - Angeles National Forest, California

Cover design & photo by Richard Taesch

Fall

  I am mature, stately, and proud – my beauty can only be seen by those who walk with me in solitude – I am summer's memory ...

Summer's Memory
The Autumn Sequel

Richard E. Taesch
A Fall Remembrance

"Summer's Memory" ...*is currently in progress.*

              - R.T

Richard Taesch is founder and retired chair of Braille Music Division at Southern California Conservatory of Music - Est. 1971-2013. He founded *Music Education Network for The Visually Impaired* - MENVI in 1997, and authored "An Introduction to Music for the Blind Student" series, "A Blind Music Student's College Survival Guide," and textbooks for the guitar while serving as Guitar Department chair for the SCCM since 1976. A music educator since 1961, he has been listed in "Who's Who in America" since 2003, and recognized as Recipient for the *Albert Nelson Marquis Lifetime Achievement Award* in 2017.

CPSIA information can be obtained
at www.ICGtesting.com
Printed in the USA
BVHW090504150521
607370BV00009B/1346

9 781499 907100